Mastering

Business Law

Macmillan Master Series

Mastering

Business Law

Second edition

Terry Price

MACMILLAN

First published 1982 by Pan Books as
Practical Business Law
First published as *Mastering Business Law* 1989
Reprinted four times
Second edition 1995

Published by
MACMILLAN PRESS LTD
Houndmills, Basingstoke, Hampshire RG21 2XS
and London
Companies and representatives
throughout the world

ISBN 0–333–62048–8

A catalogue record for this book is available
from the British Library.

10   9   8   7   6   5   4   3   2   1
04   03   02   01   00   99   98   97   96   95

Printed in Great Britain by
Mackays of Chatham PLC
Chatham, Kent

Contents

Acknowledgements

Acknowledgements are due to the following:

Deborah Nicholson, my daughter, a solicitor who made many constructive suggestions and kept me well informed regarding changes in the law; Rachel Tennant and Julie Price, my daughters, who assisted me in the preparation of the index and various tables; Simon Beckwith, barrister, for some interesting suggestions regarding judicial precedent and insurance law; Dr Angela Conyers, Director of Library Services at Canterbury Christ Church College and her staff for the help given in locating so much information; Norma Featherstone who provided considerable secretarial assistance; and finally to my wife, Sheila, who assisted me greatly in the preparation and whose encouragement made the work so much easier.

   Any mistakes or omissions remain of course my sole responsibility.

TERRY PRICE

The author and publishers wish to thank the following who have kindly given permission for the use of copyright material: The Controller of Her Majesty's Stationery Office for extracts from the Sale of Goods Act 1979, Courts Act 1971 and the Unfair Contract Terms Act 1977 and SI 917; the Solicitors' Law Society plc for the Standard Agreement form and other material; and Times Newspapers PLC for 'Women's Entitlement to Equal Pay', *The Times*, May 1988, 'Estate agent owes duty of Care', *The Times*, February 1994, 'Battle of the leyland cypresses', *The Times*, September 1994.

Introduction

Mastering Business Law incorporates changes in the law that have been made up to December 1994 and is intended for anyone who wishes to gain an understanding of some of the legal aspects relating to business.

The book will be very useful for anyone studying business courses which include business law, and is of particular relevance to GNVQ/BTEC, NVQ/RSA/LCCI/City and Guilds courses. In addition, the book will be of considerable value to students preparing for GCSE, A Level and professional examinations in business studies and law.

It is important to remember that many changes take place in the law which reflect the changes taking place around us. Readers should try to ensure that they keep up to date. *The Times* and *Guardian* publish regular accounts of decided cases and will also provide reliable information on new legislation.

⬡ Table of cases

Table of statutes (Acts of Parliament)

Law and the courts in England and Wales

1.1 Criminal and civil law distinguished

Michael Moore is a technical representative with a steel firm known as Swaleness Steel. He is returning from a sales visit in the Midlands, having obtained a valuable contract for the supply of a large quantity of steel rope to an engineering company, Peak Dale Engineering plc. He is driving through a small Midlands town on route for the motorway and, no doubt thinking of this big order, allows his concentration to lapse. John Martin steps onto a pedestrian crossing and Michael fails to see the red light and knocks John down. John sustains quite serious injuries and both the police and an ambulance are called. The police take a statement from Michael and ask him to take his licence and insurance certificate to his nearest police station. They indicate that they are likely to press charges. On the advice of his solicitor, John decides to sue Michael.

Michael is certainly in trouble with the law. On the one hand he is being threatened by the police with prosecution and on the other John has decided to sue. In this section we will be dealing with the meaning of the terms 'prosecute' and 'sue' and at the same time bringing out the important differences between the two major branches of our law, *criminal* and *civil*.

When the police say they will prosecute what they are really saying is that they believe that the person in question has committed a crime. In our situation the police could argue that Michael has committed the crime of driving a motor car on the highway 'without due care and attention'. The case would be heard in one of the criminal courts and in this situation it is most likely that it would be heard in a Magistrates' Court. If Michael is found guilty, he could be fined and have his licence endorsed. Michael then would have been punished for his wrong-doing. Criminal law is concerned with conduct of which the state so strongly disapproves that it will punish the wrong-doer.

Activity _____

Think for a moment about other crimes and about the punishments which the state imposes.

1

Many of you no doubt will have thought of theft as an example of a crime. Our society could not work if people were allowed to help themselves to the property of others and so the state imposes a punishment such as imprisonment. It is hoped that this threat will deter persons from committing the crime of theft.

The branch of law which deals with crimes is known as criminal law.

You will remember, however, that Michael is also threatened with being 'sued' by John Martin. When we talk of suing we are concerned with that branch of law known as civil law. Civil law is concerned with settling disputes between persons, groups of persons or organisations such as companies or local authorities and providing a *remedy*, often compensation to the person wronged. Thus John Martin who is the person wronged would be anxious to receive compensation from Michael Moore for the hurt and suffering as a result of the accident. The case that John is bringing against Michael would be likely to be heard in the County Court, which is one of the civil courts. The branch of law concerned with disputes between persons is known as civil law.

In the two cases which could be brought against Michael Moore, the criminal case could be referred to as *R.* v. *Moore*. *R.* stands for Regina, which is a Latin term for Queen and signifies that it is the Crown which prosecutes on behalf of the community. It is likely in this sort of case that the prosecution would be referred to as CPS, or the Crown Prosecution Service. This service was set up in 1986 and indicates again that it is the Crown which is prosecuting on our behalf. CPS recruits qualified solicitors and barristers for this work.

In the civil case the parties would be referred to as *Martin* v. *Moore*. This indicates that this is a dispute between two individuals in which John Martin or his lawyer would be trying to prove that Michael Moore had been negligent and had thereby caused injury to John. In this situation John Martin would be the plaintiff (he is making a complaint) and Michael would be the defendant.

We will be returning to the important subject of negligence in Chapter 11.

Exercise 1

1 See if you can write a short description of criminal law.
2 See if you can write a short description of civil law.
3 In each of the two cases which Michael Moore is likely to face, he would of course be the defendant. What would the other party be known as in (a) the criminal case, (b) the civil case?

The main differences between criminal and civil law are summarised in the chart below.

Criminal law	Civil law
1 A set of rules dealing with conduct of which the state disapproves.	1 A set of rules dealing with disputes between individuals or businessmen.
2 A breach of the rules may lead to prosecution.	2 A breach of the rules may lead to the defendant being sued.
3 Cases heard in criminal courts, e.g. Magistrates' Court.	3 Cases heard in civil courts, e.g. County Court.
4 Parties involved: *R.* (Regina) v. *Defendant*.	4 Parties involved: *Plaintiff* v. *Defendant*.
5 Fines and/or imprisonment may result from prosecution	5 Compensation/damages may have to be paid by the defendant to the plaintiff.

We have identified five differences between criminal and civil law. Try to remember the five by seeing if you can note them without reference to the book. If you cannot do this read the sections again and then try to remember the five differences.

___ **Exercise 2** _____

In each of the following, say whether you think the situation would involve criminal or civil law.

1 Brenda Jardine is injured while shopping when some heavy packages fall against her.
2 David McCarthur owes a garage £395 for some motor car repairs it has done.
3 Deborah Prince has been stopped by the police for driving a car which does not display a tax disc.
4 Colin Richardson has been arrested and charged with having committed burglary.

1.2   Criminal and civil courts in England and Wales

We have already learned that criminal and civil cases are heard in different courts. In the situation relating to Michael Moore the criminal case was heard in the Magistrates' Court while the civil case was heard in the County Court. In this section we will be dealing briefly with the system of courts in this country and at the same time learning about their various functions.

The present system of courts in England and Wales was set up in 1971 by the Courts Act, as the extract below shows. Although there have been changes since that time the structure and system have remained basically the same.

Courts Act 1971

ELIZABETH II

1971 CHAPTER 23

An Act to make further provision as respects the Supreme Court and county courts, judge and juries, to establish a Crown Court as part of the Supreme Court to try indictments and exercise certain other jurisdiction, to abolish courts of assize and certain other courts and to deal with their jurisdiction and other consequential matters, and to amend in other respects the law about courts and court proceedings.   [12th May 1971]

B E IT ENACTED by the Queen's most Excellent Majesty, by and with the advice and consent of the Lords Spiritual and Temporal, and Commons, in this present Parliament assembled, and by the authority of the same, as follow:—

PART I
INTRODUCTORY

1.—(1) The Supreme Court shall consist of the Court of The Supreme Court. Appeal and the High Court, together with the Crown Court established by this Act.

(2) All courts of assize are hereby abolished, and Commissions, whether ordinary or special, to hold any court of assize shall not be issued.

Criminal courts

Magistrates' Court. First of all let us look at the system of criminal courts in this country. All criminal cases are heard in the first instance in the Magistrates' Court. The magistrates only have the power, however, to try less serious cases and thus many driving offences are tried in the Magistrates' Court. The power of magistrates is governed by the rule that they can only impose fines up to a maximum of £5000 and imprisonment up to a maximum of six months for any one offence but no more than one year for two offences or more. If, however, the magistrates in a summary trial or in a case 'triable either way' (see below) feel that the crime merits a more severe sentence than they have the power to give, then, following the conviction, they can send the person convicted to the Crown Court for sentence. It is clear, therefore, that more serious cases must be heard elsewhere. However, even such serious cases as murder or rape will go in the first instance to a Magistrates' Court for what is called a preliminary hearing. The task of the magistrates in a preliminary hearing is to examine the evidence to decide whether or not a reasonable case can be made. If they decide that a reasonable case does exist they will send the accused to the Crown Court for trial or, to use the legal term, 'commit the accused to the Crown Court'.

Certain criminal offences are known as intermediate offences. These offences, which include theft, may be tried 'summarily', that is at the Magistrates' Court, or 'on indictment', that is at the Crown Court. These offences are therefore known as offences 'triable either way'. The Magistrates' Court will decide in this category of offence whether it appears more suitable for summary trial or for trial on indictment. However in this category of offence the defendant has the right to insist on trial by jury and if he or she insists then the case will be an indictable offence. This choice of course is only available in the case of offences 'triable either way'. However, as the case *R.* v. *Brentwood Justices ex parte Nicholls* (1990) shows, where a defendant is charged with other defendants with an offence triable either way and where one of the other defendants elects trial by jury, then all the defendants will have to be committed to the Crown Court even though the others had elected to be tried summarily.

The famous case in 1981 involving the so-called Yorkshire Ripper began in the Magistrates' Court in Dewsbury, West Yorkshire. Following the preliminary hearing the magistrates committed the accused to Leeds Crown Court, although, as you will no doubt remember, the case was actually heard at the Central Criminal Court, the Old Bailey in London. The Old Bailey is, in fact, a Crown Court which has become famous because many well-known cases have been heard there. Cases which have attracted a lot of publicity will often be heard in the Old Bailey rather than the nearest Crown Court. The Yorkshire Ripper was in fact Peter Sutcliffe and the case is referred to as *R.* v. *Sutcliffe* (1981).

Of all criminal cases in England and Wales, 98 per cent begin and end in the Magistrates' Court; this gives some indication of the importance of this court. In sittings of the court there must be at least two magistrates and more usually there are three. Magistrates are not usually legally qualified and are unpaid. They do have the services of a clerk who will always have a legal qualification and offers advice to the magistrates. In some very busy Magistrates' Courts there are stipendiary magistrates. These are legally qualified solicitors or barristers who are, as the name suggests, paid. Stipendiary magistrates count as two 'lay' magistrates and therefore, as explained above, could in theory sit alone.

Activity

In the next few days have a look at your newspaper to see if you can find reports of magistrates holding preliminary hearings.

Crown Court.   The Crown Court, which always has a judge presiding, will hear all those criminal cases which are too serious for the Magistrates' Court. In some cases for the most serious crimes, such as murder, the judge will be a High Court judge, but less serious cases such as burglary will be tried at the Crown Court but may be presided over by a circuit judge or a recorder. Criminal offences are divided into four groups for the purposes of the trial. Class 1 offences are very serious and will always be heard before a High Court judge. Whether before a High Court judge or circuit judge or recorder, when the accused pleads 'not guilty' the case will always be heard in the presence of a jury. It is the jury guided by the judge who gives the verdict of guilty or not guilty. If a verdict of guilty is given then the judge will pass sentence. If the defendant pleads guilty then the judge passes sentence and the jury is not required. There are Crown Courts in most of the larger towns in England and Wales which are usually open to the public and if it is possible to make a visit this will help you to understand this branch of the law more easily.

Appeals against decisions of the Magistrates' Court

It is possible for a defendant to appeal against a decision of a Magistrates' Court. He may feel that he has been convicted wrongly. For example, a person convicted of a speeding offence may feel that the evidence produced by the police was neither sufficient nor accurate. It may also be that a defendant could think that, while he may have been fairly convicted, the sentence he had been given was far too severe, for example too heavy a fine or too long a term of imprisonment. In each of these situations, that is an appeal against conviction or an appeal against sentence, the case would go before the Crown Court and be reheard before a circuit judge sitting with magistrates. There would be no jury. The Crown Court sitting as an appeal court in these situations could reverse the decision of the magistrates in respect of the decision and also could reduce the fine or length of imprisonment. The Crown Court could equally uphold (keep the same) the decision of the Magistrates' Court.

There are, of course, occasions where the prosecution, often the police, feels that the defendant has been wrongly acquitted, which means he has been found not guilty by the magistrates. In some cases the police may feel that the sentence given has not been severe enough. The prosecution has no right of appeal in either of these situations. Thus the right to appeal to the Crown Court is available only to the defendant, not to the prosecution. There are, however, circumstances where both prosecution and defence can appeal against a decision of the Magistrates' Court where it is felt that in coming to the decision the magistrates made a mistake in their application of the law. The appeal is made to the High Court, to the Divisional Court of the Queen's Bench Division, and it is made on a point of law.

The Divisional Court consider the details of the case and, if the judges feel that the magistrates have interpreted the law incorrectly, they will order the case to be reheard by the magistrates and at the rehearing the magistrates must apply the Divisional Court ruling. The following example of the sort of appeal which might be made to the Divisional Court from the magistrates may help you to understand this better.

R. v. *Marylebone Justices ex. p. Yasmin Farrag* (1980)

In a case before a Magistrates' Court at Marylebone, Yasmin Farrag had pleaded not guilty to an alleged offence of soliciting for the purposes of prostitution. The police acting for the prosecution gave evidence and were cross-examined by the barrister for the defendant. The defendant then gave evidence and the chairman of the magistrates indicated that the prosecuting police officer did not need to cross-examine and, turning to the other magistrates, said 'case proven' before the defence barrister had closed her case or addressed the magistrates. Yasmin was found guilty and sentenced.

The defendant's barrister decided to appeal as 'a case stated' because a defendant or the barrister acting for the defendant must be allowed an opportunity to address the magistrates. The Queen's Bench Divisional Court, after considering the situation, ordered a retrial because the magistrates clearly had wrongly applied the law.

When an appeal is made on a point of law as in the above example, it is known as an appeal by way of 'Case Stated', which means simply that the details of the case are laid before the divisional court.

A more recent case provides another good example of an appeal by way of 'Case Stated'.

Erewash Borough Council v. *Ilkeston Consumer Co-operative Society Ltd* (1988)

The Queen's Bench Divisional Court in this case decided that the magistrates had wrongly convicted the society for trading on Sunday in contravention of the Shops Act 1950. It was held that the society was acting as a travel agency and that this was not a shop in the ordinary sense of the word, that is 'a place where anything is sold'. Unless this decision is challenged in a higher court, for example the House of Lords, then travel agents will be able to open on Sundays without risking prosecution.

As you know, Parliament has changed the law relating to Sunday trading and the importance of this case for the travel agents will be not so important.

However it is a good illustration of the way in which appeals are made on a point of law which is known as 'Case Stated.'

Appeals against decisions of the Crown Court

In the case of more serious offences which, as we know, are heard in the Crown Court, the defendant may appeal against conviction or against sentence to the court of appeal (Criminal Division), as the following example illustrates.

Rachel Davis has been convicted in the Crown Court for the manslaughter of her husband and she has been sentenced to four years' imprisonment. Her lawyers feel that the sentence of four years is far too severe in view of the evidence of severe provocation by her husband. The lawyers seek leave to appeal; permission is granted and the case is reheard in the Court of Appeal (Criminal Division). Three judges review the case by looking at a record of the Crown Court proceedings from tapes or shorthand notes. They also examine carefully the Crown Court judge's notes. After careful consideration the three judges decide that the sentence imposed upon Rachel was far too severe and Rachel's sentence is reduced to one year. Since Rachel has already served six months of her sentence while awaiting the appeal we can see that she has only a short time further to serve.

From this example we can see the way in which the Court of Appeal (Criminal Division) operates. An example of a case heard by the Court of Appeal (Criminal Division) is *R.* v. *McIlkenny* (1991). This case, as you may remember, involved the so-called 'Birmingham Six' whose convictions were quashed in the light of fresh scientific evidence and fresh investigation of police evidence. The three judges who heard the appeal felt that the convictions were both unsafe and unsatisfactory.

In almost all cases the decision of the Court of Appeal (Criminal Division) is final, though where it is thought that a point of law of considerable general public importance is involved the prosecution or the defence may be given leave to appeal to the highest court in the English legal system, the House of Lords. When the House of Lords sits as a court, a minimum of three, but more usually five, judges, known as Lords of Appeal in Ordinary, sit to review the case in much the same way as described in relation to the Court of Appeal (Criminal Division). Very few criminal cases ever come to the Lords but since the House of Lords is the highest court its decisions are final.

Although criminal appeals to the House of Lords are rare, there was in 1981 an appeal in a case relating to 'causing death by reckless driving'. The case *R.* v. *Lawrence* concerned a motorcyclist who ran into and killed a pedestrian who was crossing the road. The prosecution alleged that Lawrence was driving at between 60 and 80 mph within an area restricted by a 30 mph limit. In coming to their decision in this important case the Law Lords stated what constituted 'driving recklessly' and indicated that two elements must be proved: (i) that the driving in question created what an ordinary and prudent driver would regard as 'an obvious and serious risk of causing physical injury to another or of doing substantial damage to propery'; (ii) that the driver was 'reckless' as to whether physical injury or substantial damage to property resulted from his driving. This means that the driver realised the risk but nevertheless took it or he failed to think about it.

In this case it was clearly felt that such was the general and public interest in what constituted 'reckless driving' that by making the appeal to the Lords it was hoped that the law could be clarified on this subject.

House of Lords decisions are binding (must be followed) on all other courts but the House of Lords is not bound by its own decisions and it will sometimes overrule (change) its previous decision and therefore the law, as the following case shows.

R. v. *Shivpuri* (1986)

In this case Shivpuri thought he was bringing into the UK prohibited drugs. In fact the material was not a drug but quite harmless and certainly not illegal.

In a previous case, *Anderton* v. *Ryan* (1985), the Lords had applied the Criminal Attempts Act 1981 and concluded that if the act itself was innocent even though the defendant thought it to be illegal he/she could not be convicted.

In *R.* v. *Shivpuri* the Lords overruled their previous decision and found Shivpuri guilty of a criminal attempt.

It may help you to understand the organisation of the criminal courts and the various steps in a criminal action if you look at Figures 1.1 and 1.2. If you are not sure of any of the terms used, read the section again and then attempt the review questions which follow in Exercise 3.

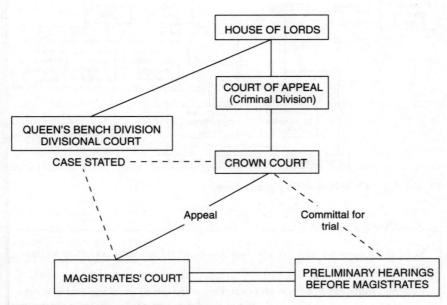

Figure 1.1 The criminal court structure

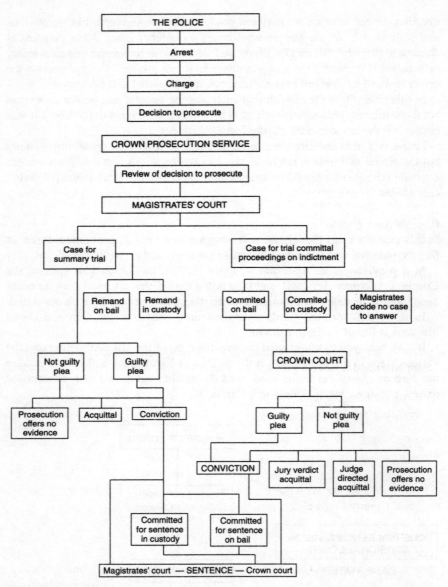

Figure 1.2   Criminal action procedure

Exercise 3

Read the following and say for each example which court is likely to hear the case.

1 Roy Goldstein has been convicted on a charge of drinking and driving. His lawyers decide to appeal because they think the magistrates have not applied the law correctly.

2 Peter Fairweather is charged by the police with having exceeded the speed limit of 70 mph on the motorway.

3 John Smith has been charged with the offence of 'causing death by reckless driving'.

4 Jennifer Jones, having been convicted on a charge of manslaughter, decides to appeal against the conviction.

5 James Johnson has been convicted for an offence contrary to the Official Secrets Act 1939. He has appealed unsuccessfully against his conviction but because of the great legal importance of the case a further appeal is allowed.

6 Cyril Rubak has been sentenced to four months' imprisonment by the magistrates for being drunk and disorderly in a public place. Cyril decides to appeal against what he regards as too severe a sentence.

Civil courts

County courts. We have now considered the main criminal courts in England and Wales but, as we have already learned, the other major branch of law is civil law and this branch also has a system of courts. Civil law is concerned, as you will remember, with settling disputes between individuals, businesses or companies and it is with such a dispute that the following example is concerned.

Peak Building Supplies Co. Ltd is a small company which supplies a range of building materials and equipment to builders. The company has supplied materials to the value of £7500 to a small building firm known as Woodruffe Renovations. Despite a number of reminders to the owner of the business, Mr Woodruffe, the bill remains unpaid and Peak Building Supplies Co. Ltd decides to take legal action to recover its money. Peak Building Supplies Co. Ltd writes to Mr Woodruffe explaining that it will start proceedings in the local County Court unless payment is made in full within seven days.

Here, then, we have an example of a dispute between a company and a small one-man business. This is a clear example of a dispute which could be settled by reference to civil law. Civil law is concerned with such disputes and providing a remedy. The remedy which Peak Building Supplies Co. Ltd is seeking is the recovery of the £7500. If Mr Woodruffe decides to ignore the letter from Peak Building Supplies then the company could begin proceedings to sue Mr Woodruffe by sending to the local County Court particulars of the claim. Because this is an action to recover money it is known as a 'default summons'. Other types of claims, such as for compensation for injury, would be by means of an ordinary summons.

This type of case would be likely to be heard in the County Court and would be referred to as *Peak Building Supplies Co. Ltd* v. *Woodruffe Renovations*. There are around 400 County Courts in England and Wales. The courts are grouped within circuits with about 15 courts in each circuit. The judge is known as a circuit judge. There are about 420 of these judges who also work in the Crown Courts. County Courts deal with a range of civil actions and, since the Courts and Legal Services Act 1990 and The High Court and County Court Jurisdiction Order 1991, there is no upper financial limit for actions, though those actions involving large financial claims are usually heard in the High Court. Before 1990 the County Court's jurisdiction was limited to £5000 in actions related to contract or tort. The administration of the County Court is in the hands of a district judge, formerly called a registrar. They have the power to try cases where the amounts do not exceed £5000.

Where a claim is for less than £1000 the district judge will arbitrate the matter using the small claims procedure. This is a very informal procedure and no costs are awarded to the successful party. The procedure which is much cheaper than a full County Court action will be presided over by the district judge or his/her assistant. The following example might help to explain this.

Medway Computer Services, a small business owned by Chris Chapman, has supplied a 486 PC computer to Katie Pullin who runs a small secretarial service. The cost of the equipment and associated software comes to £989 and despite frequent reminders Katie refuses to pay. Chris reluctantly takes action for recovery and since the amount is less than £1000 it is likely to be dealt with using the small claims procedure. Both parties appear before the district judge and present their cases. The procedure is not like a normal court and is quite informal. The district judge arbitrates (decides between the two parties). She orders Katie to pay for the equipment. Although Chris has been successful in getting the debt paid, he will not be able to recover any costs from Katie. However, since Chris did not need the services of a solicitor, the costs of the action were small.

This sort of procedure has become very popular and has persuaded many people that it is often worth taking action where, before this sort of court existed, they were often put off by the costs and the formality of the County Court.

In addition to actions relating to contract and tort, which will be dealt with in more detail in Chapters 5, 6, 11 and 12, the County Court deals with property matters, partnerships and also undefended divorce actions. It also deals with a range of family matters. The range of work in the family area has increased a great deal following the passing of the Children Act 1989. The tort of defamation will never be heard in the County Court and will always commence in the High Court. This no doubt is to discourage frivolous claims and because defamation cases are always heard before a jury.

Activity

Find out where your nearest County Court is. County Courts will supply, on application, a booklet entitled *Small Claims in the County Court*. This book will explain in more detail County Court procedure in this respect.

Exercise 4

1 In the case concerning Woodruffe Renovations and Peak Building Supplies Co. Ltd, name the plaintiff and defendant.
2 What is the main difference between a default summons and an ordinary summons?
3 Give three examples of the types of cases which might be heard by the County Court.

The High Court.   Although most civil disputes are settled without court action, of those that do come to court by far the majority are heard in the County Court. However some cases go to the High Court, particularly those involving large sums and also, as we have seen, cases involving defamation. The High Court has 26 'first tier' centres in various parts of England and Wales where almost any type of High Court case can be heard. Cases coming before the Chancery Division are heard in London or in certain centres in the North of England. The High Court is divided into three divisions and is staffed, as you would expect, by High Court judges who also have duties in the Crown Courts. The three divisions described below are presided over by the Lord Chief Justice (Queen's Bench Division); the Lord Chancellor (Chancery Division), (though in practice by the Vice Chancellor) and the President (Family Division).

1 The Queen's Bench Division (QBD) deals with cases such as failure to perform a contract, as where a pop group has failed to turn up for an engagement, causing losses of many thousands of pounds, or claims for damages in a serious road accident where injuries have resulted in permanent disability and the claim is high. The Queen's Bench Division also deals with defamation with which the County Court cannot deal.
2 The Chancery Division (Ch.D) deals with financial matters such as disputes relating to mortgages, bankruptcies and company liquidation.
3 The Family Division deals, as its name suggests, with family matters such as divorce, matrimonial property and settlements, custody of children and adoption.

A recent case heard by the Queens Bench Division which illustrates the sorts of cases heard there is *Jones and others* v. *Wright* (1991). This case concerned a disaster at a football stadium and the facts and decision of the court are as follows:

This case involved 16 people who suffered nervous shock and psychiatric disorders following a football match in which 95 spectators died. Some of these spectators were at the match; some watched on television. It was decided by the court that the defendant could not owe a duty to eye-witnesses who were not close to the victims, that is brothers, sisters, wives, husbands or parents, but did not extend to other relatives or friends.

Activity

Newspapers often carry reports on important civil cases and within the next few weeks you might find it helpful to look for those reports. *The Times* often has a special section for court business.

Exercise 5

Name the three divisions of the High Court and for each division name one sort of case which might come before it.

Appeals against decisions of the County Court and High Court

In a County Court case both plaintiff and defendant, if they feel that the decision reached was incorrect, may appeal to the Court of Appeal (Civil Division). This right of appeal to the Court of Appeal (Civil Division) is also available to plaintiff and defendant in a High Court case. A recent case which went to the Court of Appeal will help to explain how the appeal system works in civil cases.

Mr Eric Hyde, a man of 46, had been admitted to Ashton-under-Lyne Hospital suffering from acute pains in his neck and arm. Fearing that he might be suffering from cancer, Mr Hyde tried to commit suicide by jumping from a third-floor hospital window. His suicide bid failed but he was left totally paralysed. Mr Hyde sued the hospital board, Tameside Area Health Authority, claiming the hospital had been negligent in allowing him to attempt suicide. At the Queen's Bench Division Court he was awarded £200 000 damages. The Area Health Authority, in this case the defendant, decided to appeal. The appeal was heard in the Court of Appeal (Civil Division) in 1981.

Three judges hear the appeals in the Court of Appeal (Civil Division), looking through the judge's notes and the official shorthand writer's notes. In an appeal hearing the three judges never call witnesses, nor do they allow fresh evidence to be produced. The barristers representing both defendant and plaintiff may argue their cases. After considering the case the judges may reverse the decision of the court below, uphold it or change the amount of damages awarded. In some circumstances, though much less often, they may order a new trial to take place in the original court, that is County Court or High Court.

In this case, known as Tameside Area Health Authority v. Hyde, (1981) after carefully considering the evidence the judges reversed the decision of the Queen's Bench Division and stated that they did not feel the hospital had been negligent and no damages should be awarded to Mr Hyde.

This case illustrates the procedure which the Court of Appeal (Civil Division) uses in hearing appeals. It is interesting to note that in the description of the case above the defendant, Tameside Area Health Authority, is the first-named party. Usually, as we have learned, the plaintiff's name is mentioned first. Where, however, an appeal is heard the name of the party appealing is the first mentioned name. Clearly it was the health authority which was appealing against the £200 000 damages payment.

An example of a case coming to the Court of Appeal is *Morris* v. *Murray* (1991).

In this case there was an appeal against the decision of the Queen's Bench Division. The plaintiff had been severely injured in a light plane crash in which the pilot died. The plaintiff was claiming compensation from the dead man's inheritance and the QBD had awarded compensation though both men had, prior to the flight, been drinking heavily. The Appeal Court reversed the decision of the QBD, arguing that the plaintiff had willingly taken the risk.

We will be dealing with negligence, to which this case refers, in Chapter 11.

As with the criminal branch of law, the highest court is the House of Lords and where an important point of law is involved appeals may be allowed to the House of Lords from the Court of Appeal (Civil Division). The case is reheard usually before five Law Lords and majority decisions are given. Since 1969 it has been possible for cases to go directly to the House of Lords from the High Court by means of a device known as 'leapfrogging'. The device is so called because the Court of Appeal (Civil Division) is, as it were, 'leaped' over. There have, however, been few instances of 'leapfrogging' since 1969 when this process was allowed.

A good example of a case which went to the House of Lords is provided by *British Railways Board* v. *Herrington* (1972). This case involved a young boy of six who had got on to an electrified section of rail by entering through poorly maintained fences, and was injured. The boy's parents sued British Rail for negligence but British Rail claimed that since the boy was a trespasser they could not be held responsible. In coming to its decision the Lords stated that an owner of property could be responsible for injuries to trespassers, especially children, when insufficient attention had been paid to excluding or warning them. The British Railway Board's appeal failed and damages were paid to the boy. Three other recent cases provide good examples.

1.   *Hill* v. *Chief Constable of West Yorkshire* (1988)
We have already mentioned the case of Peter Sutcliffe, known as the 'Yorkshire Ripper'. The mother of one of his victims sued the police, claiming that they had been negligent in not apprehending Sutcliffe who subsequently murdered again. The House of Lords dismissed an appeal and in their judgment stated: 'as a matter of law and also of public policy an action could not be brought against the police in respect of their failure to identify and apprehend a criminal where that failure had resulted in him committing further offences'.

Decisions of the House of Lords are binding on other courts and similar cases will result in a similar decision.

2.   *Pearce* v. *Secretary of State for Defence* (1988)
The Court of Appeal sitting in 1987 had dismissed an appeal from Pearce who had suffered personal injuries when serving as a solider on Christmas Island where the UK Atomic Energy Authority were conducting nuclear tests. The Court of Appeal relied on the Crown Proceedings Act of 1947 in coming to this decision.
The House of Lords overturned this decision and stated that the Crown could not use this Act as a defence. Pearce's successful appeal may well open the door to further claims for damages from soldiers.

3.   *Alcock* v. *Chief Constable of South Yorkshire* (1991)
Another example of a case which went to the House of Lords related to a claim by friends and relatives of some of those injured in the Hillsborough football stadium disaster, who claimed they suffered nervous shock and psychiatric disorders after seeing scenes of the disaster televised. The claim was not successful and the judges decided that the defendants could not have foreseen this eventuality. This case relates to negligence.
Figure 1.3 shows the organisation of civil courts in England and Wales. You will see that the Magistrates' Court is mentioned here. This is because this court has some civil functions, particularly in respect of certain family matters and also actions related to non-payment of council tax to district authorities. Figure 1.4 is a simplified representation of the stages in civil disputes.

The European Court of Justice (ECJ)

The UK is a member of the European Union (formerly the European Community) and it is important to realise that, in addition to the various courts which we have dealt with, there is a court which sits in Luxembourg, known as the European Court of Justice, which deals with matters relating to the European Union. The court has 13 judges, one from each member of the community plus one other. Usually cases are heard by three to five judges. The following example may help to explain the sorts of matters dealt with by the court.

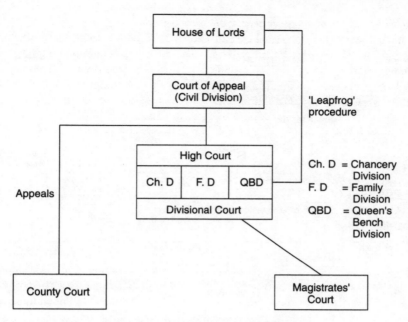

Figure 1.3   System of civil courts in England and Wales

Liam Duffy has qualified as an accountant in Cork in the Irish Republic and he applies for a post with a firm of accountants in London. He is called for interview and told that the firm does not fully recognise Irish qualifications. He is offered a post on a temporary basis until he passes an examination set by the Association of Chartered Accountants. Liam decides to take the case to the European Court of Justice. The court would examine the case in the light of articles 7, 52 and 59, which deal specifically with qualifications and their standing within any country within the European Union. It would also examine directive 89/48 which is concerned with mutual recognition of qualifications and came into effect in January 1991. It is likely that the court would find for Liam. However the ECJ has no powers of enforcement. If Liam's firm decide to insist on his taking this examination there is nothing that the ECJ could do. Liam would need to press his claim through an English court.

Another example of the sort of case coming before the ECJ is provided by an actual case, *Stoke on Trent City Council* v. *B & Q plc (1993).*

In this case B & Q plc had opened its store in Stoke-on-Trent on a Sunday and this was in contravention of section 47 of the Shops Act of 1950. Stoke City Council took B & Q to court and obtained an injunction which prevented B & Q opening. B & Q plc argued that this was against article 30 of the EEC

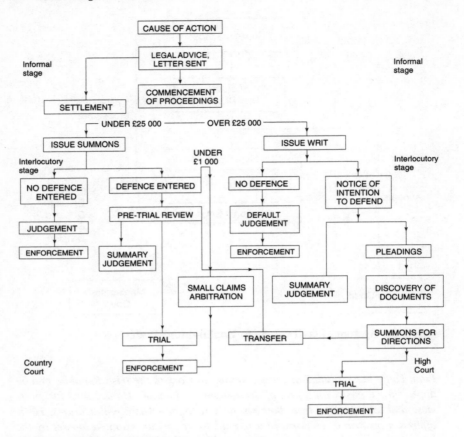

Figure 1.4   The stages in civil disputes

treaty. The case went to the House of Lords which sought a ruling from the ECJ. The European Court of Justice gave the view that section 47 of the Shops Act did not contravene article 30 and thus the injunction was not contrary to European Union law. The changes in the Sunday trading law which came into effect in 1994 will, of course, allow B & Q plc, like other large stores, to open for 6 hours on Sundays.

We will be looking at the effect of the UK's membership of the European Union on the law in detail in Chapter 3.

Tribunals and arbitration

Tribunals.   From time to time new laws are passed by Parliament and it is decided that actions arising from the new laws would be better heard by tribunals – groups of people who are specialised in this area of law. Examples of this are industrial tribunals *or* actions heard by Income Tax Commissioners. The following example may help to illustrate how such tribunals operate.

Bob Dash has been working for Industrial Chemicals plc for 6 years. Following a slight disagreement with one of the supervisors Bob is called in to see the Plant Manager and is dismissed without notice.

In this situation, Bob would have recourse to an industrial tribunal, which is usually comprised of a chairman who is a lawyer and two other people with specialised knowledge of the branch of the law. The tribunal can award compensation *or* order Bob to be reinstated.

In addition to unfair dismissal, industrial tribunals also deal with such matters as redundancy claims, discrimination on grounds of sex or race and other matters in respect of employment protection.

The procedure for industrial tribunals is usually much simpler than the courts and, for example, Bob could take a trade union officer to represent him rather than a solicitor.

The subject of unfair dismissal and other aspects of employment legislation will be dealt with more fully in Chapter 7.

Other tribunals which exist include: social security appeal tribunals, medical appeal tribunals, rent assessment committees, land tribunals, transport tribunals, VAT tribunals and the Criminal Injuries Compensation Board.

The government at any time can set up a tribunal of inquiry, as it did in 1981, following the Brixton riots. This high-powered tribunal met under Lord Scarman and it made various recommendations regarding, for example, police training.

Control over tribunals is exercised by the High Court. An example of the way this control operates is shown in *R.* v. *Criminal Injuries Compensation Board ex parte Thompstone* (1983).

In this case the applicant sought compensation for criminal injuries and the Board refused, having taken into account his history of violent conduct and his numerous convictions. The High Court held that the Board was right to take this into account and refused the applicant's claim.

Arbitration. It is possible for legal disputes to be settled outside courts by an independent body or person. Often businesses entering into legal contracts will insert a clause that, in the event of a dispute, settlement will be by an independent arbitrator. The following example may help.

North Derbyshire Haulage plc had entered into a contract with North West Civil Engineering plc for the building of a large new complex for storing and garaging. The contract was worth £2 million. There were a number of clauses in the contract related to stage payments, completion dates and so on, and the parties agreed that, in the event of a dispute, the matter would be arbitrated by William Marshalls (chartered surveyors) of Manchester.

In the contract the completion date for the building was agreed as being Friday 11 March 1994 and that, if the building was not ready by that date, North Derbyshire Haulage plc could claim compensation at a rate to be determined by the arbitrator.

In the event the building was completed six weeks late and the arbitrator (a chartered surveyor from William Marshalls) met the two parties concerned, listened to both sides and decided a rate of compensation to be paid. The contractor, North West Civil Engineering plc, paid North Derbyshire Haulage plc £23 600.

This sort of arrangement is very useful because it avoids the need for expensive and often lengthy legal action in the courts. An arbitrator can settle the matter quickly but, of course, if both parties have agreed to arbitration then the matter cannot then normally be raised in the courts.

As we have seen, there is an arbitration service available within the County Court.

Domestic Tribunal.   A number of professional associations, such as the Law Society and the British Medical Association, have disciplinary committees which have the power to expel a member, making it impossible for him/her to practise his/her profession. These are known as domestic tribunals.

> *Judith Black is a solicitor in a small country town. Her clients include a large number of elderly ladies who are wishing to sell their large houses to move to smaller houses. Judith persuades them to sell to her. She then resells them at a profit and pays her clients the agreed price. She has made over £1.5 m in this way over the past 3 years.*

This very unprofessional practice is discovered and she is asked to appear before the disciplinary committee of the Law Society. She is found guilty of unprofessional conduct and is struck off the Law Society register. This means she cannot practise as a solicitor.

Activity

You may often read examples of solicitors or doctors being dealt with in this way. Try to find an example from your newspaper over the next few months or so.

Exercise 6

Read the following examples and for each say (a) whether you think it comes within civil or criminal law, (b) which court, if any, is likely to hear the case.

1   Peakdale Engineering Ltd has been taken to court by one of its employees, John Duffy, who was injured while using a faulty piece of machinery. John is claiming compensation of £9500 for the injuries suffered.

2　A famous pop group, the Rocker Billies, have been sued by Music Productions Ltd for failing to turn up for a concert in which they were top of the bill. Ticket money had to be refunded to the audience.

3　David Lomax has been found guilty of causing death by dangerous driving and decides to appeal against the verdict.

4　Four months' imprisonment for a minor shoplifting offence is felt by Martha Jackson to be too severe and she decides to appeal against the sentence.

5　Paula Johnson, financial director of Fortrax Ltd, has been accused of fraud and embezzlement to the tune of many thousands of pounds.

6　Because of the great public and legal importance of the case, the Queen's Bench Division allow a libel case between Conway (Publishers) Co. Ltd and Edward Tagg, to go to the highest court in the land.

7　Jenny Wood has been refused promotion in her company on the grounds that the managing director prefers to see a man in a position of responsibility.

8　Hartley & Sons (Residential Homes for the Elderly) has made a claim against the Phoenix Assurance Co. The insurance company decides to use the arbitration clause in the agreement to settle the dispute.

9　Georg Füller, a qualified engineer from Lübeck, is refused employment in Oxford because he is German.

10　Norma Fairweather has been refused a disability allowance because the Department of Employment believes she is fit for work.

2 Sources of the law

1 Peter Howell and his wife Andrea have just returned from an afternoon's shopping and Andrea is anxious to try on a new pair of boots that she has purchased from a shoe shop, Town and Country Shoes Ltd. When she tries on the boots one of the heels comes apart from the boot. Andrea is very upset and Peter decides to go straight back to the shop with the boots to demand a refund of the £48.50 he had paid. The manager of the shop, though sympathetic, refuses to refund the money, but says he will have the boots repaired. Peter decides to take the shoe shop to court.

2 Pauline Beckwith is shopping in a large department store and while stepping from an escalator she trips over a metal plate which has become loose and sustains a fractured arm and serious internal injuries. Pauline is advised to take the department store to court to gain compensation for her injuries.

Look at these two situations and think for a moment what the legal position of Andrea Howell and Pauline Beckwith might be. Also try to think what might be the origin of the law in both respects. In both of these civil actions it will be necessary for the County Court judge in situation (1) and the High Court judge in situation (2) to find out what the law actually is.

In the first case, the judge would look at an Act of Parliament, the Sale of Goods Act 1979 (see below). This Act, which is the source of the law in this situation, will tell him that goods sold by shops must be of 'merchantable quality' and if they are not then shoppers are usually entitled to a full money refund. In the second case, the judge will have no Act of Parliament to guide him and he will look at previous similar cases and will reach his decision on the basis of decisions in these cases. It is previous cases which will be the source of law here. Pauline would be suing the department store for negligence and there have been many similar cases.

In these two situations we have discovered the two main sources of law in the English legal system:

1   Acts of Parliament, or in other words *legislation*.
2   Decided cases, or in other words *precedent*.

We sometimes hear the expression, 'he has set a precedent', which means that a person by his actions has provided an example for others to follow. This is exactly what judges may do when they make a decision in court: they may 'set a precedent' for other judges to follow. Of course, in making their decisions, they often follow the precedent set by other judges in previous decisions made in similar situations. It is because judges look at previous decisions that we sometimes refer to the system as 'case law'. Another expression used to describe the system is 'common law'. If there has not been a similar case then the judge will state the law as he sees it and say he is expressing the law of the 'common [ordinary] man', hence the term 'common law'.

A great deal of our law is based upon cases and this distinguishes our legal system from that in most other countries of the European Union. The only other country in the European Union which has a similar system to ours is the Irish Republic. Can you think why this is?

Sale of Goods Act 1979

1979 CHAPTER 54

An Act to consolidate the law relating to the sale of goods   [6th December 1979]

BE IT ENACTED by the Queen's most Excellent Majesty, by and with the advice and consent of the Lords Spiritual and Temporal, and Commons, in this present Parliament assembled, and by the authority of the same, as follows:—

PART I

CONTRACTS TO WHICH ACT APPLIES

1.—(1) This Act applies to contracts of sale of goods made on or after (but not to those made before) 1 January 1894. _{Contracts to which Act applies}

(2) In relation to contracts made on certain dates, this Act applies subject to the modification of certain of its sections as mentioned in Schedule 1 below.

(3) Any such modification is indicated in the section concerned by a reference to Schedule 1 below.

(4) Accordingly, where a section does not contain such a reference, this Act applies in relation to the contract concerned without such modification of the section.

PART II

FORMATION OF THE CONTRACT

Contract of sale

2.—(1) A contract of sale of goods is a contract by which the seller transfers or agrees to transfer the property in goods to the buyer for a money consideration, called the price. _{Contracts of sale.}

Of course, as we will see below, judges also use precedent when they inter-pret Acts of Parliament; that is, judges will look to see how an Act has been interpreted in a previous case.

2.1   Legislation

The word 'legislation' means a body of rules which have been formally made by Parliament and therefore have become an Act of Parliament and part of the law of the country.

Most legislation starts with the government. It usually has a majority in the House of Commons and can push through its legislation. Legislation starts as a Bill of Parliament which must be approved by both houses, the House of Commons and the House of Lords. Both houses receive plenty of opportunity to debate and discuss the Bill before voting upon it. Once it has passed both houses it must receive the signature of the Queen, which is known as the royal assent. After receiving the royal assent the Bill becomes an Act and becomes law.

Delegated legislation

This is where Parliament *delegates* to others, such as government ministers, powers to make the law. This delegation is always through an Act of Parliament.

Statutory Instruments   and Orders in Council. There are circumstances where an Act of Parliament is passed which sets out in general what is required and then gives power to a minister to make detailed regulations. These regulations are known as Statutory Instruments. The term 'Statutory Instrument' means really the instrument of a statute (in other words an Act of Parliament). These regulations have just the same force of law as legislation provided the minister acts within the power given to him by the Act of Parliament.

In a later chapter we will be considering the Health and Safety at Work Act 1974. This Act is an example of an instance where Parliament set out the new law in general terms and then gave considerable power to the minister, in this case the Secretary of State for Employment, to make the detailed regulation. On page 26 you can see an example of a Statutory Instrument based upon the Health and Safety at Work Act. This particular example, which came into force on 1 July 1982, deals with first-aid provision which must be made in places of employment. Failure to comply with this regulation may lead to criminal prosecution.

This Statutory Instrument is an example of delegated legislation. Delegated legislation is so called because Parliament has 'delegated' its power to make the law to a minister or Secretary of State. The delegated powers are contained in an Act of Parliament: in this particular case, the Health and Safety at Work Act.

There are some instances where ministers will issue Orders rather than regulations. These have the same force of law and provide another example of delegated legislation.

Bye-laws. Acts of Parliament will also delegate law-making power to local authorities. Local authorities use this power sometimes to make bye-laws. The Local Government Act 1974 gave this power to what are called district councils Each county has a number of district councils and they have limited law-making power.

An example of a bye-law is one made by Canterbury City council on 2 February 1979 and approved by the Secretary of State on 18 April 1979. This bye-law is concerned with the fouling of footpaths by dogs. A person in charge of a dog which fouls a pavement is liable on conviction to a fine not exceeding £50. Canterbury City council, by passing this bye-law, has created a new criminal offence in respect of that district. Similar bye-laws are in force in many districts in the country.

Regulations, rules and bye-laws of nationalised industries. There also are a number of examples where nationalised industries such as the British Railways Board has been given power by Acts of Parliament to make laws.

Delegated powers are only available through an Act of Parliament. Ministers, local authorities and nationalised boards can only act within the powers accorded them in the Act of Parliament. If they exceed these powers they are said to be acting *ultra vires* – 'beyond their powers' – and therefore illegally.

Statutory interpretation

When an Act of Parliament is passed or the minister issues a Statutory Instrument under delegated legislation, it is the courts which have the task of interpreting the law. This is known as statutory interpretation. When legislation is prepared to become a Bill and finally an Act of Parliament, the government employs specialists known as parliamentary drafts persons, to ensure that the Act is written in language which is clear and unambiguous so that courts can apply the literal meaning to the Act when they need to apply it in the courts.

Let us look at an example. The Sale of Goods Act 1979 is quite clear in setting out that goods sold must be of 'merchantable quality'. It is for the courts to interpret what this means. *Rogers* v. *Parish [Scarborough] Ltd* (1987) sums this up quite well.

In this case the plaintiff, Mr Rogers, had bought a new, expensive car which had considerable mechanical and bodywork faults. The court judged that, although driveable, it was not of merchantable quality and the garage was held to be in breach of contract. Mr Rogers recovered his money.

STATUTORY INSTRUMENTS

1981 No. 917

HEALTH AND SAFETY

The Health and Safety (First-Aid) Regulations 1981

Made - - - -	*29th June* 1981
Laid before Parliament	*9th July* 1981
Coming into Operation	*1st July* 1982

ARRANGEMENT OF REGULATIONS

1. Citation and commencement.
2. Interpretation.
3. Duty of employer to make provision for first-aid.
4. Duty of employer to inform his employees of the arrangements made in connection with first-aid.
5. Duty of self-employed person to provide first-aid equipment.
6. Power to grant exemptions.
7. Cases where these Regulations do not apply.
8. Application to miscellaneous mines.
9. Application offshore.
10. Repeals, revocations and modification.

Schedule 1.   Repeals.
Schedule 2.   Revocations.

The Secretary of State, in exercise of the powers conferred on him by sections 15(1), (2), (3)(a), (4)(a), (5)(b) and (9) and 49(1) and (4) of, and paragraphs 10 and 14 of Schedule 3 to, the Health and Safety at Work etc. Act 1974 ("the 1974 Act") and of all other powers enabling him in that behalf and for the purpose of giving effect without modifications to proposals submitted to him by the Health and Safety Commission under section 11(2)(d) of the 1974 Act after the carrying out by the said Commission of consultations in accordance with section 50(3) of that Act, hereby makes the following Regulations:—

Citation and commencement
  1. These Regulations may be cited as the Health and Safety (First-Aid) Regulations 1981 and shall come into operation on 1st July 1982.

Interpretation
  2.—In these Regulations, unless the context otherwise requires—
"first-aid" means—
      (a) in cases where a person will need help from a medical practitioner or nurse, treatment for the purpose of preserving life and minimising the consequences of injury and illness until such help is obtained, and

---

In this instance the court was applying one of the rules of statutory interpretation; that is, where the Act is interpreted as the term suggests 'literally'. Another case illustrates the 'literal rule' well.

In 1959 the government, anxious to deal with the problem posed by flick-knives, made it an offence under the Restriction of Offensive Weapons Act to 'offer for sale' flick-knives. The High Court, using the literal rule, held that a convicted shopkeeper had been wrongly convicted for he had merely 'invited his customers to make offers'. It is interesting to note that the Act was amended to close this loophole in 1961. The case referred to here is *Fisher* v. *Bell* (1961).

In *Wills* v. *Bowley* (1982), the House of Lords held that the term using abusive language to the 'annoyance of passengers' [as laid down in the Town Police Clauses Act 1847] had to be literally interpreted and that the prosecution had to prove this.

Courts generally would prefer to use the literal rule; however it can cause difficulties, as *Inland Revenue Commissioners* v. *Hinchy* (1960) shows.

The Income Tax Act 1952 stated that if a person should fail to declare income then the commissioners have the right to charge treble the whole tax due. Does this mean the whole tax due or the undisclosed sum? The Court of Appeal held that it was merely the undisclosed sum, but this was overruled in the House of Lords and it was held that the 'whole sum' means the whole sum according to the literal meaning. Because of this interpretation, the law relating to the taxing of undisclosed income was changed by section 4 of the Finance Act 1960.

However there are situations where the literal rule would lead to such an absurd situation that the courts will seek to avoid what is absurd by the application of what is known as the *golden rule*. A very old case, *R.* v. *Allen* (1871) illustrates this well. Section 57 of the Offences against the Person Act 1861 provided that 'whosoever, being married, shall marry another person during the life of the former husband or wife shall be guilty of bigamy'. A literal interpretation of this statute would mean than no one could ever commit bigamy since if one is already married he/she cannot marry again. In this case, therefore, the judge used the golden rule and allowed the act to be interpreted as 'going through a ceremony of marriage'.

There are a number of other rules of interpretation which judges may use in their interpretation of Acts of Parliament or other delegated legislation. Here we will consider just one, the 'mischief rule'. In certain circumstances where the literal rule leads to an absurdity and where the golden rule does not give in an appropriate result, the judge may examine the legislation to see what was the intention of Parliament in making this act. This rule goes back to 1584, in the Heydon's Case, when the judge asked four questions: (i) what was the common law before the making of the Act? (ii) what was the mischief or defect for which the common law did not provide? (iii) what remedy has Parliament resolved? (iv) what is the true reason for the remedy? The rule has thus been called the mischief rule.

A good example of the application of the mischief rule is in *Gardiner* v. *Sevenoaks RDC* (1950). In this case the Local Authority sought to prevent Gardiner storing film without fulfilling certain conditions as laid down in the Act. The Act used the expression 'premises' and Gardiner claimed that, since his film was stored in a cave, he was exempt since a cave was not premises. The court, applying the mischief rule, looked to see what was the intention of the Act and recognised that it sought to protect employees and others from fire risks. Sevenoaks RDC was successful.

Another case which illustrates the use of the mischief rule well is *Northam* v. *Barnet London Borough Council* (1978).

In this case a woman teacher was dismissed at age 61. She felt she had been unfairly dismissed and she took her case to the Industrial Tribunal. One of the rules of the Tribunal is that the right to bring a case under unfair dismissal ceases at retirement age, which is 60 for a women and 65 for a man. Ms Northam was refused permission to bring her case. On appeal Lord Denning applied the mischief rule and said that, because Barnet's own rule was 65 for both men and women, Ms Northam could take her case to the Tribunal. The judge was applying the mischief rule in saying the statutory retirement age was only applicable where no retirement age had been laid down.

Rules of interpretation tend to cancel each other out. By using one or other of these rules judges may be reformist, narrow or conservative. Pollock, in his *Essays in Jurisprudence and Ethics*, writes: 'English judges have often tended to interpret statutes on the theory that Parliament generally changes the law for the worse and that it is the business of the judges to keep the mischief of its interference within the narrowest possible bounds.' It has been said that judges are quite prepared to use their training to fill the gaps in criminal law to convict a guilty person of a crime but unwilling to fill the gaps or pronounce on welfare law which they are ill-equipped to pronounce upon.

There are thus three main rules governing statutory interpretation: (i) the literal rule, (ii) the golden rule and (iii) the mischief rule.

2.2   Precedent

This is a system where, once a court has stated the legal position in a given situation, the decision reached by this court will be followed in all similar cases. We have already learned the system of courts in England and Wales and the rule is that decisions of the higher courts will be binding on the lower courts. This means that the lower courts must follow the decision of the higher courts, so for example the decisions of the House of Lords will be binding on all other courts.

Since the decision of one court may be binding on other courts, that is, it will have to be followed, it is important that judges make it quite clear why they have come to a particular decision. If we look back for a moment to the situation relating to Pauline Beckwith, the judge, when giving his decision, assuming he agrees that Pauline has a good case, will say something like, 'I find for the plaintiff', but then he will go on to give his reasons for coming to the decision that the department store had been negligent. In his reason, known by the Latin phrase *ratio decidendi* (the reason for the decision), he will explain the legal principles he has applied in coming to his decision and he will no doubt refer to other similar previous cases.

It is, of course, possible that a situation arises where there have been no similar cases and there is no Act of Parliament to guide a judge. In this situation the judge must still come to a decision and give a reason. The decision must be followed by judges in similar cases in lower courts and may be followed by higher courts.

A good example of a case which has helped to make the law, particularly as it applies to negligence (see Chapter 11) , is the now famous *Donogue* v. *Stevenson* (1932). In this case the plaintiff suffered illness after drinking ginger beer containing the remnants of a decomposed snail. Lord Atkin, the judge in this case, established what has been called 'the neighbourhood principle' when he stated, 'who then in law is my neighbour? The answer seems to be persons who are so closely and directly affected by my act that I ought reasonably to have them in contemplation...'.

This *ratio decidendi* (reason for the decision) has been used in countless cases of negligence down to the present day and therefore used as a precedent. The court found for the plaintiff in this case – the manufacturer of the drink owed her a duty of care.

Judicial precedent

Because judges are said in such situations to be 'declaring' the law, this system of law is often known as 'judge-made law' or case law. Sometimes the expression 'common law' is used to indicate that the judge is declaring the law of ordinary (common) people.

This system of judicial precedent as it is called, is to be found in this country and in those countries which have developed from ours, such as the USA, Canada, The Irish Republic, New Zealand and Australia. It is quite different from systems in Europe, where the source of law is codes; that is, the rules are written and the task of the courts is to implement them. This explains why the status of judges in France and Germany, for example, is quite different from that of British judges.

You will often find examples of the use of case law by reference to cases published in *The Times* or *the Independent*. The two examples below show how the court has declared the law.

In the first, *Bostik Ltd* v. *Sellotape GB Ltd* (1994), the judge determined that Sellotape GB Ltd were not 'passing off', that is copying, a rival's product (see Chapter 12), in this case blue tac. As Mr Justice Blackburne put it, 'the crucial point of reference is at the point of sale'.

In the second case, *C[a minor]* v. *Director of Public Prosecutions* (1994), at the Court of Appeal, the judges laid down that it is no longer part of English law that a young person aged between 10 and 14 is incapable of committing a crime. This of course represents a quite important change in our law because before young people who had committed criminal offences could rely upon this defence.

2.3 European Community law

In addition to the two major sources of law described above, there is also an important source of law known as community law which results from our membership of the European Community or, as it is now called, the European Union.

In the next chapter we are going to consider this important area of law in more detail, but here we are merely looking at European Community law as a source. There are really three aspects of this source:

1 The various treaties establishing the community, for example, the Treaty of Paris (1951) and of Rome (1957), the Single European Market Treaty (1986) and the Treaty on European Union (1992), sometimes known as Maastricht. When the UK became a member of the European community in 1972, it agreed that its law would be amended automatically by the treaties, and of course the UK was a signatory to the 1986 and 1992 treaties. English courts must apply the various articles embodied in these treaties. The treaties are an important source of law.

2 Delegated (secondary) legislation, which is of course that legislation which is allowed by a primary act or, in the case of Europe, by the treaties. The Council of Ministers and the Commissioners can issue regulations, directives or decisions. Regulations and decisions are binding on the member states but directives require the national law-making body to make changes in the light of the directive.

3 The Court of Justice of the European Communities, sitting in Luxembourg and having representatives from each country, has the job of making a ruling which, whilst not binding on other courts, does carry a great deal of weight, and this makes it an important source.

Macarthys Ltd v. *Smith* (1981) illustrates the application of this source of law:

In this case Ms Smith claimed that she was doing a job for £50 per week whilst her male counterparts earned £60 for the same work. The Court of Appeal turned down her claim but referred the case to the Court of Justice. The court applied article 119 and held that she had a right to equal pay.

In future cases in this respect the English courts would have to take note of this ruling.

In 1988 the Community challenged in the European Court the right of the British government to grant zero VAT rating on certain goods to certain non-domestic users. In this case, *Commission of European Communities* v. *the United Kingdom* (1988), the court held that the British government's action was illegal.

Activity

Try to find as many examples as possible of cases coming before the Court of Justice of the European Communities. As mentioned before, *The Times* publishes details of these cases. To get used to the way they are published, look at the cases on page, 45 and 121.

2.4 Custom

Very occasionally a local custom is discovered and the courts, under stringent rules, may accept this. If, for example, someone could prove a right of way which had existed from 'time immemorial', then this could become a legal right of way. This source is now very rarely used. An example may assist an understanding of this.

Michael Moss has regularly taken a short cut between his house and a neighbour's which means his going across land owned by a Mr Cyril Rubeck. On one occasion he is surprised to see the pathway has been blocked. He seeks legal advice and is told that, if he can show the pathway existed from 'time immemorial', which means right back to the eleventh century, then the right of way would be legal. This is difficult to prove and so courts have taken the view that it is sufficient to show it existed within the living memory of the oldest resident of the area who has retained his/her faculties. Michael consults Olwyn Selby, who declares that it was a right of way when she was a child 79 years ago. The burden of proof lies now with Mr Rubeck who has to show that a right of way could not have existed since the eleventh century because, for example, historical records show the area was completely waterlogged for 50 years between 1715 and 1765.

Exercise 1

1 Name the three main sources of law.
2 Why is it important for a judge to give reasons for his decision in a court case?
3 Which court's decision is binding on all other courts?
4 Give three examples of persons/organisations that have been given delegated power to make law.

5   What three stages must a parliamentary bill pass before it becomes an Act of Parliament?
6   Name the three sources of European Community law.
7   In what main ways does the English system of law differ from that in France?
8   What would you have to prove to establish a custom as law?
9   Give the full name of the court which gives rulings on European Community law.

③ European Community law

Mention has already been made of the importance of European Community law as a source of law in the UK. Because of the increasing importance of the European Union in the affairs of this country and because it is likely to affect a good deal of business practice, we are going to devote a whole chapter to this topic. The following example may help you to understand this area of law.

Fairweather Business Supplies PLC of Faversham has appointed Mr Andrew Perkins as its agent for its Southern European market. The managing director, Peter Fairweather, is impressed by Andrew's energy and his knowledge of Italian and Spanish. Andrew negotiates a very good deal with a regular salary and a commission on all sales. After a very successful six months commencing 1 May 1994, Andrew's agency contract is terminated because he is suspected of working simultaneously for another company. Four weeks after the termination, Fairweather Business Supplies signs a valuable contract with two companies in NW Spain in Corunna and Santiago de Compostela. Andrew is angry because he believes he really won these contracts and is entitled to commission.

Before 1 January 1994, under English law, Andrew would have no entitlement to commission. However on that date the Commercial Agents (Council Directive) Regulations 1993 came into effect in the UK. Amongst other changes, this clearly states: 'A former agent is entitled to a commission even where the agency contract is terminated on transactions which are mainly attributed to his efforts during the period of the agency contract and which are entered into within a reasonable period after termination of that contract.' It would appear that, as a result of a regulation issued in Brussels and now effective in the UK, Andrew is entitled to some compensation.

Activity

In the last chapter the three sources of European Union law were mentioned. See if you can remember them.

They are, of course: (i) the various treaties establishing the union; (ii) the various directives, regulations and decisions; and (iii) rulings by the European Court of Justice (ECJ) in Luxembourg. Let us look at each of these elements in turn.

3.1   Treaties

A number of treaties brought the European Union into existence. They include the Treaty of Rome 1957, the Treaty of Accession 1972, which brought the UK into membership, the Single European Act 1986, which came into effect in 1992 and the Treaty on European Union 1993 known often as Maastricht. The various treaties establish four basic economic freedoms:

1   free movement of goods,
2   free movement of persons,
3   free movement of capital and
4   free movement of services.

The treaties also provide a general right to non-discrimination on grounds of nationality. In simple terms this means that citizens of any European Union country are entitled to all the rights of any country as though they were citizens of that country. The following case will, it is hoped, explain.

In Cowan v. Le Trésor (1989) ECR (European Court of Justice) Mr Cowan was attacked and robbed while in Paris on holiday. He applied for criminal injuries compensation. It was held that under an article of one of the treaties he was entitled to the same compensation as was available to a French person.

A number of countries, notwithstanding, it appears, their membership of the European Union, have tried to introduce measures to discriminate against non-nationals in employment. In one case, *Commission v. France (re French nurses)* (1984) it was held that the attempt to reserve appointments in French hospitals to French nationals was in contravention of article 48 of the 1957 treaty and, in a similar case, *Lawrie-Blum v. Land Baden-Württemburg* (1985) a German civil service training scheme could not be restricted to German nationals.

It is quite clear that, under the articles of treaties setting up the European Community/Union, every encouragement is given to ensure free movement of labour between the various countries of the Union, as the following example shows:

Gérard Croce is French and lives in Metz in eastern France. He is a qualified motor mechanic having studied at a local college (lycée professionnel) and gained his CAP (Certificat d'aptitude professionnelle) and BP (Baccalauréat professionnel) in motor vehicle technology. Gérard's mother is English and he speaks English well. He works for a large Peugeot garage on the outskirts of Metz. While Gérard's mother is visiting her mother in south London, she notices an advertisement for a senior mechanic at a large Peugeot garage in south-east London. She tells Gérard, who decides to apply. He receives a letter from the manager of the English company which owns the garage stating that it is company policy only to employ English staff and that the local job centre has issued a directive that local firms should not consider nationals from other European Union countries. It goes on to say that the company might be willing to employ him at a non-skilled rate of pay.

There is no doubt that this contravenes article 48 of the EEC treaty of 1957 which states that there must be no discrimination based on nationality between workers of the member states. This article has been implemented by regulation 1612/68 (see below). The situation regarding Gérard is clearly illegal and he could take his case to an industrial tribunal which would need to consider this aspect of European Community law.

There are many articles relating to the rights indicated above but we will just look at two more examples which relate to the right of establishment of a national of one member state in another, the right to provide services of a commercial nature and the recognition of qualifications.

1. Xavier Holingue has a business in Namur in Belgium. His company produces signs for display outside shops and on vehicles. He decides to open a branch in Kent and buys an empty property in Margate. He applies to the local authority for planning permission for the new use and for a grant and both applications are turned down because he is not English.

2. Mariá González is qualified in hotel management from a leading hotel school in Corunna in Spain. She has a diploma following a four year course incorporating one year in a top hotel in London. She now works in a hotel in Barcelona as a manager and applies for a post in Sussex as a section manager in a large hotel. Her application is rejected on the grounds that her qualifications do not match similar English qualifications. She is advised that she needs at least HCIMA, a UK professional qualification. She writes to the Hotel, Catering Institutional Management Association [HCIMA] to see if it will recognise her 4 year diploma course as an equivalent qualification. This application is turned down. Following this disappointment she decides to use a large inheritance to purchase her own hotel in Kent. She buys a country house and seeks permission to convert it into a country hotel. She applies for a business grant from the local authority and a loan from the bank and she is turned down in both applications because she is Spanish.

Articles 52 and 58 make it quite clear that there should be no additional restrictions on non-nationals setting up business in other member states. They should be afforded the same rights and privileges. Clearly for both Xavier and Mariá this has not been the case.

On the question of qualifications, directive 89/48 came into effect on 1 January 1991 which provided for mutual recognition of higher education diplomas across the European Community. These diplomas must be gained through three years' study or more.

A number of decided cases illustrate the points concerning right of establishment to provide services and to receive equal benefits. In *Commission* v.

Italy re Housing Aid (1986) it was held that the offer of cheap mortgages only to Italian nationals wishing to establish a business was in contravention of article 7.

— Activity —

The Times, in the section on decided cases, will give details of cases decided in the European Court of Justice. Try to build up a portfolio of such cases. This will help you to understand this very important branch of law.

3.2   Regulations, directives and decisions

In the previous chapter you read a little about regulations, directives and decisions. The treaties and their articles are the primary source of European Community law. They are really the equivalent of our Acts of Parliament. As we discovered in Chapter 2, just as UK Acts often delegate legislative power to ministers, so article 189 gives the Council of Ministers and the Commission the power to issue directives, regulations and decisions. These are perhaps rather confusingly referred to as 'acts' and are defined in article 189 as follows:

A regulation shall have general application. It shall be binding in its entirety and directly applicable to all member states. A directive shall be binding, as to the result to be achieved, upon each member state to which it is addressed but shall leave to the national authorities the choice of form and methods. A decision shall be binding in its entirety upon those to whom it is addressed. Recommendations and opinions shall have no binding force.

Regulations

These have the force of law immediately and in the UK a person can rely upon a regulation in a UK court. The following example may assist.

Eva Andersen has worked for 30 years in Copenhagen. She decides to settle in the UK and obtains a post as a laboratory technician. After a year ill health forces her to give up work and she claims invalidity benefit, which is refused. She takes the matter up with a DHSS tribunal. She relies on regulation 574/72 which is based upon article 4(1).

This regulation provides that, where a person has been insured under a general scheme which includes invalidity benefit in their own country, they are entitled to the range of benefits of the member country in which they are living. In our case this is the UK. Eva could claim this benefit and it is likely that she would be successful at the tribunal. This regulation applies to a range of social security benefits set out in article 4(1). Note that a regulation is secondary legislation and is dependent upon an article, in this case article 4(1). We also met the term 'regulation' in the example relating to Andrew Perkins at the beginning of this chapter.

Directives

These differ from regulations in that, although they are binding on member states, it is for the member state to choose the 'form and methods'. The directive will usually indicate the time limit for its implementation. The following example will explain:

> *Better Toys PLC is a producer of high-quality toys and prides itself on its safety record. Because of concern about standards in some branches of the industry, a directive 88/378 is passed. Under this directive all toys produced within the Community must bear a quality mark 'CE'. Better Toys refuses to comply, saying their standards have always been high.*

The directive does not become law in a member state until it is implemented and Better Toys could refuse to comply until implementation. In fact the directive was implemented on 1 January 1991, with the issue by the government of a statutory order Toy (Safety) Regulations. Better Toys now need to comply with the directive.

Decisions

These are binding immediately but differ from regulations in that they are addressed to individual member states, or individual persons or legal persons such as companies.

How regulations, directives and decisions are made

Regulations, directives and decisions are all examples of European Union secondary legislation, which means they can only be made on the basis of some primary legislation; that is, an article of one of the treaties. They are all examples of delegated legislation.

We have already explained the difference between regulations, directives and decisions. They are, however, made in the same way. Let us take one example, in this case a directive, and examine in more detail how it might be passed and become law.

> Directive 89/617 extends the use of metric units throughout the union and requires that imperial units, such as pounds, inches and gallons should be phased out by 1999. The only exceptions are the mile for road signs and the pint for beer and milk.

This directive comes from article 100A which seeks to harmonise consumer protection.

First, this directive is formulated in the European Commission. The Commission consists of 17 members, two from the UK, Spain, France, Germany and Italy, with one from each of the other countries. One of the Commission's tasks is to initiate community action.

Second, the proposal is sent to the Council of Ministers. The Council consists of one representative from each member state, the representative being the appropriate minister. In the case of this directive, for the UK it was the Secretary of State for Industry.

Third, the Council of Ministers send the proposal to the European Parliament for an opinion; this is known as the first reading. The European Parliament which sits at either Brussels or Strasbourg can recommend amendments. The Parliament is made up of 567 members and the UK has 87 along with Italy and France. Germany has 99 MEPs (Members of the European Parliament).

Fourth, the draft proposal is sent back to the Council, which votes on the measure, using one of three methods: simple majority (very rarely used), qualified majority or unanimity. The voting at present is weighted as shown below:

France	10
Germany	10
UK	10
Italy	10
Spain	8
Belgium	5
Greece	5
Netherlands	5
Portugal	5
Denmark	3
Ireland	3
Luxemburg	2
Total	**76**

A good deal of the voting for various proposals is by qualified majority (a minimum of 54) and therefore a proposal can be blocked with a vote of 23. Two of the large countries could block the vote with the aid of one of the smaller countries. Our directive (89/617) under 100A only required a qualified majority. In order to speed up harmonisation of consumer protection, it was agreed that directives under this measure would only need a qualified majority.

With the addition of four new members (Austria, Finland, Norway and Sweden) the blocking vote will be raised to 27, a change which was, as you may remember, very much opposed by the UK.

Our directive (89/617) obtained the required majority and then was sent back to Parliament for what is called the second reading. The European Parliament may (i) accept the proposal (this is by a majority of the votes cast); (ii) reject the proposal (by an absolute majority of the votes of 285 MEPs – for our directive this would have been 260 MEPs when the number of MEPs was 518; (iii) propose amendments by absolute majority. In our case the proposal was accepted by Parliament and become a directive. As you already know, directives need to be implemented by the national government.

Exercise 1

1 There are 3 ways on which the Council of Ministers may vote on legislation; what are they?
2 Who are the Commissioners from your country?
3 In what important way does the European Parliament differ from the UK Parliament?
4 What is secondary (delegated) legislation? Give an example from Europe and one from the UK.

3.3 Decisions of the Court of Justice of the European Communities

The European Court of Justice was set up to ensure that community law is enforced. The court consists of a judge from each member state; a full court consists of seven judges, though many actions are determined by three or five. The judges are assisted by advocates-general. The job of the court is to interpret European law, such as directives. Although the court is not bound by its own decisions, it increasingly follows them. Decisions of the court have become an important source of law.

Most of the court's decisions relate to interpretation of the law, though the court has powers to deal with proceedings brought by the Commission against a member state which appears to be in breach of its obligations under the treaty.

Activity

Try to find examples in daily newspapers of the operation of the various institutions of the European Union.

See if you can find references to changes in UK laws as a result of UK membership of the European Union.

In order to understand more fully the sorts of decisions made by the court, let us look at a recent decision. In *Commissioners of Customs and Excise* v. *Gerhart Schindler and another* (1994) the Queen's Bench Division had referred to the European Court of Justice a case which appeared to come under article 177 of the EEC treaty and specifically articles 30, 36, 56 and 59. Gerhart and Jorg Schindler were agents of a lottery known as Suddeutsche Klassenlotterie ('SKL') which resulted in funds for four German Länder or states. The two brothers tried to sell tickets to residents of the UK by sending letters of invitation from the Netherlands. The letters were confiscated by British customs officials as contravening the UK lottery laws.

The Schindlers argued that this was a basic interference with the freedom to provide service, one of the four basic freedoms under the various treaties. The European Court in Luxembourg ruled that the action of the customs authorities in the UK was not an unjustified interference and therefore confirmed the QBD decision.

It is important to note that the rulings of this court are *not binding* on our courts but have become *very persuasive*. It is most unlikely that an English court would depart from a ruling of the Court of Justice of the European Communities.

___ Exercise 2 _____

1   How many judges sit in a case before the European Court of Justice?
2   Write a short sentence on each of the following, explaining the differences: (a) regulations, (b) decisions, (c) directives.
3   How is a directive made?
4   Brigitta Reinartz is employed in London as a translator. She discovers her rate of pay is 75 per cent that of several of her colleagues and is told that the company employing her always pays higher rates to native employees. Does she have any redress?
5   Françoise Dubois has been in the UK for 20 months and during that time she has gained a BTEC GNVQ level 3 qualification, being offered a place at a British university to read accountancy. She applies for the same sort of grant payable to a British student but is refused because she is from Belgium. Does she have a case?
6   What are the four basic economic freedoms resulting from the European Union?

4 Procedure in civil actions and legal personnel

4.1 Procedure in civil actions

Most cases involving business are civil actions, relating to contract or tort such as negligence, and in this section we will be looking at two situations which result in civil action: in the first case in the High Court and in the second in the County Court.

High Court procedure

The following example *(Evans & Sons (Shopfitters)* v. *Tudor Rose Ltd)* may help to explain the procedure.

> *Margaret Owen runs a small chain of restaurants and tea shops known as Tudor Rose. She decides she wishes to refit one of her teashops to give it a sixteenth-century atmosphere. She employs a firm of shopfitters to do her work and a sum of £60 000 is agreed on completion. The work is completed on schedule and Evans & Sons submit their bill a week later. Margaret, however, is far from satisfied. Many of the fittings are not very realistic, several have already become loose and certain parts of the job are nothing like the original specification. The bill remains unpaid despite several reminders. Evans & Sons decide to take the matter to court.*
>
> *Mr Alex Evans goes to see his solicitor to discuss with him whether it is worth pursuing and following counsel's advice from Mr Walter Kitson, a local barrister, Alex is advised to proceed but only after sending a formal letter to Tudor Rose Ltd asking for settlement and advising the debtor that legal action was likely. Tudor Rose Ltd reply and say that they have no intention of paying for what they regard as poor workmanship. (Individuals cannot approach barristers directly but must do so through a solicitor.)*

We will assume that the case is heard in the High Court though, as we have seen in Chapter 2, even claims as high as £60 000 can be heard in the County Court. The district judge will decide where the case is to be heard and he will fix a date for the case to be heard. The district judge in what are called 'interlocutory or preliminary stages' will ensure that all the documents are in order. In some cases where one party is not willing to accept the truth of a statement by the other a sworn statement, an 'affidavit' is necessary.

The case is to be heard at the Queen's Bench Division and begins with a writ – a formal document setting out the nature of the claim. This is served on Tudor Rose Ltd, in this case by first-class post – though it could be served by hand. Tudor Rose Ltd by now have consulted their own solicitor and give notice that they have decided to defend.

Mr Kitson will now prepare a statement known as a Statement of Claim which sets out full details of what Evans & Sons are claiming and this is served upon Tudor Rose. Tudor Rose Ltd in turn prepare a defence which sets out in detail why they have not settled their bill. It really is an answer to the claims and must be made, otherwise the defendant is admitting the claim. In the defence, Tudor Rose will no doubt comment on the bad workmanship, the poor fittings and the fact that the work does not seem to come up to specification. On receipt of this, Mr Kitson will then prepare a defence in respect of Tudor Rose's counterclaim. We thus have three documents: (i) a Statement of Claim (prepared by the plaintiff or his lawyer), (ii) a Defence (prepared by the defendant or his lawyer), (iii) a Defence to the Counterclaim (prepared by the plaintiff or his lawyer).

These three documents are known as 'pleadings'.

The next stage in the matter is known as the discovery process, in which each party has to provide the other with any written evidence that either will produce in court. It so happens that Tudor Rose Ltd have a surveyor's report on the job done by Evans which supports some of Tudor Rose's complaints. This document must be seen by Evans & Sons before the hearing. The discovery process has not posed any particular problems and the two parties make a brief appearance in the court when final arrangements are made for the trial. The trial is fixed for Friday 26 August 1994 at 10 30 am. This in fact is ten months after the serving of the original writ.

The case is heard by Mr Justice Tennant and the procedure is as follows. The counsel for the plaintiff, Alex Evans, begins the case, setting out his client's claim: the unpaid amount of £60 000. The barrister, Mr Simon Beckwith, produces evidence, such as documents showing that the work has been completed and the invoices have been sent to the defendant. The defence counsel, Ms Lucy Nicholson, then presents her case, calling expert witnesses who say the workmanship was very poor. In both the plaintiff's case and the defendant's case, there are opportunities for cross-examination.

The two barristers are given an opportunity to present their cases. Mr Justice Tennant then sums up and gives his judgement, which is for the plaintiff. He awards costs against Tudor Rose Ltd but accepts the fact that some of the work was shoddy and accepts part of Tudor Rose's counter-claim. The precise settlement is as follows:

To Evans (Shopfitters) & Sons	£45 000
Costs	£ 8 500
Total	**£53 500**
To Tudor Rose Ltd	£15 000
Costs	£ 2 850
Total	**£17 850**

Evans & Sons have gained £35 650 (£53 500–£17 850). They might have done better to deal with Tudor Rose's complaints, which could have cost less than £17 850.

As we can see, Tudor Rose owes Evans & Sons £35 650, but it is one thing to get the judgment – it is quite another to enforce it. Let us look for a moment at the various ways in which Evans & Sons might enforce their judgment.

1   Evans could apply for a writ of *Fieri facias (fi.fa)* which means that Tudor Rose's goods could be seized and sold and the proceeds used to help pay off the debt.
2   Evans could apply for a *charging order*, which means that a charge could be placed upon Tudor Rose's land or other assets such as shares that the owner might have in a company. If the money owing is not paid, Margaret Owen might find that her own house could be sold. (We must assume here that Tudor Rose is wholly owned by Margaret Owen.)
3   The plaintiff could also apply for a *garnishee order*, which means that any money owed to the defendant can be paid directly to to the plaintiff. In this case the plaintiff Evans can obtain money directly from Margaret Owen's bank account.
4   The High Court could appoint a *receiver*, who could seize any rents payable to the defendant. So, if Margaret Owen had leased out one of her restaurants, the rent could be paid directly to the court to pay Evans.
5   Evans could apply for a *writ of sequestration*, though this is unlikely in a relatively small claim such as this. However in this case the court would seize all the defendant's property and manage it until the full debt is paid. You may have read of such writs being used to seize trade union property following a judgment against the union.
6   Evans could apply for a bankruptcy order against Margaret Owen. The procedure relating to bankruptcy is explained fully in Chapter 16.

We should also remember that a High Court judgment can also be enforced in the County Court. This can be very useful since the County Court can order payment by instalments, which often is a more practical method of paying off a debt.

You will remember that this case was heard in the Queen's Bench Division of the High Court. This court deals particularly with cases involving tort or contract. These subjects will be dealt with in Chapters 5, 6, 11 and 12. Our case was concerned with contract and you will find on page 45 an extract from an actual case, *McCullagh* v. *Lane Fox and Partners* (1994) in which an estate agent was held to have made negligent mis-statements relating to a very expensive property, which the plaintiffs wished to buy. This case was concerned with the tort of negligence.

___ **Exercise 1** _____

1   Name the three documents known as 'pleadings' in High Court actions.
2   In addition to the Queen's Bench Division, name the divisions of the High Court.

3   Name the ways in which a plaintiff may enforce a judgement of the High Court.
4   Explain the 'discovery process'.
5   What is a counter-claim?

Activity

An interesting case, *McCullagh* v. *Lane Fox and Partners* (1994) is shown opposite. Read it carefully and try to work out why the judge, Mr Justice Colman, reached a different decision from the judge in a similar case, *James McNaughton Paper Group* v. *Hicks Anderson & Co* (1991). The case is about negligent mis-statements made by professional organisations, in this case an estate agent.

County Court procedure

The following example may help to explain the county court procedure.

> *Terry and Norma Featherstone own a small but very good hotel, known as the Riviera Hotel, in North Cornwall. They receive a call from Stuart Dexter, a civil engineer with his own business. He has just won a contract with a company just outside Plymouth. He asks if he could have a room with full board for a period of five weeks. The Featherstones give him a special rate of £300 per week. When he arrives he asks if he could pay at the end of the period. Norma and Terry agree. At the end of his stay, the hotel send him an invoice which comes to £1650. [5 weeks at £300 plus other items such as drinks etc which come to £150]. Despite a number of reminders and a solicitor's letter, the bill remains unpaid eight weeks after Stuart's departure. The Featherstones are advised by their solicitor to take court action.*

The solicitor, Ms Janette Staton, completes a form N1 in which both the plaintiff and the defendant are named, together with the claim being made, with a brief description of it. In our example the Featherstones would indicate the dates when Mr Dexter stayed and the amount (£1650). The County Court charges a fee of £10 and this can be included in the claim.

The court then serves the summons and Mr Dexter has an opportunity to say why he has not paid. He is obliged to respond to this summons within 14 days or judgment will be entered against him. In this example, Mr Dexter claims he paid for three weeks and therefore only £750 is owed. He then completes N9B. This is disputed by the plaintiffs and the case goes to court.

This case cannot be heard in the less formal small claims court since the sum claimed is more than the £1000 limit. The parties could agree to arbitration but they decide to take the case to the full court. The district judge will then indicate to the two parties what information they must provide to each other. The district

Estate agent owes duty of care

McCullagh v Lane Fox and Partners Ltd

Before Mr Justice Colman

[Judgment January 14]

A vendor's estate agent owed a duty of care to a purchaser of property in respect of negligent mis-statements upon which the purchaser relied in entering into the purchase contract.

Mr Justice Coiman so held in the Queen's Bench Division when finding that the plaintiff, Edward McKim Lyell McCullagh, had on the evidence not established that any loss had been suffered and dismissing his action for negligent mis-statement against the defendants, Lane Fox and Partners Ltd.

Mr Philip Havers for Mr McCullagh; Mr Richard Lynagh for Lane Fox.

MR JUSTICE COLMAN said that the plaintiff bought the residential property on May 14, 1990. He and his wife saw the house advertised as having grounds of nearly an acre and viewed it briefly with Mr Andrew Scott, an employee of the defendant, on Saturday May 12.

They were impressed particularly by the size of the plot, described in the agent's particulars as 0.91acres. That was incorrect, the result of a miscalculation. It was in fact 0.48 acres.

The judge found that Mr Scott had said during the purchasers' viewing that the size was 0.92 acres.

The plaintiff, told of an offer already accepted of £810 000, made a counter offer of £875 000 and indicated his readiness to exchange contracts on the Monday. The agent's particulars contained a disclaimer as to factual representations and the need of intending purchasers to satisfy themselves as to correctness.

To succeed the plaintiff had to establish that the misrepresentation caused him to enter into the contract.

It was unnecessary for the tort of deceit that the misrepresentation should be the only consideration which caused him to act as he did but it was enough that his judgment was influenced.

The same analysis of the requisite causal linkage applied equally in negligent misrepresentation cases such as the present.

His Lordship found that the plaintiff's understanding of the size of the area originated with the advertisement. That belief was clearly confirmed and fortified by Mr Scott's oral statement. It followed that that oral misrepresentation was material and influenced the plaintiff's decision to purchase. Accordingly, he had established the necessary causal connection between the oral representation and the decision to purchase.

Negligent mis-statement required three elements before liability could arise: (i) foreseeability of damage, (ii) proximity or neighbourhood of the parties and (iii) whether it was fair, just and reasonable that the law should impose a duty of the scope contended for.

In the instant case, the ingredients of proximity and of the imposition of the duty being just and reasonable had to rest primarily, if not exclusively, on the purpose for which the representation was made; that it was made in a professional capacity to a particular potential purchaser in relation to a particular and identifiable transaction and that, to the knowledge of the representor, it was highly likely it would be relied upon by that purchaser in entering into that transaction without making his own investigation.

The course adopted by the plaintiff of exchanging before survey, although not unknown, was unusual. He did so in the knowledge of the clause in the contract by which he acknowledged that he did not do so in reliance on any statement or representation save through solicitors' enquiries. He therefore knowingly took the risk that if the estate agents had miscalculated the area he would have no recourse against the vendors.

It was that decision that put the defendant in the unusual position of being relied upon as the party solely responsible for the accuracy of the information on the basis of which

the purchaser chose to commit himself to the cotract.

In *James McNaughton Paper Group v Hicks Anderson & Co* ([1991] 2 QB 113, 126) Lord Justice Neill had said it was necessary to consider whether the plaintiff did use or should have used his own judgment or sought independent advice.

Mr Scott knew prior to exchange that there would be no independent survey and in his Lordship's judgment it was material to what was just and reasonable that it was the plaintiff's decision to adopt that unusual course which invested the representation by Mr Scott with a causal effect which it would not normally have had.

His statement confirming the area of the plot then became a matter which it would be obvious to anybody would be one of the facts which, without further investigation, a purchaser would have in mind so that it influenced his decision when he entered the contract.

It was when Mr Scott appreciated that there was to be no independent survey that the question of duty and, in particular, proximity and what was just and reasonable, had to be tested.

His Lordship concluded that at that time there did exist the neighbour or proximity relationship between Mr Scott and the plaintiff which was a necessary ingredient of the duty of care.

His Lordship was unable to accept Mr Lynagh's submission that the disclaimer of liability on the particulars of sale protected the defendant in the circumstances of an oral misrepresentation by Mr Scott. The disclaimer related exclusively to the contents of the particulars of sale.

Having considered evidence on property values in the district, his Lordship found that it was not established that the price the purchaser paid was more than the true value of the property and, accordingly, he had failed to prove any loss. It followed that he had no cause of action and his claim was dismissed.

Solicitors: Mishcon De Reya; Cameron Markby Hewitt.

judge attempts to have all matters relating to the case resolved before the hearing. These stages are known as 'preliminary or interlocutory proceedings'. A date for the hearing is then fixed and, because the amount is fairly small, the district judge rather than the County Court judge will hear it.

The proceedings in the court will be similar to those described in the High Court, though it is likely that the parties would use solicitors rather than barristers. Mr and Mrs Featherstone use Ms Staton, but Mr Dexter decides to conduct his own defence. In the event, Mr Dexter is unable to prove he has paid and the judge decides to find in favour of the plaintiffs and they are also awarded costs, which amount to £256. Mr Dexter is obliged to pay £1906 to the plaintiffs.

The chart on page 47 shows very clearly the procedure up to the court or arbitration hearing. It is important to remember that for claims of less than £1000 the much more informal arbitration system will be used. It will be the district judge who will attend the arbitration proceedings. This procedure is being increasingly used since its introduction in 1973. No costs are awarded in this type of arbitration, often referred to as the 'small claims' court, and therefore legal representation is discouraged.

Activity

Go to your nearest County Court and obtain the various leaflets available which explain the work of these courts. Try to obtain in particular the leaflets entitled 'A guide to small businesses to debt recovery through a county court'.

Look at the chart, which is obtainable from a County Court. The chart sets out the way in which a summons for a debt might be dealt with. It shows the various actions of a defendant and the way in which the plaintiff might respond.

Let us return to our case and see how our plaintiffs (known also as creditors) might be able to recover their money, because it is one thing to get a judgment and it may be another to get the money. If Stuart Dexter has no money or no assets to sell then no method of enforcement will succeed.

If the judgment debt is not paid within six weeks, Stuart's name is registered with the Registry Trust Ltd. It is possible, for a fee, to search the register to see if there are judgements registered against someone. When considering giving credit, businesses will often make a search of this register.

Stuart Dexter could pay the amount or agree to pay by instalments. If he does not, the creditors must look for other means of enforcement. Before deciding on the method of enforcement the Featherstones could ask the court to conduct an oral examination. In this case the defendant (debtor) is ordered to attend court and questions are asked about his/her ability to pay. The plaintiff/creditor or the court on his/her behalf can conduct the examination. The sort of questions which might be asked are set out below. This list is taken from a County Court

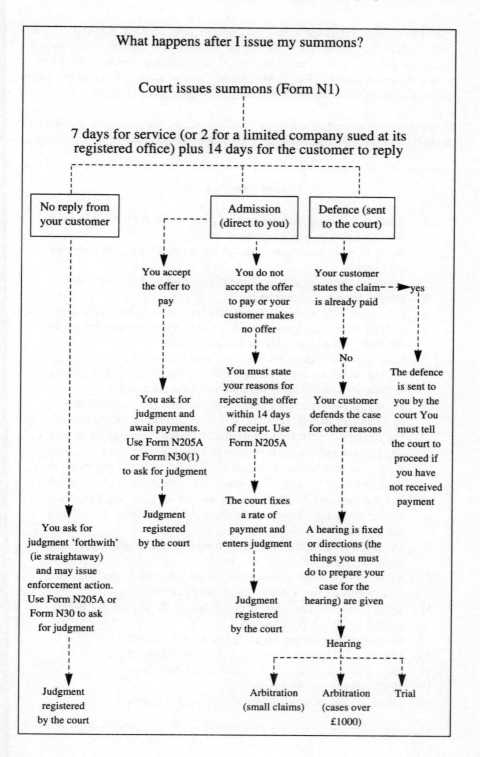

What happens after I issue my summons?

Court issues summons (Form N1)

7 days for service (or 2 for a limited company sued at its registered office) plus 14 days for the customer to reply

No reply from your customer   **Admission (direct to you)**   **Defence (sent to the court)**

You accept the offer to pay

You do not accept the offer to pay or your customer makes no offer

Your customer states the claim – – ▶ yes is already paid

No

You ask for judgment and await payments. Use Form N205A or Form N30(1) to ask for judgment

You must state your reasons for rejecting the offer within 14 days of receipt. Use Form N205A

Your customer defends the case for other reasons

The defence is sent to you by the court You must tell the court to proceed if you have not received payment

You ask for judgment 'forthwith' (ie straightaway) and may issue enforcement action. Use Form N205A or Form N30 to ask for judgment

Judgment registered by the court

The court fixes a rate of payment and enters judgment

A hearing is fixed or directions (the things you must do to prepare your case for the hearing) are given

Judgment registered by the court

Judgment registered by the court

Hearing

Judgment registered by the court

Arbitration (small claims)

Arbitration (cases over £1000)

Trial

publication, also obtainable from your County Court, entitled 'Enforcing Money judgments in the County Court'. It may be necessary for a plaintiff to supply the defendant (debtor) with 'conduct money', that is sufficient funds to allow him to attend the examination. Thus if Mr Dexter lived in Kent and the examination was in Cornwall, he could claim he had insufficient funds to attend.

If the debtor is a limited company then a director, the company secretary or another official will be asked to attend. Remember that, if it is a limited

---

Type of questions asked

1   What is the name and address of your employer? What is your works number or pay reference number?
2   What is your basic pay? Have you brought pay slips or pay envelopes?
3   What is your average take-home pay, including any overtime?
4   Do you have any other earnings?
5   Does your wife/husband have a job? How much does she/he earn?
6   Do you have a bank account? If so, state the name and branch of the bank. What is the balance in your account?
7   Have you a Building Society, National Savings Bank or Trustee Savings Bank or any other savings account? What is the balance in each account? What is the number of the account?
8   Have you any Premium Bonds? Do you have any stocks or shares, for example, British Telecom or British Gas shares? How many?
9   Do you rent or own your house/flat? (If rented) How much do you pay for rent and rates? (If owned) Is it held in your name or jointly with your wife/husband? When did you buy it? Is it registered at the Land Registry and, if so, what is the title number? How much did you pay for it? What is the present value? How much is owing on the mortgage? What are the monthly repayments? How much are the rates?
10   Do you own a motor vehicle? What is the make and registration number? How much did you pay for it and what is its present value? Is it on hire-purchase or credit sale? How much are the repayments and how much is still to be paid off?
11   Who owns the furniture in your home? Is any of it on hire-purchase? (If so) Which items?
12   Do you own any other property? (If so) Give details.
13   Does anyone owe you any money? (If so) Give details.
14   Have you any children? (If so) What are their ages?
15   What other debts do you owe?
16   Have you any other court orders? (If so) Give details.

company, it is only against the assets of the company that judgment can be enforced, not against the private assets of the directors. This is what 'limited' means; we will return to this in Chapter 16.

In the case of a partnership, it is possible to examine the partners whose liability is not limited. There are a number of ways in which Mr and Mrs Featherstone might enforce their judgment and these are set below.

1 *Warrant of execution*: this is an order directed to the bailiff to seize and sell sufficient of the debtor's goods to pay off the debt, which in our case is £1906. In the case of a business, the bailiff may enter the business premises and place a 'lien' as it is called, on certain assets with a notice to the debtor that, unless the debt is paid in full within a certain period, those goods will be sold.
2 *Attachment of earnings*: this is an order which requires the debtor's employer to deduct a sum of money on each payday from the debtor's wages. In our case this would not be suitable since Stuart Dexter is self-employed, having his own business.
3 *Garnishee*: this is an order directed to anyone who owes the debtor money requiring him/her to pay it into the court. This method is often used where the debtor has a bank account and the order can be used to tap into this asset.
4 *Charging order*: this is an order which makes it impossible for the debtor to sell his land or securities, that is bonds, stocks or shares, without paying off his debt. In some cases the court can order that securities are sold, though it is unlikely that the court would force the sale of the family house.
5 *Receivership*: the business can be declared bankrupt and a receiver appointed. For small debts this expensive method is unlikely to be used.

In our case, Mr and Mrs Featherstone use the warrant system and some of Stuart's assets are seized, including an expensive computer, printer and copier. From the proceeds therefrom his debt is paid off.

Exercise 2

1 Under what circumstances is an arbitration procedure used in the County Court?
2 What cases may a district judge try?
3 Why is receivership not often used to enforce County Court judgments?
4 How is 'attachment of earnings' organised?
5 A company director may lose his house to meet a County Court judgment: true or false?

4.2 Personnel of the law

In any legal situation it is likely that one will encounter different sorts of persons involved in the law. In this book we have already mentioned magistrates, solicitors, barristers and judges. In this section we will be looking at the work of various types of persons involved in law. In order to understand this topic, let us examine for a moment a number of different situations.

> *1. Novelty Shops Ltd is a chain of shops in the South of England. One of their lines is a range of Russian dolls imported from Russia, as is stated on the box containing the sets. A customer discovers that the dolls are made by a company in East Sussex and he makes a complaint to his local trading standards office. Following an investigation, Novelty Shops Ltd is prosecuted under the Trade Descriptions Act 1973.*
>
> *Novelty Shops Ltd is summoned to appear in the Magistrates' Court, where the managing director faces three magistrates. The company is found guilty of the offence of falsely describing goods and fined.*

In this case the personnel in the court were three magistrates and a magistrates' clerk.

Magistrates

Magistrates are normally 'lay', that is not legally qualified. They are appointed by the Lord Chancellor on the advice of a local advisory group. They will not be appointed if aged over 60 and those convicted of criminal offences will also be disqualified from appointment. They should normally be available for 35 sittings each year, for which they receive only out-of-pocket expenses. Although the local advisory committees must seek to make magistrates as truly representative of all sections of the community as possible, and representing a range of opinions, it is still difficult to get wage-earners onto the 'bench', as it is called. Sums for loss of earnings are payable, but these are not generous and employers may not be very willing to allow 35 days off each year in addition to holidays.

Magistrates are not, except in some cases, legally qualified, but they must attend a course in the essentials of procedure and sentencing and those appointed since 1980 must attend refresher courses. From 1994, only magistrates who have attended refresher courses can become chairpersons (magistrates sit in threes at the court and there will always be a chairperson). There is no doubt that there is a greater emphasis on training than ever before but the commitment to 35 days' court work plus training puts heavy pressure on these important 'amateurs'.

It is evident that magistrates are very important in our system when it is realised that 95 per cent of criminal cases begin and end in the Magistrates' Court.

Court clerk

Magistrates will have the services of a court clerk who is the principal administrative officer of the court. Deputy clerks may also be appointed. One of the clerk's functions is to advise the magistrates, but under no circumstances must they usurp (interfere with) or appear to usurp the role of the magistrates.

Stipendiary magistrates

There are in the Inner London area and in some other large cities paid magistrates known as 'stipendiary magistrates'. These are legally qualified, either barristers or solicitors. They are appointed usually in those areas where the volume of court business is considerable and it might therefore be difficult to obtain the services of sufficient numbers of 'lay' magistrates.

2. Sir Dennis Hayes is an important local businessman who has just become chairman of the county council. He finds an article in the local paper which suggests that he has seriously mixed up his business interests and his county council work and that several of his companies have gained valuable contracts from the county. Sir Dennis is incensed by this attack on his reputation and seeks legal advice. He sees his solicitor, Ms Christine Saunders who indicates that he has a good case in defamation. Ms Saunders decides to seek 'counsel', that is she consults a barrister , Ms Gladys Rumley, who endorses her view. Sir Dennis takes court action and the case is heard, as are all defamation cases, in the Queen's Bench Division of the High Court.

Barristers and solicitors

As we have seen, Sir Dennis consults a solicitor and she refers the case to a barrister. In the English system, unlike most other countries, there are two types of lawyer, solicitor and barrister. Barristers are mainly concerned with court work – arguing cases on behalf of their clients – whereas solicitors are the 'general practitioners' of the law. They give advice, do legal work in connection with house and property transfer and some limited court work. They also brief barristers, as we have seen in our example. Table 4.1 gives the main differences between the two professions. The figures given are approximate, but they do provide a general picture of the situation.

There have been discussions from time to time concerning merging the two professions and changes have allowed solicitors an extended right of audience in courts. It does not seem likely that there will be a fusion, though the Lord Chancellor's committee on education and training has suggested that there should be a merging of the education and training of barristers and solicitors.

You may have noticed that some barristers carry the letters 'QC' after their names. This means 'Queen's Counsel' and it is given by the Queen on the advice of the Lord Chancellor. Barristers may make an application for this and 20–30 per cent of applications are successful. There are therefore two types of barristers, 'QC' and junior barristers. The QC wears a silk gown, hence the phrase 'taking the silk'. High Court judges will almost always come from the ranks of QCs.

TABLE 4.1   Solicitors and barristers in England and Wales

	Barristers	*Solicitors*
Number in practice	6000 (22 per cent women) including 535 QCs.	57 000 (23 per cent women)
Mode of organisation	Independent practitioners practising from sets of chambers.	Sole practitioners or partnerships. Can be employed often by industry or local authorities.
Professional body	Bar Council.	The Law Society.
Education and training	Usually a law degree followed by a 1 year course at one of the Inns with examinations of the Council for Legal Education. 1 year pupillage.	Usually a law degree followed by a 1 year course at a university or Law Society law school with a Law Society examination. 2 years articles.
Professional discipline	Professional Conduct Committee.	Professional Standards Directorate. The Lay Observer (the solicitors' ombudsman) also investigates complaints.
Relationship with client	Through solicitor; cab-rank principle. Cannot sue for fees.	Contractual.
Professional liability	No liability in negligence in respect of advocacy in court (*Rondel* v. *Worsley* (1969) 1 AC 191). May be liable in negligence in respect of work outside court (*Saif Ali* v. *Sydney Mitchell & Co* (1980) AC 198).	Liable in contract and tort to clients (*Midland Bank Trust Co Ltd* v. *Hett, Stubbs & Kemp* (1979) Ch 384) though tort liability doubted in *Lee* v. *Thompson* (1989) 40 EG 89. See also *Gran Gelato* v. *Richcliff* (1992) 1 All ER 865. May be liable to others affected by their negligent professional actions (*Ross* v. *Caunter* (1980)
Professional etiquette	No advertising. Wig and gown in court. Must join an Inn of Court.	Limited advertising (Publicity Code 1987). Gown in courts (except Magistrates' Court) but no wig.
Number of firms	Barristers work in what are called chambers [firms] there are 378	There are 10 243 firms of solicitors

It is beyond the scope of this book to give a detailed account of the various judges and other judicial officers who are part of our legal system. Table 4.2 summarises the main position.

One of the features of the judicial system which is often regarded as very important is the independence of the judges from political control. However there has recently been some concern that this independence is being reduced. The Lord Chancellor is an important figure in our legal system and he is a political appointment. He is a member of the government. Below is a summary of an article written by a member of parliament who was obviously concerned about the interference of the Lord Chancellor in court matters. The MP, as you can see, is worried about the position of the Lord Chancellor, who is an unelected member of cabinet, Speaker of the House of Lords and Head of the Judiciary – the court system. In the article the MP describes how the Lord Chancellor tried to pressurise a High Court judge into a course of action in order, it seems, to 'save the Treasury money'.

Activity

Read the article and see if you can identify the concern of the MP in respect of judges' independence.

TABLE 4.2   **The judges, law officers and lay personnel**

Judges	*Court*
Lords of Appeal in Ordinary	House of Lords
Lord Justices of Appeal, Lord Chief Justice	Courts of Appeal (Criminal and Civil)
High Court Judges	High Court and Circuit (Crown Court)
Circuit Judges	Circuit and County Court
Deputy Judges	County Court
Political law officers	*Functions*
Lord Chancellor	Speaker of House of Lords Head of Court System
Attorney-General Solicitor-General	Law Officers of the Crown
Director of Public Prosecutions	Head of the Crown Prosecution Service
Lay Personnel	*Functions*
Magistrates	Appointed by the Chancellor on local advice Are judges in Magistrates' Court/assisted by a clerk
Jury	Juries are necessary in certain criminal cases and a very limited number of civil cases
	Jury service is a legal obligation for most UK citizens

A LAW UNTO HIMSELF?

Tomorrow Lord Mackay of Clashfern will face an unprecedented debate in the Lords over his suggestion that Mr Justice Wood should 'consider his position' if he did not toe the line on appeals procedures. Lord Mackay maintains he did not intend to invite the judge to resign; nor had he done so. The comment provoked a furore among some senior judges...

As a parliamentarian, I have the greatest respect for the principle of judicial independence – it is not for politicians to interfere with the work of judges.

Yet I have found myself asking questions of the head of the judiciary, the Lord Chancellor, Lord Mackay of Clashfern, on a matter which I think raises extremely important questions about his role in our constitution.

The Lord Chancellor is in a unique position in having a foothold in the executive, legislature and judiciary. He is an unelected member of the Cabinet, 'Speaker' of the House of Lords, and head of the judiciary. Yet to which is he ultimately responsible? And to whom is he accountable?

Lord Mackay has been accused of attempting to pressure a High Court judge, Mr Justice Wood, to change his view of the law in order to save money for the Treasury.

I raised the issue in Parliament and, with courtesy, Lord Mackay invited me to discuss the matter with him, and then agreed to release his correspondence with Mr Justice Wood. The contents reveal the conflict of loyalties that inevitably face a Lord Chancellor.

In December 1992, Lord Mackay wrote to Mr Justice Wood, who was President of the Employment Appeal Tribunal, expressing concern about the growing backlog of cases face by the tribunal. He urged Mr Justice Wood to make use of a procedural device, known as rule 3, to dismiss without any hearing cases in which there was no point of law shown in the notice of appeal. He added that he was 'unwilling' to spend extra money on setting up additional courts.

Mr Justice Wood, who had served for 16 years on the High Court bench, explained that there were cases in which the judge could be left uncertain as to whether the appellant's grounds of appeal were on a matter of law or not. In such cases, he argued, it was necessary, in order to do justice, to hold a preliminary hearing.

The Lord Chancellor's reply in March 1993 expressed 'disappointment' at Mr Justice Wood's attitude and continued: 'I did not seek further discussion of rule 3 but had sought to make it clear to you that I was not prepared to accept preliminary hearings being held where rule 3 provides a cheap and expeditious procedure for final disposal of a purported appeal.

'I ask you again for your immediate assurance that rule 3 is henceforth to be applied in full and that preliminary hearings are not being used where no jurisdiction is shown in a notice of appeal. If you do not feel you can give me that assurance,

I must ask you to consider your position.'

Mr Justice Wood responded by stating that the view he had expressed had been reached following consultation with many others on the bench and that in their collective opinion it was the correct statement of law.

He added: 'I have, of course, given the most serious consideration to my position as you required of me.

'You have demanded that I exercise my judicial function in a way which you regard as best suited to your executive purposes, but I have to say that in all the circumstances that present themselves to me and in the light of existing law, I cannot regard compliance with your demand as conducive to justice.

'You express disappointment. I express profound regret that it has ever been the uncomfortable duty of a judge in this country, in compliance with the judicial oath, to write to a Lord Chancellor refusing a demand such as the one which you have made of me.'

Two months later, in response to an enquiry from the Lord Chancellor's office as to whether he would be retiring later in the year, Mr Justice Wood confirmed that he would be. He had made the decision, he indicated, well before he had been asked to consider his position.

It is an accepted principle that Lord Mackay, despite being the country's most senior judge, does not have the power to tell a judge how to interpret the law. Yet is this not in essence a Treasury-driven attack on the independence of the judiciary?

I tabled a whole series of parliamentary questions to the Lord Chancellor's office on the matter. One answer appears to confirm that Lord Mackay has exceeded his authority.

The jury

In all defended criminal cases which go to the Crown Court, and in some civil High Court cases, there is a jury in English law. In criminal cases it is the task of the jury to decide, on the basis of what they have heard on following the directions of the judge, the verdict of guilty or not guilty. Table 4.3 provides a summary of the system of juries.

Judges in the European Court of Justice

We considered the effect of UK's membership of the European Union on the legal system in this country in Chapter 3. The UK is a member of the European Union (formerly the European Community) and it is important to realise, as was explained in Chapter 3, that, in addition to the various courts which we have dealt with, there is a court which sits in Luxembourg, known as the European Court of Justice, which deals with matters relating to the European Union. It is important to say something about the judges who sit in this court.

TABLE 4.3   The system of juries

Number of jurors	*Crown Court* (criminal cases) 12. *Queen's Bench Division of High Court* (civil cases) 12. *County Court* (civil cases) 8 (very rare). *Coroner's Court* 7 to 11
Selection	Until 1972, property qualification. Morris Committee on Jury Service 1965 *principle*: jury citizen. Since 1972 names taken from *electoral roll*. If called, jury service is compulsory (unless excused, see below).
Qualification for jury service	18–70, ordinarily resident in the UK for five years since age of 13 (Juries Act 1974, s.1).
Ineligible	Mentally ill; those whose occupations are concerned with the administration of justice or with religious vocation.
Disqualification	Any person who has served a custodial sentence (including a suspended sentence of imprisonment or a community service order) within the past ten years is disqualified. A sentence of five years' imprisonment or more disqualifies a person for life. A probation order disqualifies someone for five years (Juries (Disqualification) Act 1984). This Act is reckoned to have disqualified 250 000 people from jury service.
Excusals	(a) *As of right*. MPs and members of the House of Lords; members of the medical profession and armed forces; those who have served on a jury in the previous two years. (b) *Discretionary*. Judge may excuse a person for 'good reason', e.g. mother with small children, booked holiday etc.
Lack of capacity	Judge may decide a person may not act as juror because of doubt over capacity (deafness, poor understanding of English etc.).
Challenge	Defence's right to peremptory (without giving a reason) challenge abolished (Criminal Justice Act 1987). Right of challenge for cause (giving reasons) for both prosecution and defence. Prosecution's right to 'stand by' prospective juror (provisional challenge, putting prospective juror to the back of the queue). To be exercised sparingly: Attorney General's Guidelines (1990) 3 All ER 1086.
Jury vetting	Two types. (1) Routine police checks on prospective jurors to eliminate those disqualified. Process approved by Court of Appeal in *R.* v. *Mason* (1981) QB 881. (2) Exceptional cases (those cases involving national security, where part of the evidence is likely to be heard in camera, and terrorist cases). Checks performed on police and Special Branch records. Governed by Attorney-General's guidelines (1980) 3 All ER 786, but these have no statutory authority or judicial approval. *But* no power to empanel a multiracial jury (*R.* v. *Ford* (1989) 89 Cr App R 278).

TABLE 4.3 (continued)

Majority verdicts	Allowed since 1967, now dealt with under Juries Act 1974, s.17. Jury must strive for unanimity for at least two hours. If unanimity not possible, judge may accept the following majorities in both Crown Court and High Court cases (11–1, 10–2, 10–1, 9–1). The foreman of the jury must state in open court numbers agreeing and disagreeing with the verdict (*R.* v. *Pigg* (1983) 1 WLR 6).

The court has 13 judges, one from each member of the community and one additional judge. Usually cases are heard by three to five judges. We considered the example of Liam Duffy on page 31 and an actual case Stoke on Trent City Council 1993 which explains the sorts of matters heard by the court.

___ **Exercise 3** ___

1 What is the difference between a stipendiary magistrate and other magistrates?
2 Who is effectively the head of the judicial system in the UK?
3 Who advises 'lay' magistrates?
4 Name the professional bodies regulating: (a) solicitors (b) barristers.
5 Solicitors can never be held liable for breach of contract: true or false?
6 Explain by reference to their respective functions the difference between a High Court judge and a circuit judge.
7 What is the role of the jury in a criminal case?
8 How many judges are appointed to the European Court of Justice, where are they from and how many usually sit?

5 Business agreements (I)

5.1 Essential requirements in a contract

Ian Wood has just been made redundant and he decides to use his redundancy money to purchase a business. The business which he purchases is a shop which sells do-it-yourself materials and items of hardware. After just a few weeks in business Ian realises that he needs a van to make deliveries and to collect stock from suppliers. He notices in the local paper a nearly new van advertised at £9650. The van is being sold privately by Alan Willis. Ian goes to see the van which is in very good condition and has done only 8500 miles. Ian makes Alan an offer of £9600 for the van and Alan accepts. Ian pays Alan by means of a cheque and Alan allows Ian to drive the van away.

This agreement reached between Alan and Ian is an example of a contract and in this chapter we will be looking at the main essential requirements which must exist in a legally binding contract. We will be concentrating particularly on business contracts but much of what is included here will be applicable to any legally binding contract. You will have noticed that the agreement between Ian and Alan was made neither in a solicitor's office nor in writing. In fact, although some contracts are in writing, this is by no means a necessity and in practice only a very small percentage of contracts made are actually made in solicitors' offices. A contract is simply an agreement which the law will recognise.

Exercise 1

1 All contracts made must be made with the help of a solicitor: true or false?
2 All contracts must be in writing: true or false?
3 Give a definition of a contract.

In order for an agreement to be a contract, that is something which the law will recognise, it must contain certain essential elements and it is with these essential elements that this chapter is concerned. A contract must begin with an offer. You will remember that Ian made an offer to Alan to purchase the Bedford van for £9600. An offer may be made to a specific person. In our example the offer was made to Alan. An offer, however, may be made to a group of persons, for example when a company makes an offer to its employees. An offer may be made to the whole world, as when an offer of a reward is made. A very famous case, *Carlhill* v. *Carbolic Smoke Ball Co* (1893) illustrates the principle that an offer can be made to the whole world:

> An advertisement was placed in a newspaper by the Carbolic Smoke Ball Co, offering to pay £100 to anyone who contracted influenza after using one of the company's smoke balls in a specified manner and over a set period of time. Mrs Carlhill, the plaintiff, did this but still caught influenza. She sued for the £100 and was successful.

This case illustrates that offers can be made to the whole world and need not be to a specific group or person. However most advertisements are *not offers* and are usually 'invitations to treat': in other words, an invitation to the person seeing or hearing the advertisement to make an offer. It is important that the offer is communicated; thus in our example there is no doubt that Ian communicated his offer to Alan. When an offer is made the person making the offer is known as the offeror and the person to whom the offer is made is known as the offeree.

___ **Exercise 2** _____

In our example, name the offeree and name the offeror.

It is very important to distinguish an offer from an invitation to treat. Goods in shop windows or on display and goods advertised are usually invitations to people to come in and make offers and are known as invitations to treat. Thus, in our example, the appearance of the van in the newspaper advertisement was an invitation to readers to come to Alan to make an offer. Only offers can be accepted; it is not possible to accept invitations to treat.

___ **Exercise 3** _____

If a shopkeeper displays in the shop window, by mistake, a PC computer for £75 instead of £775, what would be the legal position of the shopkeeper if he refused to sell the computer for £75 to a customer?

A well-known case illustrates the difference between an 'invitation to treat' and an offer. *Pharmaceutical Society of Great Britain* v. *Boots Cash Chemists* (1953) was a criminal case which the Pharmaceutical Society brought against Boots. Usually criminal cases are brought by the Crown or the police acting on the Crown's behalf, but individuals or organisations can bring a private prosecution. This prosecution was brought because the society argued that Boots had offered to sell drugs to the public without there being a qualified pharmacist present. This was contrary to section 17 of the Pharmacy and Poisons Act. Boots, in their defence, argued that goods had been sold in a self-service store and that the goods on display on the shelves were merely 'invitations to treat', that is invitations to the customers to make offers which they made at the cash point. There was, Boots argued, a qualified pharmacist at the point of sale, that is at the cash desk, who could if he wished reject the offer. Boots were found not guilty and acquitted.

This case illustrates well that goods on display or goods advertised are not offers; indeed it is the customer who makes the offer and the shop proprietor or his assistant who accepts. Another case, *Gibson* v. *Manchester City Council* (1979) might help you understand the difference between 'offers' and 'invitations to treat'.

Mr Gibson, a council tenant, received a letter from the council saying that it 'may be prepared to sell the property to you at a price of £2180'. Mr Gibson made a formal application to buy but, before the matter was dealt with, the council's policy regarding the selling of council houses changed and it refused to sell. Mr Gibson took the matter to court and the court held (decided) that the letter was an invitation to treat and not an offer. Therefore there was no contract between the council and Mr Gibson and his action failed.

We have seen, then, from our example of the van that legally binding contracts must start with an offer and it was Ian who offered Alan £9600 for the van. The next stage in a contract is the acceptance, which must match the offer completely. Thus it is sufficient that Alan replies simply 'yes'. Alan's acceptance must be unconditional, that is there must be no 'ifs' or 'buts'. If Alan had said 'yes, but I want £9650' this would not be an unconditioned acceptance and therefore not an acceptance at all. When the two parties, Ian and Alan, had offered and accepted, respectively, there was an agreement.

The next stage in our agreement was the two-way exchange; Ian gave Alan the money and Alan gave Ian the van. In this example the money (£9600) and the goods (the van) were the 'consideration'. Consideration is the legal term for something of value which exchanges between the parties as a result of the agreement. Consideration must be two-way and must be of value. In the example, the consideration in both directions was of value.

Exercise 4

If Frank offered one of his employees a gift of £200 which the employee accepted, would this be a contract?

___ **Exercise 5** ___

In the following example identify the offeror, the offeree and the consideration.

Good Deal Motors Ltd have displayed in their showroom a 1993 car priced at £9100. John Hardiman, who is very interested in this car, tells the salesman that he is willing to pay £8900. The salesman agrees and John collects the car, giving a cheque for £8900.

We have now identified three essential ingredients of a legally binding contract: (i) an offer, (ii) an acceptance which matches the offer completely, (iii) two-way consideration. In addition to these three ingredients several other ingredients must be present in order for an agreement to be legally binding.

It is essential that the two parties entering into the agreement have the capacity to do so. By saying a person has the capacity we mean that he is legally entitled to enter into a contractual agreement. In English law a person who has attained the age of 18 has full legal capacity and therefore can enter into legally binding arrangements. A person below the age of 18 has not got this full capacity and there are certain agreements entered into by young people who are under 18 (to use the legal expression, who 'have not reached the age of majority') which are not legally binding because for these agreements the young person (the minor) has no contractual capacity. A good example of such an agreement is one where a young person enters into an agreement to obtain credit. This agreement is not legally binding and therefore not a contract. This important fact serves as a warning to any business that it is dangerous to afford credit facilities to young persons. If the young person should default, that is not pay, then payment can never be enforced in the court. This is so because no contract exists; the creditor could not sue for breach of contract because there is no contract. The subject of 'legal capacity' is dealt with more fully on page 74.

In our example we can safely assume that both Ian and Alan possessed full contractual capacity to enter into the agreement. If someone enters into a contract while drunk or temporarily insane then that person can 'avoid' the contract, that is cannot be bound by it, provided he/she can prove (a) he/she was drunk or insane when he/she made the contract, (b) the other party knew that he/she was drunk or insane. The following example may help to explain this part of the law.

Gaynor Curzon has had six double whiskies and in her resultant state of drunkenness she agrees to sell her nearly new Ford Monza car for £1200. Bill Usher is delighted with this deal but when he goes the next day to take delivery Gaynor refuses to hand the car over.

As we have seen, Gaynor can 'avoid' the agreement provided she is able to prove (a) that she was drunk when she made the agreement; (b) Bill knew she was drunk. It seems she is within her rights to refuse to hand it over.

English law will only recognise agreements which are legal, and therefore any agreement by one party, for example, to commit a crime in return for payment will not be recognised. Under no circumstances would a court allow a hired murderer to collect damages in the court if the person hiring him had refused to fulfil his side of the bargain, that is refused to pay for carrying out this illegal act. The hirer would not be in breach of contract because no legally binding contract exists.

There seems, however, nothing illegal in the arrangement to sell the van mentioned earlier and therefore it would appear to have the ingredient of legality.

Exercise 6

We have now established the existence of five essential elements necessary to make a legally binding contract. Before we go on to consider the other essential elements, try without reference to the book to list these five elements.

Although an agreement may contain each of these five elements the court may still not recognise it because, as it is sometimes put, there is between the two parties to the agreement 'no meeting of the minds'. This means that one or both parties had entered into agreement either unwillingly or perhaps not knowing all the facts because they had been misled. For example in the van agreement, if the van was much older than suggested, that is it displayed false number plates because in fact it had done 27 500 miles, not the 8500 indicated, then it is clear to see that Ian was entering into an agreement having been misled; indeed Alan had misrepresented the facts to Ian. There is little doubt that Ian would not have entered into the agreement had he the true facts before him. There would have been certainly no 'meeting of the minds' between Ian and Alan. The court would not uphold this agreement. In some cases of misrepresentation, courts will uphold the contract but award damages to the injured party.

Similarly courts would not uphold agreements where one party had been forced against his will to enter into an agreement. Agreements will not be legally binding where there is clearly no 'meeting of the minds'. Often you will come across, in law books, a Latin phrase to describe this 'meeting of the minds': *consensus ad idem.*

As we have already seen, contracts need not be in writing; in fact in the majority of cases the law is not concerned with the form in which the contract is made. There are, however, several situations where the form of contract is an essential element, and where if an agreement is not in a particular form it is not legally binding. The list below gives three examples where the form of contract is an essential element.

1   A document to transfer ownership in land (for example, a house) must be in a special form known as a deed otherwise it is not legally binding.

2   A hire purchase agreement must be in writing to be legally binding.
3   Some contracts are legally binding without being in writing but if not in written form will not be enforceable in the courts, for example an agreement to sell land. If you are buying a house or a shop, the first stage is a contract and this must be in writing to be enforced. The second stage is the actual transfer of ownership and this stage must be supported by a special form of contract. This subject relating to the purchase of land is covered by the Law of Property (Miscellaneous Provisions) Act 1989 and is dealt with more fully in Chapter 18.

Agreements may contain all the seven elements as above, that is offer, acceptance, consideration, capacity, legality, *consensus ad idem* and be in the correct form, but nevertheless still not be legally binding. This is because there is one final element which must be present. Was there 'legal intent'; that is, did the parties to the agreement intend that their agreement should have legal consequences? There is no doubt that Ian and Alan intended this and in fact the rule in English law is that in business agreements which contain all the seven essential elements it is assumed that 'legal intent' is present unless it is specifically removed. In some agreements one party states that the agreement is 'binding in honour only' and in this case the legal intent has been specifically removed.

Exercise 7

A football pool coupon is an agreement lacking this essential element of legal intent. Obtain a coupon and try to find the clause which is contained in all football pools which removes the legal intent.

Appleson v. *Littlewoods Ltd* (1939) sums this up well. The plaintiff sued to recover money which he claimed to have won on a football pool. His action failed, because the printed entry form contained a statement that the transaction was 'binding in honour only'. Although it is assumed that in most agreements 'legal intent' is present unless specifically removed, in domestic and social arrangements the assumption is the opposite, that is the court will assume the absence of legal intent unless it is specifically included. Thus if a father promises his son an extra £1 a week for digging the garden and then refuses to pay even though the son has fulfilled his side of the agreement, there will be no breach of contract because no contract exists because of the absence of legal intent.

Exercise 8

Write down the eight elements essential in a legally binding contract. Check your answers. If you have missed any from your list, go over this section of work again.

It is important that you understand the elements necessary in a legally binding contract because a number of the chapters which follow are concerned with the law of contract. An understanding of contract forms a good basis for a number of topics included in later chapters. The following review exercise is an attempt to test your understanding of legally binding agreements and the essential elements within them.

Exercise 9

In each of the following examples there is one element missing; try to identify in each case why the agreement is not legally binding by stating the missing element.

1   Jim Frezier offers his wife £10 per week if she will clean his two cars regularly. Thelma, his wife, accepts the offer but Jim will not pay the £10, even though Thelma has performed her side of the bargain by regularly cleaning the cars.
2   Keith Martin buys a second-hand car from Good Deal Motors Ltd for £8400. The purchase is on a hire-purchase agreement, £2400 down and 24 monthly instalments of £286.66, which includes 10 per cent per annum interest. The manager explains the agreement to Keith, saying that his firm does not believe in unnecessary paperwork. The agreement is a verbal one.
3   Woodruff Renovations Ltd offer to paint a customer's house free of charge. The customer accepts this offer but Woodruff Renovations refuse to do the job.
4   Michael finds a wallet belonging to Frank Dolman, a wealthy director, Frank's address is in the wallet and Michael takes it to Frank's house, unaware that there is an offer of a £50 reward. Frank refuses to pay up despite getting his wallet back.
5   The Hotel Regal advertises two nights' bed and breakfast, double room with bathroom, for £55. John and his wife Barbara write asking for the first weekend in August. They do not hear from the Hotel Regal but, assuming a booking has been made, arrive at the hotel to find it fully booked.
6   Graheme Browne is a technical representative for a machine tool company. He persuades Low Peak Co. Ltd to buy a lathe which he describes as a new German lathe of the most advanced design. In fact, it is an old lathe which has been reconditioned. Low Peak Ltd order the machine at a price of £14 000.
7   Carol Latham (aged 17) has passed her driving test and buys a second-hand Mini for £4700 from Carsales Ltd. She signs an agreement to pay £700 deposit and the balance over two years at £200 per month, which includes 10 per cent interest per annum.

8 Anxious to find more information about a rival firm's new revolutionary machine, Jack Lawrence, managing director of Engineering Developments Ltd, pays John Davey £2000 to break into the development office of the rival firm to obtain a photocopy of the plans for the new machine. John obtains this information but Jack refuses to pay the £2000.

If you have not correctly identified the element which was missing in any of these examples then read through this first section again, so that you understand the eight essential elements.

5.2 The main contractual elements

Offers

Commercial Vehicles Co. Ltd, which deals in the sale of both new and second-hand commercial vehicles, offers to sell Roger Kent, a market gardener who is visiting the showroom, a one-year-old lorry for £19 500. This is rather more than Roger wished to pay but he is impressed by the lorry's condition and asks the salesman if he can have a couple of days to think about the offer.

As we have already seen, all legally binding agreements must begin with an offer which must be communicated to the offeree. In this example, Commercial Vehicles Co. Ltd have communicated an offer verbally to Roger Kent. An offer has then been made. Offers, however, cannot last indefinitely and we will be examining the ways in which an offer may come to an end by looking at our particular example:

1 If Roger decides to accept the offer of the lorry for £19 500 then the offer has ended by acceptance.
2 An offer can also come to an end if the offeror, in this example Commercial Vehicles Co. Ltd, decides to withdraw it. Sometimes the word 'revoke' is used instead of 'withdraw' but it means exactly the same. The rule relating to revocation (withdrawal) is that the offeror may withdraw his offer at any time before it has been accepted. If this withdrawal is communicated directly or indirectly to the offeree, for example Roger, then the offer comes to an end. There must, however, be a definite communication of the revocation. Roger must hear that the offer has been withdrawn from a 'reliable source', that is by letter or by a telephone call from the offeror. It would not be sufficient for Roger to hear by chance, for example in his local pub, where the barman in conversation indicates that he had heard that Commercial Vehicles Co. Ltd has agreed to accept a higher price for the vehicle.

In our example you will remember that Commercial Vehicles Co. Ltd gave Roger a couple of days to think about the offer, yet despite this Commercial Vehicles Co. Ltd would be perfectly within their rights to withdraw the offer as soon as Roger left the showroom, as long as the fact of the withdrawal has been brought to Roger's attention. The company may decide to sell the vehicle to another customer and they could do this because this would be the same as withdrawing the offer.

There is, however, one situation where the company would be prevented from withdrawing their offer before the allotted time of a couple of days had lapsed. This is if Roger had asked them to keep the offer open and he had paid Commercial Vehicles Co. Ltd, let us say, £300. In this case a contract has come into existence, as shown below:

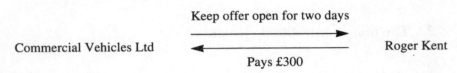

Keep offer open for two days

Commercial Vehicles Ltd   Roger Kent

Pays £300

As you can see, this contract is supported by two-way considerations. The company keeps the offer open and Roger pays £300. In business practice the £300 is used as a deposit and deducted from the purchase price. If Roger decides not to accept the offer then Commercial Vehicles Co. Ltd could keep the £300, since they kept their side of the bargain, keeping the offer open.

Exercise 10

1 Name two ways in which offers may be brought to an end.
2 Offers may be revoked at any time before...
3 How can an offeree ensure that an offer remains open for a specific period of time?

There are two additional ways in which offers may be brought to an end. If after thinking about the offer Roger decided that he could not really afford £19 500, or if he did not really think the vehicle was worth that, he could do one of two things. He could notify Commercial Vehicles that he did not wish to accept the offer – in other words he would be rejecting the offer. Or he could ask the company if they were willing to accept £19 000; here Roger would be making what is called a counter-offer and he would be rejecting the first offer. In fact, Roger would become the offeror because he is now making the offer and Commercial Vehicles would be the offeree. Offers may come to an end by rejection, by the offeree saying 'no' to the offer or making a counter-offer. This situation is summed up well by an old case, *Hyde* v. *Wrench* (1840).

A farm was offered at £1000. The offeree thought this was too much and offered £950, but this was refused. The offeree, anxious to obtain the farm, then suggested £1000. The court decided that the offer of £950 was a counter-offer and was the same as a rejection.

An offer may also come to an end by what is called lapse. If a specific time is put upon an offer, in our example two days, then when the two days have expired the offer comes to an end unless before that time it has been accepted, withdrawn or rejected. Where no time has been stated then the offer will come to an end after the expiry of a reasonable time. In a dispute it is for the courts to decide what is reasonable and clearly this will depend upon the subject of the offer. An offer to buy fresh fruit cannot remain open for too long for obvious reasons, whereas an offer to buy a motor car may remain open for a longer period.

The Motor Agents' Association, to which many garages belong, has produced a standard form for motor car sales, which lays down certain time limits in respect of car sales.

Activity

Go along to your nearest motor car dealership and see if you can obtain or see a copy of these standard conditions of sale relating to motor vehicles.

The other way in which an offer can lapse is through death of the offeree before acceptance. Thus, if Roger should die before accepting the offer of the vehicle, the offer would lapse and no other member of his family could accept. The offer will also come to an end if the offeror should die.

Exercise 11

1 Name the four ways by which an offer may come to an end.
2 If Roger offered to buy the lorry for £19 000 this would be a _____ and Roger would become the _____.
3 Name two ways in which an offer might lapse.

Acceptance

All agreements must start with an offer but, equally important, offers must be accepted. In our example, Commercial Vehicles Co. Ltd have made an offer of a lorry for £19 500. For Roger to accept it means that he must do so unconditionally, that is without conditions. As we have seen, it is not sufficient for him to say, 'I accept but I can only pay £19 000'. There must be no 'ifs' or 'buts'; Roger must say 'yes'. If he says 'no' or 'yes but' this is a rejection of the Commercial Vehicles Co. Ltd offer. The acceptance must match the offer completely. *Hyde* v. *Wrench* showed that a counter-offer could not be an acceptance.

There are, however, special rules relating to postal acceptance, that is where the offeree decides to accept an offer by letter. The following example will help to illustrate this.

Arthur Williams is a technical representative working for Computer Power plc, a firm producing computers and word processors. On a visit on 1 June to a large firm of chartered accountants, Jordan & Sons, Arthur offers to sell the firm two computers, each costing £2500, for £4000. Arthur explains that the offer will remain open for one week; he leaves full details of the offer and suggests that Jordans write to his firm if they wish to accept the offer. On 2 June in the morning the partners of Jordans meet and decide to accept the offer and post a letter to this effect to Computer Power plc. The letter is posted at 11.30 am. In the afternoon of the same day, Arthur is severely reprimanded by his boss for making too 'good' an offer and is asked to ring Jordans to withdraw the offer. Arthur does this at 3.30 pm, but Mr Philip Jordan who answers the phone replies, 'Too late ; we have already accepted'.

In this case Jordans have accepted the offer and a legally binding contract has come into effect between Jordans and Computer Power even though Computer Power has not yet received the letter of acceptance. The law, as it relates to postal acceptance, is quite clear; acceptance takes place at the time of posting, that is at 11.30 am, provided the letter has been correctly addressed and prepaid, that is has a correct stamp on it. Withdrawal takes effect when it is brought to the attention of the offeree, that is at 3.30 pm, but this was clearly too late because, as we have learned, an offer cannot be withdrawn if it has been accepted.

The rules relating to postal acceptance are only applicable where either postal acceptance was suggested, as with Jordans and Computer Power plc, or where it is a normal means of acceptance. If the offeror specified other means of acceptance, such as telephone, then the acceptance would be effective from the receipt of the telephone call and the letter would be irrelevant. It is for the offeror to specify if he wishes a particular form of acceptance. This is summed up well in the following case.

In *Holwell Securities Ltd* v. *Hughes* (1974), an offer to sell required that acceptance be made 'by notice in writing to the intending vendor' within six months. Notice was posted but never arrived. It was held that there was no contract. The words of the offer showed that the offeror was not prepared to be bound until he *received* the written notice.

The rules relating to postal acceptance were laid down in the judgement in *Byrne* v. *Van Tienhoven* (1880).

In *Byrne* v. *Van Tienhoven* (1880), a firm in Cardiff offered by letter to sell tin plate to a firm in New York. Later, the firm sent another letter revoking this offer, but while this was in transit and before its delivery, the New York firm posted a letter of acceptance. It was held that the parties clearly intended the use of the post to communicate acceptance, and posting the letter of acceptance, therefore, brought the contract into existence, since this was done before the revocation arrived.

Exercise 12

1 An acceptance must match the offer completely: true or false?
2 Postal acceptance takes effect from the time the letter is received by the offeror: true or false?
3 The offeree can accept the offer by whatever means he wishes: true or false?
4 Withdrawal of an offer takes place when it is posted: true or false?

Consideration

As we have already learned, all legally binding agreements must be supported by consideration in both directions.

Exercise 13

Identify the consideration in the following example:
Commercial Supplies Ltd are selling a laser printer to Highgate Televisions Ltd for £1200.

Normally, therefore, a promise of a gift cannot be enforced because a gift is one-way consideration. It is possible, however, to make legally binding an agreement to give a gift by incorporating the promise of the gift into a deed which is simply a document which has been signed, sealed and delivered. For example, if Yvonne Hill, a grocer, promises to give one of her employees, Michele Ashton, a gift of £200, the courts will not give any remedy to Michele if Yvonne breaks her promise. However, if Yvonne signs a document, such as the one below, the document becomes a deed and is enforceable against her in the courts.

I, Yvonne Hill, promise to pay Michele Ashton within seven days of the date on this deed, the sum of five hundred pounds (£500).

Signed and Delivered

by the said Yvonne Hill **Signature** _____

in the presence of

Name Julia Price   **Signature** _____

Address 56 Whitstable Road, Canterbury Kent CT1 1QU

Occupation Midwife

Date 9 December 1994

Until recently such documents required a seal (a small red wafer was attached to the document near the signature) and they were 'signed, sealed and delivered'. The Law of Property (Miscellaneous Provisions) Act 1989 has abolished the need for the seal. The document is still called a deed and contracts which must be made in this form are known as 'specialty' contracts. Other contracts are known as 'simple' contracts.

The rule, therefore, is legally binding agreements must be supported by consideration in both directions unless the agreement is made on a deed. This allows consideration to be only one-way.

There are, however, four more rules which must be understood relating to consideration and the four following examples will help to illustrate these rules.

1 Adam Bradd is a qualified accountant who has, on two occasions, helped a friend, Roy Spencer, who runs a small furniture and carpet business, with his tax returns. There has never been any mention of payment but Roy decides to make his friend a gift of a carpet and goes to Adam's house to measure up the lounge. However, Roy, before fitting the carpet, falls out with Adam and the carpet is never delivered. Adam thinks of suing.

We have seen that consideration must be two-way and in this case Adam has done the tax returns and Roy is going to supply the carpet. However, the consideration supplied by Adam, that is the tax return, is in the past and the courts will not recognise past consideration. As far as the courts are concerned, the promise by Roy of the carpet is merely one-way and as suggested in the example merely a gift; Roy's promise is not legally binding.

Consideration can be present, if Adam had done the tax return and Roy had given him the carpet, or it can be future: Roy provides the carpet and Adam does the tax return in the future. It must, however, never be in the past. Promises for services rendered in the past are not legally binding.

If, therefore, you decide to assist a friend in some activity and you want payment for this it is always wise to discuss this at the outset. There are, however, many examples where work is done and payment made afterwards. If someone takes his car to the garage for repair the payment made after the repair will not be for past consideration for, in commercial dealings of this sort, there is an implied promise to pay for the repairs; the car repair is present consideration and the payment is future consideration because of the existence of the promise to pay.

2 Peter Hurwell is a hotel manager with a large hotel chain known as Leisure Hotels Ltd. He is, at present, manager of the Royal Hotel, a large hotel in the South West of England. There have been for some time certain problems at the Royal and the company feel that a lot is due to Peter's casual attitude to work. Peter is called to a meeting at Leisure Hotels Ltd in which he promises to give up this casual attitude and to work to the best of his ability. In return the company agree to pay him a bonus of £2000 at the end of the year. When the company conducts its review at the end of the year there is no doubt that considerable improvements have taken place and Peter's new attitude has been the major contributory factor. Nevertheless, Leisure Hotels Ltd refuse to pay the promised bonus and Peter decides to sue his company.

It would seem that this agreement is based upon a two-way consideration – Peter's promise to work to the best of his ability and the company's promise of a £2000 bonus. If, however, we examine Peter's side of the bargain in more detail we will discover that, in fact, Peter was only promising to do something which he ought to have done anyway. In other words, Peter was promising to fulfil an existing obligation and that in law is not consideration. Therefore the agreement between Peter and Leisure Hotels Ltd is based only on one-way consideration; only the company is giving consideration and therefore the agreement is not legally binding and Peter could not sue.

The third rule, therefore, relating to consideration is that it must not be an existing obligation.

In *some* circumstances a court may decide that a person *can* be rewarded for fulfilling an existing obligation, and this was the case in *Williams* v. *Roffey Bros and Nicholls* (Contractors) (1990).

A carpenter had contracted to do work for £20 000 but it became clear that he could not complete the work in time at that price. The builder knew that the delay would result in a loss and he promised an extra amount for prompt completion. However, when the carpenter completed the work on time the builder refused to pay, saying it was an existing obligation. The court held that the carpenter was entitled to the extra money although it was an existing obligation. The court came to this decision because it felt that the avoidance of the penalty payment for non-completion and the fact that the builder did not have to engage another subcontractor was sufficient consideration.

However a court would never agree to this if there was any hint that the plaintiff knew of the difficulties of the builder and exploited the situation. This is well illustrated in *D & C Builders Ltd* v. *Rees* (1966).

Exercise 14

Mary Goodwin has borrowed £400 at 20 per cent interest per annum for one year from East Credit Ltd. Her agreement is that she pays this sum off by means of 12 x £40 monthly payments = £480. By the end of the year Mary has paid just six instalments, making £240 in all. The credit company suggest she pays a further £160 and they will let her off the interest. Mary pays this but East Credit Ltd decide to sue for the £80 interest.

What would your advice be to Mary, remembering what we have learned about consideration not being an existing obligation?

---

3 Tony Hurnford and his wife Celia own a large detached house with a market value of about £120 000. Wishing for a quick sale because of financial problems they are in, Tony and Celia advertise the house at £90 000 and get a buyer immediately. Contracts are exchanged between the Hurnfords and the buyer, Timothy Lomas. The Hurnfords refuse to complete the sale because they argue the price was too low. Timothy decides to sue.

In fact, Timothy would be successful and it is likely that the court would order the Hurnfords to complete the sale. This is because, while consideration must exist in both directions, the court will never concern itself with the value of consideration. Timothy and the Hurnfords have entered into the agreement willingly and the court will not interfere with bargains unless there is any evidence that the agreement was obtained by Timothy unfairly, for example by threats. As we have seen, this was not the case and the agreement was willingly entered into. This then establishes our fourth rule, that courts are not concerned with the adequacy of a consideration; they are only concerned with its existence. As long as consideration is two-way and is of some value the court will accept it.

___ **Exercise 15** _____

We have now learned four rules relating to considerations. State these four rules.

_____

There remains just one more rule relating to consideration which can be explained by reference to this example:

4 XYZ Co. Ltd decide to give ten of their senior staff a special thank-you present for their efforts in a successful year. A weekend is booked for each of the ten staff and their wives or husbands. XYZ Co. book with the Regal Hotel on the south coast and pay in advance the bill which amounts to £2000. When the staff arrive at the hotel they find that the rooms are all fully booked. Keith Martin, one of the senior executives on the trip, threatens the Regal with legal action.

In fact, Keith could not sue the hotel since normally only the person supplying the consideration may sue on a contract. So XYZ Co. Ltd could sue because they supplied the consideration. Thus the final rule for us to learn is that only parties providing consideration can sue on the contract; in other words, only parties to a contract can sue on it. This rule is known as 'privity of contract', which means that an agreement is private to the parties who make the agreement. There is an important exception to this rule. This applies to motor insurance. A third party injured by a motorist can sue the motorist's insurance company even though the injured person was not a party to the insurance contract. Also the Road Traffic Act 1972 allows a person driving a car with the owner's consent to recover compensation from the insurance company with which the owner is insured. This is another example of an exception to the privity of contract rule.

___ **Exercise 16** _____

The following examples are provided to test your knowledge of the rules relating to offer, acceptance and consideration. Study each carefully and advise the party in italics of his legal position. Try to do this review exercise without reference to the text. Check your answers and if you have found difficulty with any of the exercises reread the relevant section.

1 Marchant Machine Tools Ltd offer to sell a computerised milling machine to *Sterndale Engineering Ltd* for £15 500. Sterndale ask for a week to think the offer over and pay a deposit of £1500 and this is accepted. Subsequently, Marchant Machine Tools decide they cannot wait a week and sell the machine for £15 000 to another firm.
2 *The Palace Hotel* receive a letter from Deepdale Cash Registers Ltd wishing to book a suite of rooms for three days for a sales conference.

The manager of the Palace writes a letter confirming the booking. Before receiving the letter Deepdale cancel the arrangements.

3 *Harpur Builders Ltd* decide to give each of their five employees a £100 Christmas gift. They send a written statement to the employees saying this gift will be in the next week's pay packet, but in fact no gift is given.

4 *Paul Caffery* owns a cottage on the south coast and he decides to offer his solicitor a week's holiday in the cottage free of charge to thank him for legal work the solicitor has done in the past. The solicitor accepts the offer but when he presses Paul for a date Paul changes his mind.

5 Reg Pullin sells a two-month-old luxury 2.6 litre car for £6000 to *Kearings Motor Supplies Ltd*. Reg then tries to recover the car, saying £6000 is not nearly enough for a luxury car of this sort.

6 *Julian Cartwright* is injured while driving his friend's car. He tries to recover compensation from the Norwich Assurance but is refused because he has not made any contract with Norwich.

Capacity

We have already seen that one of the elements necessary in a legally binding agreement is capacity. In other words each party must be fully capable of entering into the agreement. The general rule is that everyone has full capacity but there are certain restrictions placed upon young people below the age of 18 and upon drunks and insane persons.

Minors.   In a legal sense a person who has not reached the age of majority, 18 years, is known as a minor. Minors do not have full contractual capacity. The following examples will distinguish those agreements made with minors which are legally binding from those that are not.

Agreements which can be enforced against minors

Simon Beckwith (aged 16) orders a made-to-measure suit for his new job in a bank from Easifit (Tailors) Ltd. The tailors deliver the suit to Simon's house but Simon refuses to accept it, saying he has changed his mind about the colour. Easifit decide to sue.

A legally binding agreement has come into operation and Easifit would be able to sue. Minors can make contracts for what the law calls 'necessaries', that is things which a minor needs. A suit for working in a bank is a 'necessary'. It is important to distinguish 'necessary' from 'necessity'. A 'necessity' is something which is essential, such as food and water. The courts will judge 'necessaries' against the criteria:

1 Is the article suitable to the minor's position in life?
2 How many items of this article does he have?

On these two grounds the suit would be regarded as a necessary.

This rule relating to necessaries is neatly summed up in a famous case, *Nash* v. *Inman* (1908) where a minor (in those days under 21) was sued for £145 for the cost of 11 fancy waistcoats. The supplying firm could not recover this money because the court held that these were not necessaries. The boy's father had already supplied him with a full wardrobe of clothes.

Michael Pullen (aged 16) works for a large engineering company as an apprentice fitter. After a trial period of six months Michael is asked to sign an apprenticeship agreement which stipulates that he must remain with the company for four years, attending technical college one day per week, and for this he will receive a wage of £100 per week rising by £20 per week each year. Michael signs this agreement but after a year he decides to leave. The company sue Michael for damages for the money they have spent on his training.

This is an example of a legally binding agreement because, although Michael is a minor, the law lays down that agreements relating to employment, apprenticeship or education are for the minor's benefit. The company is likely to be successful in claiming damages, although in practice the company would be unlikely to sue.

Exercise 17

Name two types of contract which a minor can make.

Contracts which are not enforceable against minors

Terence Clapham (aged 17) borrows £400, at 10 per cent interest for two years, from a credit company. After paying the initial payment of £20 Terence defaults and the credit company take him to court.

Unfortunately for the company no contract exists between Terence and the company because any agreement made by a minor relating to credit lacks capacity and therefore is void. It is easy to understand why shops will never enter into hire-purchase or credit agreements with minors. Under the Minors Contract Act 1987 a court has the discretion to order a minor to transfer to the other party property or goods which he/she has acquired under a void contract. The following example may help to explain.

Oliver Harrop aged 17 buys a motor cycle from Sports Bikes PLC for £750. Agreeing to pay by instalments, he indicates he is 18 years old. The company, quite keen on the sale, agrees without doing any sort of check on his status. Oliver is taking a business course at his local college. He realises the agreement is a void contract and refuses to pay any instalments. Sports Bikes tries to recover its money or the goods in the court.

It is likely that the court would use its discretion under the 1987 Act and order Oliver to hand back the motor cycle, especially since Oliver had misled the company regarding his age.

As we have seen, another agreement with a minor which is void by virtue of lack of capacity is any agreement to supply goods which are not necessaries.

Thus there are two types of agreement relating to minors: those which are valid and those which are void. There is, however, another type of agreement which, if made by a minor, is enforceable against him when he reaches the age of 18. We call this category of agreements 'voidable', which means they can be avoided by the young person before he reaches 18 or a reasonable time thereafter. Three examples of such voidable contracts are:

1   Agreements to lease a flat or house.
2   Agreements to enter partnerships.
3   Agreements to buy shares in companies.

In the situation regarding these voidable contracts it is necessary for the minor to ratify the agreement when he reaches the age of majority, that is 18. The contract then becomes binding. This is not possible with void contracts.

Exercise 18

Give one example in each case of an agreement made by a minor which is (1) valid, (2) void, (3) voidable.

Insane and drunken persons

We have already seen that this may affect a contract. The following example will underline the legal position.

Frank Browning owns a sports car worth about £8500. At a party at his office one of his employees, seeing that he has had too much to drink, persuades Frank to sell him the car for £850. Frank even signs a document to this effect. Frank, however, when he sobers up, realises his mistake and refuses to release the car even though the buyer produces the £850.

In this situation, Frank could avoid the agreement because the court would say that at the time he made the agreement he lacked capacity. Frank must prove that (1) he was drunk; (2) the buyer knew he was drunk.

The same rule applies to someone who was temporarily insane, provided he can prove he was insane at the time he made the agreement and, secondly, that the other party realised this fact.

In certain cases persons suffering from mental illness cannot make any agreement because their property is subject to the control of the court. This device, introduced by the Mental Health Acts of 1960 and 1983, is to protect the mentally sick from unscrupulous persons and removes completely their contractual capacity.

Legal intent

Fortrex Office Supplies Co. Ltd draw up an agreement to supply a range of office machinery, value £35 000, to Trenchard Manufacturing Co. Ltd.

Mrs Lynne Jones orders a bedroom suite at £785 from Fairfield Furnishings Ltd.

Both these agreements would, on the face of it, seem to contain the elements necessary to make them contracts and therefore legally binding. You will no doubt remember that one of the essential elements is the presence of legal intent: did both parties to the agreement intend that the agreement should have legal consequences? It would be fair to assume that each of the four parties concerned here – Fortrex, Trenchard, Mrs Jones and Fairfield Furnishing – had this intent. Indeed the courts in this country will always assume that in commercial and business agreements the parties had legal intent. This assumption can only be removed if a clear statement accompanies the agreement, such as: 'This agreement is binding in honour only and it is not intended that it should have any legal consequence.' An agreement containing such a clause could not become a contract for it would lack the essential element of legal intent.

Football pools coupons always contain a clause such as: 'This transaction is binding in honour only.' Therefore no contract exists between the punter and the pools company. If anyone feels he has won a large dividend he cannot sue the company for recovery should they refuse to pay because no contract exists for him to sue. Remember the case of *Appleson* v. *Littlewoods* (1939).

There are some instances where an Act of Parliament has removed the legal intent. For example:

1 The Post Office Act 1969 removes legal intent from agreements between Post Office and sender in respect of letters and packets. You might consider the implication of this if a valuable article is lost in the post.
2 The Law Reform Miscellaneous Provisions Act 1970 takes out the legal intent from promises to marry and therefore makes it impossible nowadays for a jilted fiancée to sue for 'breach of promise'.
3 Section 18 of the Trade Union and Labour Relations Act 1974 lays claim that an agreement between an employer and a trade union is presumed not to have legal intent unless the agreement is in writing and contains a statement that the parties intend that the agreement will be a legally enforceable agreement.

Although apart from the exceptions mentioned the court will assume legal intent in commercial and business arrangements unless there is a statement to the contrary, in domestic arrangements, such as between husband and wife, the court will assume the absence of legal intent unless there is a statement to the opposite effect which is in writing.

> *Rachel Jackson has entered into an agreement with her husband John whereby she will decorate the lounge for half what it would cost if John employed a professional decorator. The sum agreed exclusive of materials was £120. Rachel completes the task to John's satisfaction but he refuses to pay the £120 and Rachel decides to sue him for breach of contract.*

There is little doubt that Rachel would lose her case because the court would assume the absence of legal intent unless Rachel could produce strong evidence to the contrary. The courts may enforce agreements between husband and wife which are non-domestic – where, for example, a husband is in business, supplying his wife, also in business, with goods or services. This will be a normally legally binding agreement and intent will be assumed. The situation is neatly summed up in *Balfour* v. *Balfour* (1919):

> A husband promised his wife an allowance before he left to take up a post abroad. When he stopped the payments, an action by the wife failed on the ground that this was not a binding contract but merely a domestic agreement with no legal obligations attached to it.

Exercise 19

1 Business and commercial agreements are always legally enforceable because legal intent exists: true or false?
2 If a parcel posted at the post office is lost in transit the sender can claim the full value by suing in the courts: true or false?
3 Domestic agreements between husband and wife are assumed to be 'binding in honour only'. Therefore they are not legally enforceable: true or false?

Legality

In the first section of this chapter we learned that an agreement could never be legally binding if it had within it any illegal element. Consider the following.

> *Francis Smythe is employed as an assistant director of finance by a well-known local authority. The post of director becomes vacant and Francis makes an application. He is desperate for this promotion and agrees to pay*

the chief executive of the local authority and the chairman of the county council £1000 each if he gets the post. Francis is appointed but refuses to pay the two £1000 each, as promised.

It is quite obvious that the court would never enforce this agreement because it was entered into for an illegal purpose and therefore lacks one of the essential elements, legality. Agreements tending to the corruption of public life are always illegal and the above agreement would fall into this category. Other types of agreement regarded as illegal are as follows:

1 Agreements to commit criminal acts.
2 Agreements involving sexual immorality; therefore, agreements between prostitutes and their customers are never enforceable. A decided case *Pearce* v. *Brooks* (1866) sums this up well.
3 Agreements to defraud the Inland Revenue, for example where a person contracts with a company not to disclose payments made to him to the tax authorities.
4 Agreements affecting public safety – therefore all contracts with persons living in enemy territory would be illegal.

Contracts in restraint of trade

Certain contracts are only partly illegal but may be declared void by the courts because they are said to be in restraint of trade. These sorts of contract fall into three categories, as the examples below illustrate.

1 Deborah Price works as an articled clerk (trainee solicitor) with Dennett, Rooke-Naylor and Bright, a firm of solicitors in Dover (Kent). Deborah has signed an agreement that, when she qualifies, she will not work within a three-mile radius of this firm. On quali-fication, Deborah gets a job about two and a half miles from her former firm's office and Dennett, Rooke-Naylor and Bright sue her for breach of contract.

This is an example of a contract in restraint of trade and the court will only uphold it if it is reasonable. In other words, is it necessary to protect Dennett, Rooke-Naylor and Bright's business? Each case is treated on the basis of the cir-cumstances. It is likely that this agreement would be enforced. However, if the restraint were too wide, for example covering the whole of Kent, then if Deborah worked next door to her former firm, the court would not find for Dennett, Rooke-Naylor and Bright.

It is important in these situations for employers drawing up such agreements to ensure that they are reasonable and do not impose unnecessary obstacles upon employees.

2 Gerald Nicholson has decided to purchase a newspaper and tobacconist shop near his home. He purchases the business rather than the shop itself, which he will rent. The cost is £80 000 and he insists that the seller of the business signs an agreement that he will not start up in a similar business within a two-mile radius. You will appreciate that it is important that this sort of arrangement is possible because, if the seller started up a new business nearby, the £80 000 payment would be a waste. The court will apply the same ruling. Is it reasonable? This is another example of a contract in restraint of trade which will, in some instances, be enforced but, if it is too wide, it will be held to be illegal.

The important aspect of transfer of business is dealt with again in Chapter 18.

3 Davis & Sons is a small paint shop in Kent. The owner, Bob Davis, signs an agreement with a leading paint manufacturer that, in return for a grant for shop improvements, he will sell only this brand of paint for 25 years.

This is known as a 'solus agreement' and the courts will again, if it comes to a dispute, apply the rules of reasonableness.

Various Acts of Parliament have been passed, for example The Fair Trading Act 1973 and the Restrictive Practices Act 1976, to assist in the regulation of arrangements and agreements to restrict competition.

It is important to remember that the courts will interpret 'contracts in restraint of trade' very differently depending on the circumstances. It is important when entering into such an arrangement to be sure that one does not put oneself in a difficult position. If an agreement in restraint of trade is regarded as too restrictive then the whole agreement falls. It is not up to the court to adjust it.

Consensus ad idem

We have already met this short Latin phrase; try to remember what it meant in relationship to agreements. It is quite clear that agreements depend on both parties to the agreement entering into it willingly. We have already seen that where one party misleads the other and causes him to enter into the agreement then there would not really be a genuine 'meeting of the minds' and therefore no legally binding agreement.

There are three types of circumstances which prevent a genuine 'meeting of the minds'. The following three examples will help to explain them.

1 Gillian Smythe is anxious to purchase a genuine George III giltwood mirror and she is delighted when she finds one of these displayed at the showrooms of Peter Hanson (Antiques) Ltd. The owner of the business, although aware that this is a reproduction, assures Gillian that it is genuine and persuades her to buy it for £2500. Some weeks later Gillian discovers that the article she has bought is not genuine. She decides to sue the antique dealer.

This is a very good example of misrepresentation and the court will order Hansons to pay back the £2500 to Gillian. It is clear that there was no genuine meeting of the minds because Gillian was misled into thinking she was buying the genuine article.

2 Ernest Leigh is managing director of a printing firm which has recently advertised the post of foreman. One of his employees, David Mellor, a former boxer, has applied for the post and before the selection he threatens Ernest with a severe beating if he (David) is not successful. Despite some other very good applications Ernest, who fears for his safety, offers David the job and David accepts.

Again, there was no genuine meeting of the minds because Ernest did not really have a free mind when making his decision. The threat of force put him, as the law says, under duress and if necessary the court would uphold the situation if David was removed from the post.

We now have two examples of situations where *consensus ad idem* (meeting of the minds) is not present: (1) misrepresentation, (2) duress. In the second example we were concerned with force or the threat of force but there is a more subtle form of persuasion which might cause a person to enter into an agreement which was unfavourable to him. For example:

3 Mrs Beckford is an old lady of 72 who has extensive properties in the South of England. Her son wishes to borrow a large sum of money from her to set up a business and Mrs Beckford decides to sell some of her properties. She goes to see her solicitor of many years, Mr Graham Brooke, and asks him to dispose of several properties. Graham, anxious to make some money, decides to buy the properties himself and suggests to Mrs Beckford that she should accept his offer of £250 000 for the three properties. Mrs Beckford accepts this advice and the sale goes through. In fact, the properties were worth at least £450 000.

Although we have seen that the courts are not concerned about the value of consideration, in circumstances such as this where one party, Graham Brooke, has used his influence to get the agreement and where clearly Mrs Beckford trusted him, the court will allow Mrs Beckford to get her properties back on the ground that 'undue influence' occurred. Undue influence may occur where one party has a dominant position over the other, as with doctor/patient, accountant/client, solicitor/client, father/son. Undue influence will only exist, however, where the dominant party uses his influence unfairly.

The courts have also shown a willingness to interpret 'duress' to include what has been called 'economic duress', where one party knows that the other is in financial difficulty and uses this knowledge to exact terms which are disadvantageous to the other party. The courts may disallow what has been exacted by duress. The following decided case may assist an understanding of this.

In *Atlas Express Ltd* v. *Kafco* (1989), Atlas Express, knowing that Kafco needed to make deliveries to Woolworths to fulfil a big order and that the company (Kafco) would be in difficulties if the deliveries were not made, tried to get extra payment for the deliveries, Kafco refused to pay the extra and the court agreed that Atlas Express were using 'economic duress'.

Exercise 20

1 Under what three circumstances might a court agree that there was no *consensus ad idem*?
2 List five types of agreement which might be void by reason of illegality.
3 What is a solus agreement? Is it illegal?

Form of contract

Generally, parties to an agreement can make this agreement in any form they wish and so, for example, they may make a verbal agreement or they may decide to set down the details of their agreement in writing. There are, of course, advantages in setting out an agreement in writing because if a dispute should arise it is easier for the party suing in the court to prove that the agreement did exist if he has written evidence. However, there are certain agreements which must be made in a certain form.

1 Certain agreements must be made by a *deed*. We have already come across the term 'deed' on page 70 and you will remember that it is a document which is signed as a deed Examples of agreements which must be made by deed include:
   (a) Agreements supported by only one-way consideration such as a gift.
                                    and
   (b) Agreements to transfer land.

   We will be dealing with the subject of property transfer in Chapter 18.

   (c) Agreements relating to leases of three years or more. It is possible to rent a house or a piece of land. This procedure is often called a lease. Many home owners, in fact, have the land on which the house is situated on lease. These are usually for long periods, often 999 years.
2 Some agreements must be in writing because if they are not the contract is void, that is empty, and therefore not legally binding. Three examples of agreements which must be in writing are:
   (a) contracts to buy and sell shares in a company,
   (b) contracts of marine insurance,

(c)   contracts to buy certain consumer goods such as televisions by instalments, for example hire-purchase agreements.

3   There are some agreements which need to be in writing to make them enforceable in the court. The absence of writing does not render the contract void but if one party does not fulfil his side of the bargain then the other party cannot sue. Probably the best known example of an agreement in this category is a contract to sell land. An agreement to buy or sell a house can only be enforced if it is in writing.

Exercise 21

Examine 'for sale' notices outside houses; some of them will have included the phrase, 'sold subject to contract'. What do you think this phrase 'subject to contract' means?

Exercise 22

1   What is a deed?
2   Give two examples of agreements which must be made by deed.
3   Give two examples of agreements which must be in writing.
4   Give one example of an agreement which will only be enforced if it is in writing.

Exercise 23

We have now covered in some detail the main elements of contract and in this exercise you will be tested on your understanding of this important part of law. If you have any difficulty with any of the following six review questions go back over the text.

1   Give four ways in which an offer can be brought to an end.
2   The Hotel Metropole receives a booking from an Alan Harrison and his family: one week, two double rooms, full board, cost £650. The hotel accepts Alan's offer by post, which confirms the booking. Alan, before receiving the letter, decides to withdraw his offer but the Hotel Metropole say that the contract is binding on Alan. Advise Alan.
3   (a)   Consideration may be past: true or false?
    (b)   Courts are always concerned with the value of consideration: true or false?
    (c)   Consideration must never be an existing obligation: true or false?

4   Bob Walkden (aged 17) borrows £100 from his friend's father and says he will pay this back in a month's time. Bob, however, cannot pay this debt and the friend's father decides to sue. Advise Bob.

5   What three factors may cause the absence of a meeting of the minds (*consensus ad idem*).

6   (a)   Agreements between husband and wife which are related to domestic arrangements are never legally binding: true or false?

(b)   Give your reasons for your answer to (a).

6 Business agreements (II)

6.1 Terms and conditions

Excelsior Engineering Ltd is a small but very successful company producing a range of engineering products. The managing director Mr Kirkham is keen on buying a new up-to-date fully computerised lathe at a price of £34 350. He orders this from a firm of machine tool suppliers, Goodwin Machine Tools plc.

As we have already learned, an agreement such as this will be a legally binding contract provided all the essential elements are present. Goodwin Machine Tools plc decide to send to Excelsior Ltd a written agreement in which all the terms are included in connection with delivery dates, fitting and installation and so on. The new machine is quite a complicated one and Mr Kirkham is happy to see that the supplier will be responsible for fitting and installation and also for a training programme for his employees. A number of terms are written into the agreement, including the following:

1 Goodwin Machine Tools plc undertake to deliver the machine to the premises of the purchaser by 31 August 1994.
2 Goodwin Machine Tools plc undertake to fit and install the machine and to provide at its expense a three-day training programme for up to three employees of the purchaser company. This undertaking to be effected within three weeks at least of the delivery.

The two terms which have been quoted here are examples of express terms. These are known as 'express' because they have been expressed, in this case in writing, though there would be nothing to prevent the terms being expressed verbally. Express terms are, then, those which have been mentioned and agreed by the parties at the time of reaching the agreement, whether this be done in writing or by word of mouth.

___ Exercise 1 _____

Express terms in a contract must always be in writing: true or false?

┌─ **Activity** ──┐

You will find terms included in many contractual documents which you may have. For example, look at an insurance policy, or a hire-purchase/credit sale agreement and find the terms which are included.

└──┘

The terms relating to a credit sale agreement with a company are shown here and you will see that the company uses the expression, 'terms and conditions'.

Extract from an agreement

Terms and Conditions

1   The Company shall sell and the Buyer shall purchase the goods at the credit sale price specified in the Schedule hereto.

2   The Buyer shall on the signing of this Agreement make the initial payment and thereafter shall make the subsequent payments specified in the Schedule hereto.

3   If the Buyer shall fail to pay any instalment within five days of its due date or in the event of any other breach by the Buyer of the terms and conditions hereof, the whole of the balance of the credit sale price then outstanding shall immediately become due and payable forthwith.

4   The property in the goods shall pass to the Buyer on delivery after which the Company shall not be responsible for any loss of or damage to the goods howsoever caused.

5   If the Buyer shall intend to vacate or shall vacate the said premises he shall forthwith inform the Company thereof and shall state his new address and shall during the period of this Agreement inform the Company immediately of any further change of address.

6   If the Buyer is the Tenant of premises in which the goods the subject of this Agreement are to be installed by the Company then the Buyer hereby indemnifies the Company against any claims of non-negligent damage to the said premises or Landlord's fixtures or fittings therein caused during the installation or removal of the said goods by the Company.

7   The Buyer hereby acknowledges that previous to the making of this Agreement he was informed of and knew the cash price of the goods.

8   The Company hereby grants the Buyer the option to pay the cash price for the goods and installation stated on the face of this Agreement within three months of the date of signing this Agreement.

9   Any forbearance or indulgence shown by the Company to the Buyer shall in no way prejudice or affect the strict rights of the Company hereunder or otherwise.

10 Nothing herein contained shall affect diminish or extinguish any right or interest whether statutory or otherwise vested in the Company as an electricity undertaker.

11   This Agreement having first been signed by the Buyer shall become operative and binding upon the parties only upon being executed by or on behalf of the Company and shall be dated accordingly.

Although the document uses the words 'terms and conditions', in law 'condition' has a special meaning. Let us for a moment return to the two terms relating to the agreement between Goodwin Machine Tools and Excelsior. Both these terms are an important part of the agreement but there is a difference in the degree of importance as between (1) and (2). You will remember that in term (1) Goodwins agreed to deliver the machine on or before 31 August 1994. If delivery was delayed by one day and in fact took place on 1 September 1994, do you think that Mr Kirkham of Excelsior could treat the contract as breached? If the case went to court it is most certain that the court would judge that Goodwins had not really broken a term which lay 'at the heart of the contract' and the failure to deliver by 31 August was a breach of warranty for which Excelsior could sue if they could show that they had lost money as a result of late delivery.

If, then, a term is not considered important enough to affect the very basis of the contract it is regarded as a 'warranty'. However, some terms are so vital as to go to the heart of the contract itself. These will be considered to be 'conditions' and a breach of a condition will be treated in the same way as a breach of contract. Consider the following situation. You will remember that in term (2) of the Excelsior/Goodwin agreement it was undertaken by Goodwins to fit, install and provide training in the use of the new lathe. If despite delivery on 1 September the machine had not been installed by December 1994, then Mr Kirkham would be correct to assume that this really was affecting the whole basis of the agreement. Indeed he would doubtless argue that he would have been unwilling to spend £34 350 of his firm's money had he known of such delays. If the case went to court the court would almost certainly treat this as a breach of condition and could order Goodwins to pay Excelsior back its £34 350.

Terms of an agreement may be conditions or warranties and this will be determined by their importance. It is important to realise that the mere using of the word 'condition' in an agreement does not in any way guarantee that it is a condition. The test is, will 'non-observance' of the term affect the main purpose of the agreement? If the answer to this question is yes then it is a condition.

Two old cases in the same year sum up the difference up very well. In *Bettini* v. *Gye* [1874–80], an opera singer agreed to attend for rehearsals six days before the first performance. He did not arrive until two days beforehand. This was held to be only breach of warranty, which entitled the management to recover damages but not to terminate the contract. Conversely, in *Poussard* v. *Spiers & Pond* (1876), Madame Poussard, a singer, failed to turn up for the first few performances. This was held to be breach of condition, which entitled the management to end her contract.

Exercise 2

1 Examine the terms and conditions of a sale credit agreement on page 86 and identify any which you would regard as a 'condition' in the legal sense in which we have used the word.
2 (a) Explain the meaning of the word 'warranty'.
   (b) What will happen if a warranty is breached?

Exercise 3

Examine the four following examples and indicate whether you think the defendant is in breach of warranty or breach of condition.

1 John Martin, a promising young cricketer, has signed a contract to play for a well-known English county cricket club. One of the terms of the contract is that he must attend six practice sessions before the start of the playing season. John misses one practice session and the club threatens to sue him for breach of contract.
2 Michael Pullin signs a one-year contract to play for a First Division football club. One of the terms of the agreement is that he must play for any of the club's teams if selected. Michael decides to take his wife for a winter break and misses six key fixtures. The club decide to sue Michael for breach of contract.
3 Andrew Perkins has a small but busy insurance broker's office. Anxious to increase efficiency he orders a small computer. One of the terms of the agreement reached with the suppliers, Computer Supplies Ltd, is that a programme will be supplied with the machine which will allow a more efficient accounting system. Although the computer is delivered on time the programme is not supplied and Andrew decides to sue.
4 H. & G. Heavy Haulage Ltd orders from a well-known truck manufacturers a tip-up lorry capable of dealing with lime supplies. The agreement which is drawn up between the two firms expressly mentions the tip-up facility. When the lorry is delivered H. & G. Ltd find that the tip-up mechanism will not work. The firm decide to sue the manufacturers.

Implied terms

We have been considering express terms, that is terms which are stated either in writing or verbally. There are, however, instances where even though the parties to an agreement have not made express provision on a point the courts nevertheless will imply a term. The following example will perhaps illustrate this.

Keith Robinson owns a smallholding and he decides he needs the use of a tractor for a couple of weeks. He hires the tractor from Agricultural Hire Equipment Ltd at a cost of £560, payable in advance. When the tractor is delivered Keith finds that he is unable to use it owing to a number of serious transmission faults and its unsafe condition. Keith decides to ask for the return of his £560. Agricultural Hire Equipment Ltd refuse, saying that they had given no express undertaking that the vehicle was safe or suitable.

In fact in this instance, if a case of this sort went to the courts, the courts would say that this undertaking (term) existed by implication, or in other words there was in existence an implied term because clearly the agreement would make commercial nonsense without it. It is fair to assume that Keith would think that the goods would be fit for the purpose for which he was hiring them. This is summed up well by the following example. In *Liverpool City Council* v. *Irwin* (1977), the written tenancy agreements in a tower block of flats imposed no express duty on the landlord to keep the lifts and stairs in good repair! The court nevertheless implied such a term.

There are a number of examples where an Act of Parliament has stipulated that in certain agreements terms are implied. The best known example, which we will consider in detail in Chapter 9, is the Sale of Goods Act 1979, whereby it is implied that goods sold by a shop, for example, shall be of 'merchantable quality'; for example, if you bought a new camera from a shop for £185 which you later discovered had such a serious fault that it would not take pictures, you could claim a full money refund because the shop had breached one of the essential implied terms, that goods must be of merchantable quality.

Another example of terms implied by an Act of Parliament is where furnished houses which are let to tenants must be fit for human habitation. This is laid down by the Defective Premises Act 1972. We have therefore two types of implied terms: (i) terms implied by Statute (Acts of Parliament); (ii) terms implied because it is necessary to give commercial sense to a business agreement.

Exercise 4

Advise the party in italics as to whether he/she would have a case in the following situations:

1 *Rachel Martin* buys a new motor car which has two defective tyres, faulty brakes, broken headlights and badly chipped paintwork.
2 *Precision Engineering* hire a high-quality lathe which has such a serious fault in it that a number of jobs are ruined, with the consequent loss of materials.
3 *Mr and Mrs Goldstraw* rent a furnished flat which is rat-infested. The landlord, Real Estates Ltd, refuses to refund the advance monthly rent of £150.50.

6.2   Exclusion clauses

__ Activity _____

During the course of the next few days look around to see if you can find
examples of notices of the sort shown below:

Vehicles and their contents are parked at the owner's risk and no liability is accepted for loss or damage to vehicles or persons howsoever
caused.

The wording of notices you may see may be different but they all amount to the
fact that one party to the agreement, the proprietor of the car park in this
example, has excluded liability, that is taken out liability, by the introduction of
what is called an exclusion clause.

The following example will help to explain the law relating to exclusion
clauses. (Sometimes these clauses are known as 'exemption clauses'.)

*Roger Lewis works as a representative for a pharmaceutical firm. As part of
his work he has to spend three days at a seaside resort in the South West of
England and he decides to book into a guest house which is owned by Mr Neil
Nickson. When Roger arrives he is asked to sign a form which contains,
amongst other things, a notice which reads:*

The proprietors of Maxstone Guest House cannot accept liability for
personal injury to guests, loss or damage to guests' property howsoever
caused which might arise during the guests' stay at this guest house.

*This notice is also displayed very prominently at the reception desk in
such a way that it would be difficult to miss. Roger has always been
very careful and he reads the form carefully before signing. He feels that
nothing is likely to happen to him in three days. However, this particular
week must have been his unlucky one; on the first morning of his stay he
leaves his wallet with £100, an expensive suit and some pharmaceutical
samples in his room which he locks before going down to breakfast.
When he goes back to his room he discovers the loss and reports the
matter to Mr Nickson. Mr Nickson is sympathetic but draws Roger's
attention to the notice he has signed. He does, however, agree to make an
investigation.*

*The following evening Roger, having spent a day on business, has taken a
shower prior to having dinner. While walking from the bathroom to his room*

Roger trips on some loose carpet outside his room and falls awkwardly. He sustains a broken arm. Mr Nickson is informed and is most apologetic but again draws Roger's attention to the notice that he has signed.

What, then, is Roger's legal position? There is little doubt that at the time of making the contract to stay at the hotel Roger had agreed to the exclusion clause. Let us for a moment examine the first situation. If Roger took the guest house to court for recovery of his loss, Mr Nickson would draw the attention of the court to the existence of the exclusion clause and the court would apply a number of rules to the situation to establish whether or not Mr Nickson could reply upon it:

1 Was it part of the agreement? The fact that it was incorporated in a form which Roger had every opportunity to read is a good indication that it was part of the contract. The general rule is that if a contract is drawn up in a written document which is signed by the party concerned then everything contained therein will be binding upon the signer, whether he has read it or not.
2 If there is no signing involved then the court would need to be sure that everything reasonably had been done to bring to the attention of the other party the existence of the clause.
3 Was the clause introduced at the time the agreement was made? Under no circumstances will courts allow exclusion clauses to be relied upon if they have been introduced after the agreement has been made. In our situation Roger signed the form containing the exclusion clause at the time he booked in and therefore had an opportunity to say to Mr Nickson, 'I do not agree to your terms.' If, for example, the notice had not been signed and was displayed in guests' rooms then this would be after the agreement was made and therefore could not be relied upon. For example, in a decided case, *Olley* v. *Marlborough Court Ltd* (1949), the defendant tried to rely upon a notice in the guest room but the hotel was course unsuccessful. The exclusion clause in this case was introduced too late.

In fact in this situation the guest house had introduced the exclusion clause in the right manner. Roger had been required to sign a document but, even if he had not, the guest house could still have relied upon it because the notice had been prominently displayed at the reception, that is, it was introduced at the time the contract was made.

Unfortunately Roger could not recover from the guest house the value of his lost property even though he might be able to prove that the guest house staff had been careless in leaving his room unattended and the door open while cleaning the rooms on his corridor. Mr Nickson had carefully indemnified himself against this claim. (The exclusion clause is sometimes called an indemnity clause because it indemnifies the party introducing it.) Here 'indemnifies' means that it protects him against the possibility of any claim being made upon him. You may hear these clauses being referred to also as 'disclaimer' clauses because they disclaim liability.

Exercise 5

1 An exclusion clause in a contract is sometimes known as an ____ clause or a ____ clause.
2 An exclusion clause, to be relied upon, must always be part of a signed document: true or false?
3 Exclusion clauses may be introduced at any time during the operation of a contract: true or false?

It seems, then, that Roger would have little chance of success in an action to recover the value of his loss. However you will remember that on the second day of his stay he fractured an arm tripping over some loose carpet. You will also remember that the exclusion clause which he signed sought to indemnify Mr Nickson against claims in respect of personal injury. If we applied the same rules to this second situation as to the first then it would appear that Roger would have no claim. This would have been the position prior to 1977. However, as a result of the Unfair Contract Terms Act 1977, section 2(1), no one acting in the course of business can either by contractual terms or by notice given or displayed exclude his liability in contract or tort for death or personal injury arising from negligence.

In this second situation, Mr Nickson has attempted to exclude liability for personal injury. He has done this with a notice and in the course of business. There is little doubt that Mr Nickson was negligent in leaving loose carpeting in the guests' rooms and Roger could successfully sue him for compensation for suffering resulting from his fractured arm and for any other loss incurred thereby.

The Unfair Contract Terms Act 1977, although it prevents a business from excluding liability for death or personal injury, still allows it to exclude liability for any other loss due to his negligence. Thus the notice given to Roger excluded Mr Nickson's liability for personal loss, that is in respect of the first situation, but not from liability for personal injury, that is in respect of the second. Therefore Roger would most likely be successful in an action based upon his personal injury – provided he could show that the guest house had been negligent. The law as it relates to negligence will be explained more fully in Chapter 11.

A section of the Unfair Contract Terms Act is shown below.

ELIZABETH II

Unfair Contract Terms Act 1977

1977 CHAPTER 50

An Act to impose further limits on the extent to which under the law of England and Wales and Northern Ireland civil liability for breach of contract, or for negligence or other breach of duty, can be avoided by means of contract terms and otherwise, and under the law of Scotland civil liability can be avoided by means of contract terms.   26th October 1977]

B E IT ENACTED by the Queen's most Excellent Majesty, by and with the advice and consent of the Lords Spiritual and Temporal, and Commons, in this present Parliament assembled, and by the authority of the same, as follows :—

PART I

AMENDMENT OF LAW FOR ENGLAND AND WALES AND NORTHERN IRELAND

Introductory

1.—(1) For the purposes of this Part of this Act, 'negligence'   means the breach —

    (a) of any obligation, arising from the express or implied terms of a contract, to take reasonable care or exercise reasonable skill in the performance of the contract ;

Scope of Part I.

Activity

As we have learned, these exclusion clauses, sometimes known as indemnity clauses, may also be referred to as disclaimers – disclaiming liability. If you look around you will often find examples of these. Many still disclaim liability for personal accident but, while it is not illegal to display such a notice, it cannot be relied upon. Have a look for notices excluding liability and in the light of your reading of this section on exclusion clauses try to work out the protection afforded to the business seeking to rely upon the notice.

You may notice that in a number of cases notices have been changed to bring them in line with the 1977 legislation. An example of a notice displayed by Torbay District Council is shown below:

The Corporation will accept no responsibility for any loss of or damage to any articles including articles of value brought into or left in this building whether such loss or damage is caused by the negligence of the Corporation, its officers or servants or otherwise.

You will note that in this example there is no attempt to exclude liability for personal injury. Even though it is possible to exclude liability for losses, in deciding whether an exclusion clause can be relied on, the court will attempt to see if it is reasonable. The cost of the service being provided will probably be taken into account, as the following case shows. In *Photo Production Ltd* v. *Securicor Transport Ltd* (1980), Securicor contracted to guard the plaintiff's factory where paper was stored. The patrolman deliberately started a fire, and it destroyed the premises. It was held that an exemption clause in the contract protected Securicor. Both parties were established businesses that had negotiated the terms freely. The price of the patrol was modest. Both parties were insured, the plaintiff against loss of the building, Securicor against liability. The court was satisfied that both sides had intended Photo Production (or its insurers) to bear the risk.

The Unfair Contract Terms Act lays down guidelines which help the court to determine what is reasonable in these exclusion clauses. These guidelines will, of course, also help those who are drafting the exclusion clauses. The following points are examples of these guidelines:

1   the relative bargaining strength of the two parties: if one party is in a strong position, the court might take a different view of reasonableness;
2   whether the customer was given some inducement to accept the terms, such as a price reduction;
3   whether the goods were made to a special order;
4   whether it was reasonable to expect compliance, for example where complaints have to be made within a certain number of days.

In *R. W. Green* v. *Cade Bros* (1978) a farmer bought seed potatoes and the contract stipulated that any complaint re the goods had to be made within three days of delivery. The court held that three days was unreasonable because within such a short period it would not be possible to identify any problems with the product.

Exercise 6

Examine the following examples and explain whether you think the person suffering the loss would successfully sue for compensation.

1   *Veronica Clapham* has to make a business trip to Austria and she books a flight with a British airline. Her luggage is put in the hold of the plane

and during the early part of the flight from Manchester to Vienna she is handed a ticket which explains that the management cannot accept liability for any loss or damage of goods while in transit. Veronica's luggage is badly damaged owing to the negligence of airline staff and she loses about £550 worth of property. She decides to sue the airline.

2 *Francis Harris* hires a touring caravan from Caravan Hire Ltd and at the time he makes the contract he signs a form indemnifying the company from claims in respect of personal injury resulting from the use of the caravan. Owing to the negligence of one of Caravan Hire Ltd's staff, Francis is badly injured and he sues the company, who draw his attention to the form he signed.

3 *Electrical Components plc* has decided to move its head office from Derby to Ilkeston but for a short period they have to store office machinery in a furniture store known as County Store Ltd. The managing director of Electrical Components has to sign a document indemnifying County Store from claims should there be any loss or damage to the equipment while it is in the store. The rental for the storage is very low. As a result of some very unusual storms some of the equipment is damaged. Electrical Components decide to sue County Store Ltd.

6.3 Discharge of contracts

Concorde Car (Sales) plc is a large car distributor with branches throughout the country. Anxious to boost sales it decides to hold a three-day sales conference for 60 of its senior sales personnel. The company decides to hold the conference at the Sceptre Hotel, which has excellent conference facilities and is situated on the south-east coast. Terms are agreed whereby full board and conference rooms will be available at a total cost of £13 500. The dates agreed are 21 September to 24 September 1994.

As we can see, a legally binding contract has come into existence between Concorde and the Sceptre Hotel. In this section we will be using this example to show how contracts may be discharged, that is brought to an end. There are basically four ways in which contracts may be ended (discharged).

1 If the conference goes ahead as planned and the bill of £13 500 is paid by Concorde then the contract will be discharged by performance. Each side has performed his side of the bargain, or to use the expression used in Chapter 5, each side has given consideration. Sceptre Hotel has provided accommodation and food plus full conference facilities for 60 persons and organisers and Concorde have paid the bill of £13 500. One way, then, in which a contract may be discharged is by performance – both parties fulfil their sides of the bargain.

2 It may be that at some time prior to 21 September Concorde decide that they do not wish to go ahead with the sales conference, perhaps because a number of their senior sales personnel cannot attend. If the hotel agrees to cancel

the agreement then the contract is said to be discharged by agreement. It is important to remember, however, that the agreement must be by both parties. If Concorde cancelled the conference but the hotel did not agree then the hotel could sue Concorde for the cancelled booking.

If the Sceptre Hotel had already spent some money on the arrangements then the hotel might still release Concorde but only if Concorde gave some consideration; for example, the Hotel Sceptre might agree to the cancellation provided Concorde paid £400. Obviously the nearer to 21 September it was the more likely it would be that the hotel would lose money by the cancellation, for it would give them less time to make alternative bookings.

It might be that the Sceptre, because of a number of problems, might wish to cancel the booking. If Concorde had time to make alternative arrangements it might agree to this. Thus a second way in which a contract might be discharged is by agreement, but the agreement must be two-way; it can never be one-sided (unilateral) for example where Concorde cancelled but the Sceptre did not accept.

3   There are circumstances where an event takes place, for which neither party to an agreement was responsible, which makes the agreement impossible or produces a radically different situation. In such circumstances it is possible that the court will regard the agreement as discharged by frustration:

(a)   If prior to 21 September a fire occurred at the Sceptre Hotel which completely gutted the building then the hotel would find it impossible to perform the contract and it would be discharged by frustration. However, as a result of the Law Reform (Frustrated Contracts) Act 1943, Concorde would recover money if they had incurred expense in arranging the conference prior to the discharge.

(b)   Let us assume that Concorde are a major supplier of Japanese cars and prior to the conference, as a result of government legislation, there is a total ban on the import of Japanese cars. It is easy to see that the basis of the contract has been removed. There is little point in holding a sales conference to sell new cars when no more new cars will be forthcoming, and the courts might well allow the contract to be discharged by frustration. If the Sceptre Hotel had spent money on arrangements for the conference then this might be recovered.

A decided case will help to illustrate the law as it relates to frustration.

In Krell v. *Henry* (1903), the contract was for the hire of a room in Pall Mall so that the coronation procession of Edward VII could be seen. The coronation was postponed owing to Edward VII's illness. The landlord tried nevertheless to recover the rental. However, the court held that the contract was discharged by frustration since the basis of the contract had been removed.

The third way in which contracts may be discharged is by frustration. However it must be remembered that courts will only allow a contract to be discharged by frustration exceptionally. It must be *impossible* to perform because some external event has so fundamentally changed the situation that the very basis of the contract has been removed. The courts will never allow frustration merely because it is difficult. For example:

Dr Robert Bown, who runs a business agency in Bristol, agrees to provide a consultancy service to a firm in Kent. The charges are £500 per day together with travelling expenses of £750 for eight journeys. The rail strike means Robert has to hire a vehicle and travel costs will be more than £750 and he writes to his customer indicating that he believes that, owing to the strike, the contract is impossible to fulfil and therefore frustrated.

The court would not regard the agreement as frustrated but merely as difficult and Robert could be sued for non-performance.

4　Finally one or other of the two parties may refuse to perform their side of the bargain. In our example, if on 21 September Concorde's employees did not turn up and when the manager of the Sceptre rang the Concorde office he was told that Concorde had cancelled the conference, then if Concorde refused to pay their £13 500 the company would be in breach of contract; that is, it had broken its side of the bargain. Similarly if the Sceptre Hotel refused to provide full facilities as agreed for the conference the hotel would be in breach of contract. Breach of contract could take place earlier than 21 September if one party unilaterally decided not to fulfil its side of the bargain before that date – if the Hotel Sceptre, for example, indicated before 21 September that it would not accept the conference.

The fourth way of discharging a contract is by breach. We will consider the remedies that a court may award for breach of contract in the next section.

Activity

During the next few days think of different contracts which you have made and then think of the way in which they have been discharged.

Exercise 7

1　List the four ways in which a contract may be discharged.
2　Name the Act which allows a party in frustrated contracts to recover some of the expenses incurred in respect of the contract.
3　Name a decided case which illustrates the law relating to frustration.

Exercise 8

Study the four examples below and explain in each how the contract has been discharged.

1 *Nigel Welch* has signed a contract with a well-known football club to play for three seasons. Before making an appearance he is injured in a car accident and loses the use of his right leg, which has to be amputated.

2 *Stanley Davey* is managing director of a large building firm; he orders timber from a timber merchant, Timber Supplies Ltd, at a cost of £9000. However, owing to a downturn in trade, Mr Davey asks Timber Supplies Ltd to be released from the contract and the timber merchant agrees.

3 *Precision Engineering Ltd* buys two large guillotines from Western Machines Ltd. The total cost is £12 500, including VAT. The machines are delivered on 1 August and Precision Engineering settles the account in full by cheque.

4 *Derek Scales* is sales manager for a large firm producing leather, Leather Supplies Ltd. He signs a contract on behalf of his company to supply a consignment of leather to a company producing fashion shoes in the East Midlands. Delivery is agreed for 1 October 1994. Derek's firm cannot meet the delivery date and he rings the shoe manufacturer to say that delivery will not be until February 1995. As a result the shoe manufacturer loses important business.

6.4   Remedies for breach of contract

Damages

Let us return for a moment to our example of the contract between Concorde Car (Sales) plc and the Sceptre Hotel. We will assume for a moment that Concorde has made all its arrangements for the sales conference and has employed the services of a firm of marketing consultants to organise the conference on its behalf. On 20 September, that is one day before the conference, the manager of the Sceptre, Andrew Collier, rings Concorde to say that, owing to administrative errors, overbooking has taken place and that he has no alternative but to cancel the conference arrangements.

Clearly the Sceptre Hotel is in breach of contract and Concorde would sue for compensation for expenses incurred. It is obvious that Concorde has no chance of arranging alternative accommodation and the court will award damages, as they are called, to compensate Concorde for the loss incurred. If the cancellation had been made earlier and had provided Concorde with an opportunity to make alternative arrangements for their conference then the level of damages awarded would be reduced. It has always been the rule that the injured party (here Concorde) should do what it can to minimise the loss. This is known as mitigation (reduction) of loss.

Concorde's management would argue that, because they have not been able to hold the planned conference, sales of new cars will not increase as expected; as you will remember, this was the objective of the conference. However, courts will only award damages in respect of (i) losses that might be fairly and reasonably considered as arising naturally from the breach and (ii) losses that might have been anticipated by both parties when the contract was made. It is unlikely that the courts would award damages in respect of possible loss of sales. This would be considered too remote. The following case, *Victoria Laundry (Windsor) Ltd* v. *Newman Industries Ltd* (1949), illustrates the rules relating to remoteness of damage quite well.

The laundry firm ordered a new boiler which arrived late. The court awarded damages for loss of normal profits which should have been anticipated by Newman Industries. The court would not award damages for loss by Victoria Laundry of a lucrative contract because the supplying firm could not possibly have known about this.

The three rules relating to the award of damages for breach of contract are as follows:

1 Damages are awarded so that the plaintiff will be compensated for the loss he/she has suffered.
2 Damages will be awarded only for loss that arises naturally from the breach and might have been anticipated by the two parties.
3 The injured party must do his/her best to minimise the loss resulting from the breach.

Another case which illustrates the way in which the courts assess the level of damages is *Heron II* (1969):

A shipowner was late in delivering a consignment of sugar to Basrah and the price of sugar went down sharply. The plaintiff sued for loss of profits and the court allowed this because it was held that this possibility should have been in the minds of both parties when they entered into the agreement.

Sometimes courts will award damages even though there is no contract but where one party has supplied goods or services. This is known as a 'quantum meruit' (for so much as he deserves) award.

The following case, *British Steel Corporation (BSC)* v. *Cleveland Bridge and Engineering Co Ltd* (1984) might help to explain.

BSC supplied steel to Cleveland while a contract was being negotiated. In fact there was no contract and BSC sued for recovery of the cost of the steel. The court awarded a *quantum meruit* payment.

Specific performance and injunction

Courts may at their discretion provide alternative remedies for breach of contract.

i)   A Specific Performance order which requires the defendant to do something.

and

ii)   An Injunction which requires a defendant **not** to do something

These two remedies are equitable remedies and will only be awarded if:

i)   damages are not an adequate remedy

and

ii)   the court can adequately supervise enforcement

The following examples will help to illustrate a specific performance order.

Alan Wilson is 37 and he has already had a very successful spell with a leading American electronics company. A British electronics company, British Electrics plc, wishes to employ him and offers him a salary of £125 000 per annum plus a house of his choice in any part of England. Alan and his wife wish to live in Kent and they view four very expensive houses near Canterbury. They decide on one particular house which they like so much that Alan makes its ownership a condition of employment. The house costs £220 000 and the company immediately signs a contract to purchase it from the present owner, Mrs Angela Duffy. Angela, however, changes her mind and refuses to complete the sale. British Electrics plc do not want damages, they want the house.

Courts have the power in such circumstances to award a 'specific performance order', that is an order which compels Mrs Duffy to specifically perform her side of the bargain, in this case to sell the house.

Specific performance orders will only be granted where damages would not be an adequate remedy. In this case British Electrics plc did not want money, they wanted the property. Specific performance orders will never be granted for any contract of a personal nature. Thus a person who contracts to work for a company and then refuses will never be made to do so. The company will only be able to claim damages.

___ **Exercise 9** _____

You might care to think for a moment why a specific performance order will never be awarded in employment contracts.

Entertainments Ltd have signed a contract with a well-known pop group, the Rocker Billies, whereby the group will give a live concert in a large Midlands town on 30 November 1994. The concert is a sell-out but one week before the event the Rocker Billies' agent, John Beckwith, rings Entertainments to say that the group will not be appearing because they have received a more valuable offer to appear in London.

Rocker Billies are clearly in breach of contract but, as we have seen, the court will never award a specific performance order for contracts of a personal nature. It is possible, however, for the court in this situation to award an injunction. An injunction is a court order directing a person not to do something. In this case an injunction would be awarded to prevent the Rocker Billies appearing elsewhere on 30 November. This order of course might persuade the group to appear for Entertainments Ltd, but if they decide not to then Entertainments will still get damages for any losses incurred. The situation is neatly summed up in the following case. In *Warner Brothers Pictures Incorporated* v. *Nelson* (1937), an actress had contracted with the film company not to work as an actress for anyone else during her present contract. It was held that she could be restrained by injunction from breaking this undertaking.

When describing the two remedies, specific performance and injunctions, we used the phrase 'the discretion of the courts'. This means that, in a breach of contract case, the court, if it finds for the plaintiff, must award damages, but it may award the other two remedies at its discretion. We call the order of specific performance and injunction, therefore, 'discretionary orders'.

Exercise 10

1 List the three remedies which might be available to a plaintiff in a breach of contract.
2 Specific orders may be awarded to enforce contracts of employment: true or false?
3 What is an injunction?
4 Explain the term 'discretionary' as it applies to specific performance and injunction orders.

Exercise 11

Examine the following examples and say what sort of remedy the court is likely to award for breach of contract.

1 Dovedale Motors Ltd agree to sell to John Bennett a new car for £1000 below the list price, which was at that time £9500. When the buyer, John Bennett goes to collect the car he is told it has been sold to another buyer at the list price. John claims £9500 damages.

2   Chris Oliver has signed a lucrative contract to play for a well-known football club. However, prior to his first appearance he decides to sign for a club offering him better terms.

3   United Antique Dealers Ltd agree to sell a rare piece of furniture for £17 500 to Tony Guest, but when Tony arrives to pick up his furniture he is told that the company has decided to sell it for a higher price.

4   Associated Properties Ltd sign a contract to sell Mr and Mrs E. Disdale a three-bedroomed house for £102 500. The company refuses to complete the sale and Mr and Mrs Disdale seek a specific performance order. On the same estate there are about six similar houses for sale from another company for £102 500.

Transnational contracts

Many contracts are made in a modern business environment which involves more than one country. In recent years, as a result of the UK's membership of the European Union, increasing numbers of contracts are now made involving one or more European Union countries. The difficulty lies, of course, in knowing which law of contract applies. German, French, and Spanish law, for example, are quite different from the system of common law which applies in the UK. The following example may help to explain how contracts between different European countries might be affected by different systems of law.

Katy Pullin and her brother Matthew have just completed business courses at their local college. Both are very keen on football and, following a visit to Spain, they hit on the idea of producing football kits with the shirts bearing the names of certain players. They start off just producing kits for the Bristol Rovers football club but the concept proves popular and they are approached by a number of other clubs in the West Country to produce kits for them which are sold in their clubs' shops. Soon sales of these very cheaply produced products reach a level which persuades Katy and Matthew to form a private company, which they decide to call Twerton Associates, and soon they are producing kits for clubs all over the country.

Twerton Associates enter into a number of contractual agreements with a number of football clubs and also a number of sports shops and these agreements are based on the English law of contracts. However news of this successful product soon reaches Europe and a number of clubs and sports shops in France, Germany, Spain, Belgium and Holland write to the company asking for supplies in their chosen colours and motifs. This proves something of a problem, but fortunately the Pullins' grandfather, Dr Daniel Jones, is fluent in several major European languages and he is able to help the company in its dealings with its new European customers.

The trade with Europe means that contracts have to be made with a range of organisations, each with their own legal systems. In England, of course, contracts are regulated by the system of common law (see Chapter 2). All of our European partners' systems of law are based upon civil codes and this results in different applications in relation to contracts and other aspects of the law.

In 1980 the member states of the European community signed the Rome Convention on the Law Applicable to Contract. This Convention has been brought into force in England by the Contracts (Applicable Law) Act 1990. Let us see how this Convention and Act might apply to a contract made by Twerton Associates with a European customer.

One of Twerton Associates' first European customers is a small chain of sports shops operating in the Rheinland-Pfalz region of Germany. This chain is known as Henry Kaspar GmbH. They require a supply of kits representing the colours of one of the Bundeslega teams. In entering into this arrangement, Twerton Associates offer the following contractual arrangement to their customers.

A CONTRACT

between

TWERTON ASSOCIATES Ltd and H KASPAR GmbH

A contract between *Twerton Associates Ltd* (hereinafter known as the supplier) and *H Kaspar GmbH* (hereinafter known as the customer) wherein the supplier agrees to supply 1000 kits in three specific sizes with the colours and motifs of *Kaisersläutern FC*.

The supplier agrees to deliver the goods on or before *August 26th 1994*.

The customer agrees to pay for each kit the sum of *£25* making a total sum of *£25 000* payable in *Deutschmarks (DM)* at the currency rate prevailing on the day when the goods are received by the customer.

The customer agrees to make the payment within 4 weeks from the date of receipt of the goods by means of a direct payment into the suppliers account, Midland Bank, Wells Road, Bristol, code 40-16-11, account number 21184507.

This contract will be governed by the laws of contract applying in the UK. Disputes in the first instance will be referred to the London Court of Arbitration and any dispute arising therefrom will be held in the County Court in the City of Bristol UK. This court will have exclusive jurisdiction relating to any matter arising from this contract.

K Pullin

As you can see, Twerton Associates Ltd have specifically indicated that they would wish any dispute arising from the agreement to be settled according to English law. The company has also appointed an arbitrator, the London Court of Arbitration, to try to reach a settlement.

The Convention (1980) and Contracts (Applicable Law) Act 1990 lay down three rules:

1   the parties are free to choose the law applicable to their contract by adopting a choice-of-law clause;
2   if a choice-of-law clause is not inserted then the contract will be governed by the law of the country with which it is most closely connected (usually this will be the party who has to deliver the goods);
3   the contract will be formally valid if it satisfies the formal requirements of the law applicable in accordance with the two previous rules or it satisfies the formal requirements of the law of the country where the contract is concluded.

In our contract, Twerton Associates Ltd have specifically adopted a choice-of-law clause and have specified English law and English courts. If they had not done so it is likely that English law and English courts would be inferred (see clause 2 above). There is nothing, it would seem, in the arrangement which is contrary to English contractual law or against public policy. The Convention (1980) preserves the right to reject a choice-of-law option where it is manifestly against the public policy of that country.

Two other matters, concerning arbitration and courts, remain to be examined.

Arbitration.   The European Union convention on arbitration was never signed by the UK and therefore never ratified and arbitration rules differ in different EU countries. However if Kaspar GmbH accept the arrangement then probably there will be no problem. Any dispute will be referred to the London Court of Arbitration which is not a court in the legal sense. A meeting is held and the arbitrator, on the evidence he has, makes the award: for example, if Kaspar GmbH refuse to pay the full price for the goods because of a dispute over quality, the arbitrator will make a decision.

Courts.   There are no specific EU rules on this matter but, if the parties specify the court and indicate it in the choice-of-jurisdiction clause, together with a statement that that court has exclusive jurisdiction, then provided that one of the parties is not seriously disadvantaged by this it will be followed. In our case the court has been established and it has been given exclusive jurisdiction.

___ **Exercise 12** _____

1 Explain the effects of the Contracts (Applicable Law) Act 1990.
2 Where do you think disputes in the following situation would be heard
  and what national law would be applied in the following situation,
  assuming no choice-of-law or choice-of-jurisdiction clauses had been
  introduced?

*Ziegler AG, a German company producing wine, enter into a contractual
relationship with an English supermarket chain to supply a wide range
of German wines.*

⑦ Employment law

7.1 Nature of employment contracts

Brian Webb is 29 years old and has been employed as a workshop foreman for three years with Universal Machines Ltd. He is a very ambitious man and has been studying at the local technical college, where he has been successful in gaining good engineering qualifications. While reading through the local newspaper he notices the following advertisement:

High Peak Engineering PLC

A prosperous company producing machine tools in the North West of England require a man or woman as:

WORKSHOP ENGINEER

£20–23 000 per annum to supervise the workshop. You should possess at least a degree or a NVQ qualification in engineering at level IV, and have had broad-based experience in practical engineering and management.

Applications in writing should be made within 14 days of the appearance of the advertisement to:

> J. F. Honeywell
> Personnel Manager
> High Peak Engineering PLC
> Castle Road
> Dove Holes (Nr Buxton)
> Derbyshire

You will note that the company has been careful to indicate that it requires a man or woman. It is important that every employer of labour is aware of the Sex Discrimination Act 1975 and the Race Relations Act 1976, which make it unlawful for a person in relation to employment in England, Wales or Scotland to discriminate against a man or woman on ground of sex, marital status, colour, race, nationality or ethnic or national origin:

1. in the arrangements made for the purpose of deciding who should be offered the job; or
2. in the terms on which the job is offered; or
3. by refusing or deliberately omitting to offer the job.

Not only in recruitment but also during the operation of a contract of employment an employer can face legal action if he practises discrimination on grounds of sex, marital status, colour or race. The following decided case illustrate this.

In a redundancy case, *Nemes* v. *Allen* (1977), the employer dismissed female workers when they married. One such worker, Mrs Allen, was offered alternative employment which she refused and she was dismissed. It was held that Mrs Allen had been unlawfully discriminated against, contrary to the Sex Discrimination Act 1975, because she was a woman and was married.

Discrimination is possible where it can be shown that it is a genuine qualification to be of one sex or of an ethnic origin. So, for example, it is regarded as lawful to reserve posts in Indian restaurants for Indians. Some jobs require a man or woman, for example actors or actresses. Physical strength may not be regarded as a quality to justify discrimination. The following case sums this up well.

In *Shields* v. *Coomes* (1979), male counter-hands in a betting shop were paid more than women doing the same work, allegedly because it was the men who would have to deal with trouble or violence. This was held to be discrimination, because the men had no special training and, in any event, properly trained women could deal with violence equally well. The Court of Appeal upheld this finding.

Brian Webb decides to make an application for the post advertised in High Peak Engineering PLC and writes a letter which gives details of his qualifications and experience. A few weeks later, Brian is invited for interview with the managing director, the chief engineer and the personnel manager. Following the interview, Brian is asked to wait in an adjoining office while the managing director and his colleagues discuss Brian's application. Deciding that Brian is the sort of man they are looking for, the managing director asks Brian to see him again and explains the terms and conditions relating to the job. The managing director then offers Brian the post and Brian accepts immediately, agreeing to commence work in a month's time, on 26 September 1994.

A legally binding contract has come into existence between High Peak Engineering and Brian even though, as yet, there has been nothing in writing between the two parties to the agreement. Contracts of employment are simple contracts which need not be in writing, though it would be usual practice for High Peak Engineering to send a letter confirming the offer and asking Brian to reply confirming his acceptance.

For any agreement to be legally binding it must contain, as we have already learned, seven elements. It will be useful to examine this particular agreement to make sure that these elements are present. First, the managing director made an offer which Brian Webb accepted. The consideration, which is in the future, is Brian's services as workshop engineer and the wage of £21 000 paid to Brian by High Peak Engineering. As we have already discovered, in the absence of any statement to the contrary there is an assumption in situations of this sort that both parties intended their agreement to have legal consequences. There is nothing illegal about producing machine tools and we can assume that there is nothing illegal about this agreement. On the question of legal capacity, a man of 29 has full legal capacity to enter into a contractual relationship of this sort, and we must assume that the managing director of High Peak Engineering had the right to act for his company in offering Brian the post. There is then just one final element which must be satisfied for this agreement to be legally binding and that is to ascertain whether the agreement between the two parties was real; was there *consensus ad idem*? Did Brian and High Peak Engineering enter into the agreement freely and in possession of the necessary information? We can assume that neither party felt threatened in any way and that both partners freely entered into the agreement, but on the second point are we sure that there was no misrepresentation on either side which might have persuaded the other party to reach an agreement? You will remember that in the advertisement it mentioned the need for a degree or NVQ level IV in engineering and if Brian had stated he was in possession of this qualification when, in fact, he had not obtained it, then the company when they discovered this could dismiss Brian or, if they knew in time, avoid the contract before Brian commenced work. It is important to remember that misrepresentation may cause an employee to lose his job. The following decided case, *Torr* v. *British Railways Board* (1977, illustrates this point very well.

In 1974 Torr stated on his application for a job as a guard that he had never been found guilty of a criminal offence. This was untrue since he had been imprisoned for three years in 1958. When his employers discovered this Torr was suspended and then dismissed He was told that the dismissal was fair since this position is one of trust and responsibility.

As you will appreciate, it is often difficult for people who have been in prison to obtain work, and to assist them the Rehabilitation of Offenders Act 1974 was passed. By this Act, it is possible for persons who have been convicted of offences for which sentences of up to two and a half years have been imposed (suspended or otherwise) to treat these as 'spent'; that is, they need not declare them even if asked. In the case just quoted, Mr Torr was outside the scope of this Act because his sentence was three years.

However, if a person is within the scope of the Rehabilitation of Offenders Act 1974, he/she can reply 'no' quite legitimately to the question about a criminal conviction where that conviction has been 'spent'.

In *Property Guards* Ltd v. *Taylor* (1982), two applicants for jobs as security guards replied 'no' to the question whether they had had previous convictions. When the company discovered they had in fact had convictions they were dismissed. The court held that the dismissal was unfair because the convictions were 'spent'.

It is important to note that certain types of employment fall outside the scope of the Act, for example an application for the post of schoolteacher. However, in these cases, the fact of the exemption must be brought to the notice of the applicant.

We have now seen that a contract of employment, as any other simple contract, must contain the following seven elements:

1 offer;
2 acceptance;
3 two-way consideration;
4 legality;
5 each party must have capacity;
6 there must be legal intent;
7 there must be a real agreement, that is one not based upon duress, undue influence or misrepresentation.

We have also learned that a contract of employment need not be in writing. Thus, if Brian decided, because, for example, his present firm were willing to make him a better offer, that he would not after all be joining High Peak Engineering, he would be in breach of contract even though there had been nothing in writing. If High Peak Engineering decided to sue Brian for breach of contract, the company could be awarded damages. The court will never in these circumstances order Brian to work for High Peak Engineering because, as we have already seen, specific performance orders will never be awarded in respect of personal services.

There are just two exceptions to the rule that a contract of employment need not be in writing. Under the Employment Protection (Consolidation) Act 1978 young people entering an apprenticeship must be given a written contract; and under the Merchant Shipping Act 1970 a written agreement must be signed by both parties for the engagement of a seaman on a ship registered in the UK.

Although apart from these two exceptions contracts of employment need not be in writing, it has now become necessary as a result of the Employment Protection (Consolidation) Act 1978, as amended by the Trade Union Reform and Employment Rights Act 1993 which brought together legislation under the 1963 and 1972 Contracts of Employment Acts, for an employer to give each employee within two months of his starting date a statement regarding his employment. This document is *not* a contract of employment. Thus it will be necessary for High Peak Engineering to give Brian Webb a written statement either when he begins his job or some time within the specified two-month period. Certain particulars must be given and the following document gives an indication of the type of document which Brian might be given; it will also serve to show the requirements of this part of the Act. The requirement to provide this statement applies equally to part-time workers working eight hours a week or more.

EMPLOYMENT PROTECTION (CONSOLIDATION) ACT 1978
High Peak Engineering Co. Ltd

Name: Brian Frank Webb   Date of commencement of employment:
26 September 1994
Date when particulars were
given: 10 October 1994

1   You are employed in the service of this Company and your appointment is to the post of Workshop Engineer.

2   Your current salary is £21 000 per annum within the salary scale
£20–23 000 per annum, rising by four annual increments of £750. Your
salary will be paid at monthly intervals on the 25th of each calendar
month and will be by direct transfer to your bank.

3   *Working week.* The normal working hours will be Monday – Friday
8.30 a.m.–5.00 p.m. with one hour lunch break to be taken between
12.30 p.m. and 2.30 p.m.

4   *Holiday entitlement.* This is calculated at the rate of two days' holiday
for each month's completed service, representing a total annual holiday
entitlement of 24 days in addition to the normal statutory holidays. If an
employee's contract is terminated the company will pay that employee
a sum equal to the holiday entitlement due to date.

5   *Sickness allowance and procedures.* Entitlement to sick pay is based upon
30 days' full pay and 30 days' half pay except where sickness or injury is
directly attributable to your employment with the company in which case
a minimum of 6 months' full pay and 6 months' half pay is payable.

6   *Pension.* A pension scheme operates in the company which is contributory. Full details of this are set out in the company's Pension Scheme
booklet, a copy of which is attached. A contracting out certificate is in
force in respect of the company's pension scheme.

7   *Notice.* Except in cases of serious breaches of conditions the employment to which these particulars refer is terminable by one month on
either side or such time as is laid down in existing employment legislation.

8   *Disciplinary arrangements.* Disciplinary arrangements applicable to
this employment are to be found in the booklet 'Disciplinary
Procedures in Relation to Salaried Staff, High Peak Engineering 1992'
which is available from the Personnel Office.

9   *Grievance procedure.* If you have any grievance relating to this
employment, contact in the first instance Mr K. Martin, Works
Manager.

10   *Changes.* Details of changes to these particulars will be notified to you
or will appear in the Company's monthly staff bulletin.

Please note that this document is not a contract of employment. Your contract rests upon your letter of appointment and other implied terms and conditions relating to this post.

Signed: B. Hamilton,
Company Secretary
Date: 10.10.94

The above document, which refers specifically to B.F. Webb and his employment with High Peak Engineering gives some idea of the sort of information
which these particulars must provide. It has now become necessary for all
employees to receive such a document, with the following exceptions:

1   Part-time employees working less than eight hours a week.
2   Where an employee works wholly or mainly outside the UK.
3   Where written particulars have already been embodied in a written contract,
    for example, as required in apprenticeship contracts.

It is very important to understand the significance of the written particulars
which must now be provided in most cases to employees. As our example
stated, the particulars are not a contract and a binding contract of employment is
still in existence even though an employer fails to provide the particulars within
the designated two-month limit. If Brian Webb had not been supplied with this
document he could make an application to an industrial tribunal; once the tribunal had ruled on the particulars to be supplied then they would become part of
Brian's contract of employment. It is in the interest of both employer and
employee that a written statement is provided because either party could find
himself at a serious disadvantage in any legal proceedings which might arise
out of the contract. In the particulars supplied to Brian Webb, reference was
made to the company's monthly bulletin in which details of changes might be
given. Alternatively it was suggested also under point 10 of the document that
changes would be notified directly to Brian. However it must be emphasised
that, even where the changes have not been notified, they still may be operational and part of a legally binding contract. This important point is neatly
summed up in *Parkes Classic Confectionery* v. *Ashcroft* (1973).

The written particulars of Ashcroft's employment stated that she was required
to work for 22 hours a week. When she was dismissed for redundancy her
employers contended that the redundancy payment should be based upon the
shortened number of hours she now worked, written particulars of which had not
been given to the employee.

It was held that the employer's failure to give the appropriate notice of the
changed conditions of employment as required by the Contract of Employment Act
1972 (now replaced by the 1978 Act) did not make the change ineffective; thus her
redundancy payment should be based upon the current number of working hours.

As well as emphasising that the changes need not be notified to be part of a contract, this case also illustrates well that the particulars are not part of the contract.

Exercise 1

Read the following examples and say whether or not a legally binding
contract exists.

1   Matthew Brown is an accountant and he agrees to prepare the accounts
    of his father's small retail business. He does not intend to make a charge

for his services, saying it is a way of saying thank you for all the help his father has given him. A few weeks later, following a family dispute, Matthew refuses to fulfil his promise and his father decides to take legal action against him.

2 Vic Woodruffe sees an advertisement for a foreman bricklayer in his local paper and he writes to the firm of builders in question agreeing to work for them at a wage of £235 per week.

3 Keith Robinson is a works engineer at Harpur Engineering Ltd. Knowing that his firm is about to advertise for a workshop supervisor, he decides to interview a friend and neighbour, Roy Spencer, who is a qualified engineer. Keith offers his neighbour the post and Roy accepts.

4 Michelle Bennett, a graduate in Arabic Studies and a fluent speaker, accepts a post as translator with a consortium of government scientists who have made arrangements with an Arab State to send that state regular information regarding British government defence research.

5 Tony Green applies for a job as a heavy goods lorry driver, a condition of which is that the person appointed should have an HGV (Heavy Goods Vehicle) licence. Although Tony is a competent driver, he does not have this licence, but at his interview he claims that he does. Two months later his firm discovers that he does not, in fact, hold this licence and he is threatened with dismissal.

6 Frances Hollingsbee has been offered and accepted a post as secretary to the personnel manager at Trenchard Industrial Holdings. Two days before she is due to start she phones the firm saying that she has changed her mind about the post and, since she has received no confirmatory letter, she is not bound by her agreement.

__ Exercise 2 _____

In the following cases, advise the party in italics of his/her legal position.

1 *Peter May* has been a computer operator with a firm of merchant bankers for two years but he has never received a statement of particulars relating to the post. He decides to leave the firm without giving notice and decides to sue the firm for breach of contract.

2 Because she has received no written particulars in relation to her post as accounts clerk with Boston Furnishings Ltd, even though she has been with the firm for one year, *Audrey Worsley* decides to take the matter to the industrial tribunal, which endorses a statement containing details of a monthly wage of £110.50 based upon a 34-hour week. The firm accepts this but two months later seeks to reduce her wage to £100.50 and increase her hours to 37 per week.

> **3** In his application for a post as foreman joiner with Boscombe Builders Ltd, *Vivian Phillips*, a West Indian by origin, is told that because of his background he needs higher qualifications than British-born applicants.
>
> **4** After accepting a post with a travel company, *Anne Moore* is told that the 50 per cent holiday discount is only available to married male employees.

Employees and independent contractors

It is very important to distinguish between an employee and an independent contractor. The courts have used various tests to try to define employment.

At one time a simple test was that, if a person could be told by the employer what to do and how to do it then he was an employee. However this simple test proved inadequate: for example, can a hospital trust chief executive tell a surgeon how to do his/her job? Two tests are used nowadays:

1 If a person is an integral part of the organisation he is an employee, but if he performs work for the organisation but remains outside it he is an independent contractor. For example, a painter and decorator painting an office could be part of the company's maintenance team or could be an independent person who is performing the work for an agreed price.

> In *Cassidy* v. *Ministry of Health* (1951), a patient suffered damage to his hand as a result of the negligence of the surgeon. The court ruled that the surgeon was an employee of the hospital and the employer, then the Ministry of Health, was 'vicariously [indirectly] liable' and therefore should pay the compensation awarded.

This is in fact a negligence case; we will be looking at this topic in more detail in Chapter 11.

2 In recent years courts have taken a wider view than just the 'integration' test and have taken into account a range of factors:
   (a) the powers to appoint, suspend and dismiss;
   (b) the method of payment;
   (c) whether deductions are made for PAYE income tax and national insurance;
   (d) whether the person provides his own tools;
   (e) whether the person works on his own or the firm's premises;
   (f) independence as to hours of work;
   (g) whether the person receives or is entitled to receive sick pay;
   (h) the general economic reality of the situation.

The second test has often been called the 'multiple' or 'economic reality' test. Two cases may illustrate the distinction.

In *Ready Mix Concrete Ltd* v. *Ministry of Pensions and National Insurance* (1968), the company engaged drivers and sold them lorries on hire purchase, they were given uniforms and the lorries were in company colours. The driver/owners were responsible for maintenance and fuelling of their lorries and received payment on the basis of the number of loads carried and delivered. The court determined using the multiple test that the driver were not employees and therefore the company did not have to deduct national insurance from the payments.

In another case, *O'Kelly* v. *Trust House Forte* (1983), it was held that casual waiting staff were not employees because, although there was considerable supervision, there was no obligation on the part of THF to provide work or for the waiter/waitress to accept it.

The second case illustrates well the difficulty in making the distinction, which is, however, important because a company has certain responsibilities for employees but not to contractors. For example:

1   the company may be liable vicariously for the negligence of an employee but nor for the negligence of a contractor, (*Cassidy* v. *Ministry of Health* (1951));
2   there are certain rights laid down by statute available to an employee, such as redundancy, period of notice, unfair dismissal rights, statutory sick pay, maternity benefits;
3   an employer must deduct PAYE tax from his/her employees;
4   if a business fails employees' rights re unpaid wages and redundancy are greater for employees than for contractors.

The Finance Act 1980 rules, which were introduced to ensure subcontractors paid tax, laid down that a main contractor must deduct tax and national insurance from subscontractors unless they hold an exemption certificate, which only the Inland Revenue will issue and only where the subcontractor can prove he has kept satisfactory tax records for three years previously.

7.2   Terms of contracts of employment

Pat Browne is employed as a typist for Associated Food Supplies. Her wage is £185.00 for a 37-hour week. From time to time, as part of her duties, Pat has to operate a guillotine machine which does not have the required guard attached to it.

Pat has never really hit it off with the office manager, Mrs. E. Smythe, and Pat shows her dislike on frequent occasions by outright disobedience in respect of Mrs Smythe's instructions and also by completing tasks given to her by Mrs Smythe both carelessly and incompetently. Mrs Smythe reports the problem to the firm's chief executive, who has overall responsibility for the work of the office. He sees Pat and warns her of the consequences of her disobedience, carelessness and incompetence. Pat replies by pointing out that the company is not fulfilling its duty to her by asking her to operate an unguarded guillotine. The chief executive concludes the interview with Pat by warning her that the company has been considering terminating her contract because of her continued membership of a trade union when she has had ample opportunity to join the company's own clerical staff association.

Terms relating to the employee

All contracts of employment will have within them express terms. These terms form the basis of the contract and if not upheld may lead the other party to the contract to treat the agreement as breached. Express conditions, as the words suggest, are those conditions which are actually expressed or stated either verbally or in writing. Thus in the example we have just read an express condition would be the £185.00 for a 37-hour week. There are, however, existing in contracts of employment a number of implied conditions. We have already learned that some contracts contain implied terms and what they are: these are terms which are not stated but nevertheless they exist and failure to uphold them may lead to breach, just as with express terms.

Implied term: to obey lawful instructions. When a person takes up employment he is bound by the implied term that he must obey reasonable and legal orders given by his employer or someone designated by the employer. It is quite obvious that Pat has a legal duty to obey orders and continued failure to do so could lead to her contract being terminated. This fact is well illustrated in *Pepper* v. *Webb* (1969).

> Pepper, a head gardener, refused to obey an order to plant flowers to prevent them deteriorating over the weekend while he was off duty. When questioned on weekend arrangements for the care of the greenhouse, Pepper replied, 'I couldn't care less about your bloody greenhouse or your sodding garden' and walked away. There had been complaints about inefficiency and insolence preceding this incident. Pepper was instantly dismissed without notice or payment in lieu of notice. He claimed damages for breach of contract of employment which specifically provided for three months' notice.

It was held that, by wilfully disobeying a lawful order, Pepper had shown his intention not to fulfil his contractual duties, which together with his previous conduct justified instant dismissal. It is important to remember that disobedience is permissible when the instruction from the employer is illegal or unreasonable. For example, in *Morrish* v. *Henlys (Folkestone) Ltd* (1973), a driver was sacked for refusing to obey his manager's order to make false claims for petrol expenses. Disobedience was held justified, and his dismissal was unfair. However in *Cresswell* v. *IRC* (1984), where an income tax officer had refused to work with new technology, it was held that this involved a lawful instruction to require an employee to 'adapt himself to new methods and techniques introduced in the course of employment'.

Implied term: to work competently and carefully. A second important implied term is the requirement that the employee works competently and carefully, and if Pat insists on producing incompetent, badly typed, careless work she is clearly in breach of this term and therefore, in breach of contract of employment. The standard of care and competency expected of an employee will vary in the light of what is expected of the particular occupation. Higher standards may be expected of professional persons such as doctors, solicitors or architects. This is summed up well in the following case. In *Harmer* v. *Cornelius* (1858), a man who accepted a job as a scene painter proved quite incapable of painting scenes, and was lawfully dismissed without notice. Another more recent case illustrate this point well:

> In *Tayside Regional Council* v. *McIntosh* (1982), a vehicle mechanic was disqualified from driving and was dismissed from his employment even though there was nothing in the express terms about his having to drive as part of his employment. The court decided that the dismissal was fair because this 'competency' was an important part of the job and was an implied term.

Implied term: to obey the rules of the organisation.   It is a further implied term that an employee accepts the rules of the organisation by which he or she is employed. An employee who breaks the rules can be said to be misconducting himself and may be at risk of being dismissed for breach of contract. Thus if Pat arrived for work each morning at 9.30 a.m. instead of 9.00 a.m. and insisted on taking two hours for lunch instead of the allocated one hour, then her employer would be quite justified in dismissing her without notice.

Implied term: to show good faith to the employer. Finally all contracts of employment contain the important implied term that an employee shows 'good faith' to his employer. 'Good faith' covers a whole range of aspects but it will suffice to give just two examples. In an office a good deal of confidential information is available, especially among those engaged as typists; and if Pat decided to pass on information about her employer's new plans to a rival, then this would clearly be regarded as a breach of faith. Secondly, if Pat was aware that one of her colleagues was involved in financial activities detrimental to the firm's interest, such as embezzling the firm's money, she would have a duty to her employer to pass on this information. Failure to disclose this information could be regarded as a breach of faith and therefore breach of an implied condition. Three cases sum this up very well. In *Hivac Ltd* v. *Park Royal Scientific Instruments Ltd* (1946), the appellants manufactured midget valves for hearing aids. Certain of their highly skilled workers began to work on Sundays for the respondents, a competing business which had been set up nearby. It was held that the workers were in breach of good faith and an injunction was granted restraining the respondents from employing them. In *Reading* v. *Attorney General* (1951), an army sergeant serving in Egypt used to accompany lorries which were smuggling liquor. Because he was wearing uniform, the lorries were not searched. It was held that the 'profits' accruing to him from this enterprise (some £20 000) belonged to the Crown. In *Stevenson, Jordan and Harrison Ltd* v. *Macdonald & Evans* (1952) the court ruled that an accountant who sold the copyright of a manuscript of a book on business management had no right to do so since the work was done as part of a project he had carried out for his employers. The accountant was said not to be acting in 'good faith' to his employers. This case is important because many employees, especially in universities, might develop work as part of a project or part of their lecturing duties. If they contract with a publisher, are they not acting 'in good faith'?

Thus, in addition to any express terms in a contract, an employee is bound by implied conditions. An employee who breaks his contract of employment terms may be dismissed. As we shall see, though, any employee who feels he has been unfairly dismissed may appeal to an industrial tribunal.

Exercise 3

List the four implied terms that are always implied in a contract of employment which apply to an employee.

Terms relating to the employer

Not only is the employee subject to express and implied terms but employers are also in a similar position. It is, of course, necessary for Associated Food Supplies to pay Pat a weekly wage of £185.00 because this is an express term. The employer is also bound by certain implied terms. First, the employer has to provide a safe system of work and the absence of the regulation guard protecting the guillotine would suggest that this term is not being adequately fulfilled. The law states quite clearly that an employee must not be discriminated against or dismissed because he is a member of a trade union. The mention of trade union activity by Associated Food's chief executive would clearly be inconsistent with this condition. Under the Employment Protection (Consolidation) Act 1978, and as amended by Employment Acts 1980, 1982, 1988 and 1990, it is unlawful for an employer to discriminate against an employee because he joins a trade union or refuses to join a trade union. In *Carlson* v. *Post Office* (1981) the refusal to issue a parking permit to Mr Carlson because he was a union member was held to be discrimination.

As pointed out earlier, employees also must not discriminate on grounds of sex, race, or national origin.

Where an employee incurs expense in carrying out business on behalf of his employer, then the employer has an implied duty to reimburse the employee. Thus, if Pat is required to travel to a branch office in a nearby town for her employer, her company must pay her reasonable travelling and out-of-pocket expenses. It is an obvious but nevertheless an implied duty that an employer must deduct PAYE tax and national insurance contributions. Employers must provide a reasonable system of management.

Thus, in addition to any express term which is stated, an employer is bound by implied terms.

Exercise 4

List the implied terms to which an employer is bound.

It is interesting to note that an employer is not obliged to give any employee a reference for another post. If, however, the employer does give an employee a reference it is usually confidential between one employer and another and is not, therefore, normally seen by the employee. If the employee does learn of the contents of the reference the employer is protected from a defamation action as long as there was an attempt to state his honest opinion and there was no malice. From what we have read, it is unlikely that Associated Food would give Pat Browne a glowing reference, but even if some of the statements they made about Pat were not completely true, if Pat discovered this she would not be successful in suing the firm. The law as it relates to defamation will be dealt with in Chapter 12. Provided an employer makes his remarks in a reference in good faith, he is protected, as we shall see, from any action in defamation. An employer who wishes to get rid of an unsatisfactory employee might be tempted to give the employee in question a good reference if he applied for another post. However, in giving references, an employer owes the other, prospective employer a duty of care; if he makes a statement negligently or dishonestly, and on the basis of this statement the employee gets another job, then, if the employee is unsatisfactory and causes his new employer some loss, the first employer might be sued for negligence. The case of *Hedley Byrne* v. *Heller* (1964) was a powerful reminder to employers that they must be careful in making statements in references and therefore it is sensible to add something like, 'The Company in giving this reference accepts no responsibility for its accuracy.' An employer who gives a good reference to get rid of someone may run a risk within his own organisation. In *Haspell* v. *Rostron & Johnson Ltd* (1976), the employer who gave a favourable reference was estopped from relying on inconsistent allegations when he later tried to justify dismissing the employee. 'Estopped' is a legal term meaning 'prevented from'.

Sex and race discrimination

The Sex Discrimination Acts 1975 and 1986 and the Race Relations Act 1976 make it unlawful to discriminate on grounds of sex (or against married persons) or race in the fields of employment, education, housing, grants, facilities, services and advertising.

These Acts also cover discrimination by employers in recruitment and in relation to existing employees. There are some examples where employers can show that it is necessary for a job to be done by a person of one sex (for example, a warden of a female hall of residence should be a woman) or of one particular racial group (the employment of Chinese in Chinese restaurants). In these instances discrimination in selection is permitted. Decency or privacy may require discrimination. The courts will look closely at any case of discrimination, as the following shows. In *Wylie* v. *Dee & Co. (Menswear) Ltd* (1978), an employer refused to employ a woman as sales assistant in a menswear shop. This was held to be unlawful discrimination. It could not be justified on decency grounds, because customers could change in a private cubicle. Contact such as inside-leg measurement was rarely required, and could be carried out by one of the other seven assistants, all male, if need be.

The Sex Discrimination Acts 1975 and 1986 as amended by the Employment Act 1989 which now provide the law relating to sex discrimination are also subject to European rules on equal pay (Directive 75/117) and equal treatment (Directive 76/207). Two European Court of Justice decisions, *Dekker* v. *VJV Centrum* (1991) and *Hertz* v. *Aldi Marked* (1991), provide protection to women who seek leave for reasons of pregnancy.

The European Court has also ruled, drawing on article 119, in *Marshall* v. *Southampton Area Health Authority* (1986) and *Barber* v. *Guardian Royal Assurance* (1990), that employers must adopt common retirement ages for men and women.

It is important to remember that some cases of sex or racial discrimination can be indirect, as where a height restriction applies to a job which has the effect of denying certain racial groups. In *Price* v. *The Civil Service Commission* (1987), it was held to be an indirect case of sex discrimination to set applicant age limits between 17 and 28. This was held to be discriminatory against women because these limits often covered the 'child-bearing' period.

The Equal Opportunities Commission and the Commission for Racial Equality can conduct formal investigations and both Commissions have issued Codes of Practice for employers and employees.

Equal pay

Following the Equal Pay Act it is necessary for employers to treat men and women equally in terms of pay and conditions. A man or woman can appeal to the Industrial Tribunal under the Equal Pay Act.

House of Lords

Woman's entitlement to equal pay

Hayward v Cammel Laird Shipbuilders Ltd

Before Lord Mackay of Clashfern, Lord Chancellor, Lord Bridge of Harwich, Lord Brandon of Oakbrook, Lord Griffiths and Lord Goff of Chieveley.

[Speeches May 5]

A woman was entitled under the equal pay legislation to have the same term as to basic pay as her male comparators irrespective of whether she was as favourably treated as the man when the whole of the benefits of their contracts were taken into account.

The House of Lords so held in allowing an appeal by Miss Julie Hayward, a cook at Cammell Laird Shipbuilders Ltd, from the decision of the Court of Appeal (Lord Justice Purchas, Lord Justice Nicholls and Sir Roualeyn Cuming-Bruce; The Times March 5, 1987; [1988] QB 12) to uphold the dismissal by the Employment Appeal Tribunal of her appeal from the order of an industrial tribunal that she was not entitled to a declaration under section I(2) of the Equal Pay Act 1970, as amended by the Sex Discrimination Act 1975 and the Equal Pay (Amendment) Regulations (SI 1983 No 1794) that she should receive a higher rate of pay.

Mr Anthony Lester, QC and Mr David Pannick for the employee; Lord Irvine of Lairg, QC and Mr Charles James for the employers.

THE LORD CHANCELLOR said that the issue was whether in terms of the Equal Pay Act 1970, as amended, the woman who could point to a term of her contract which was less favourable than a term of a similar kind in the man's contract was entitled to have that term made not less favourable irrespective of whether she was as favourably treated as the man when the whole of their contracts were considered.

There was no definition of the word 'term' in the legislation. The natural meaning of the word in the present context was a distinct provision of part of the contract which had sufficient content to make it possible to compare it from the point of view of the benefits it conferred with similar provision or part in another contract.

For example the employee had been employed on her accepting terms set out in a letter which included the following: 'We can offer you a position on our staff as a cook at a salary of £5.165 per annum. The base rate on which overtime is based is £4.741 . . .'. The letter had set out the normal hours of work, providing that the overtime payment should be plain time rate plus a third (two-thirds on Saturday and Sunday).

The corresponding provision with regard to basic pay in the men's contracts was less specific and referred to a national agreement from which the rate of wages and overtime payments were to be determined.

The natural application of the word 'term' in her contract was that it applied for example, to the basic pay, and that the appropriate comparison was with the hourly rate of basic pay.

But the respondents said that this was not correct and that the use of the expression in section I(2) defining an equality clause as a provision which 'relates to terms (whether concerned with pay or not) of a contract' showed that Parliament had in mind that all provisions relating to pay were to be considered as a single term and that accordingly it was only by taking account of all the contractual provisions relating to pay that one could make the comparison which was envisaged.

They went on to say that if that was not correct, many difficulties were likely to arise. For example, where a woman was paid less than a man but had the use of a car, it would be wrong to say that she was entitled to have the term dealing with basic pay put up and the man on applying under the same legislation would be able to say that there was no term in his contract giving him the use of a car and therefore he was entitled to one.

The employers submitted that the only way out of that difficulty was to consider together as one term all matters relating to pay however expressed, in order to produce a result that the woman was put up to equality with the man and no further, and the man put up to equality with the woman and no further, so that there was no general enhancement of their total remuneration.

It had been difficulties involving that and similar examples that had weighed with the Court of Appeal and the Employment Appeal Tribunal in deciding in the employees' favour.

While one could envisage difficult examples, in the ordinary case such as the present no such difficulty arose and it would be wrong to depart from the natural reading of the words Parliament had used because of the difficulty in their application to particular examples, especially when those examples did not arise in actual cases.

The difficulty of reconciling the employers' construction with the words used in the Act was emphasized when one considered the provisions of part (ii) in each of the sub-clauses (a), (b) and (c) of section I(2) as was pointed out by Lord Bridge in the course of the hearing.

It was impossible to believe that Parliament had envisaged a contract with no provision for pay at all and therefore if the employers' construction was adopted, part (ii) in each of the sub-sub-sections could apply only to other benefits.

That seemed a most unlikely construction when one noticed that the introductory words of subsection (2) which applied to parts (i) and (ii) spoke of 'terms (whether concerned with pay or not)'.

The employee's construction of section I(2) was to be preferred and the case would be remitted to the industrial tribunal for determination in accordance with that opinion.

On that view of the matter it was not strictly necessary to consider the question of Community law. His Lordship concluded, however, that there was nothing in the European legislation which detracted from the force of the employee's argument on the domestic legislation.

Lord Goff delivered a concurring speech and Lord Bridge, Lord Brandon and Lord Griffiths agreed.

Solicitors: Brian Thompson & Partners, Manchester; Davies Arnold & Cooper for Davis Campbell & Co, Liverpool.

The case above, which is an extract from *The Times*, shows very well the working of this Act. It also is an example of a case from the House of Lords. As you will see the case was heard in the Industrial Tribunal where Miss Hayward was unsuccessful and on appeal it was heard at the Employment Appeal Tribunal and at the Court of Appeal. Both these Appeal courts dismissed Miss Hayward's appeal. In May 1988 she was finally successful in what has become a very important case.

In two more recent cases, *British Coal* v. *Smith and others* (1994) and *North Yorkshire County Council* v. *Ratcliffe and others* (1994) it was established that in order to compare her pay with that of a man employed at the same or similar conditions, a woman had to show that the conditions of employment for men of the relevant class had to be the same, *not* broadly similar.

Article 119, which is part of European Union law, has often been used by employees in the UK and some important decisions have been made, such as *Barber* v. *Guardian Royal Assurance*(1990) which was referred to on page.119.

Maternity rights

In October 1994 a system of statutory maternity pay was introduced. To qualify a woman must:

1   have been in continuous employment with an employer for 26 weeks;
2   have been in employment up to the fifteenth week before the expected date of confinement (the birth). This fifteenth week is known as the qualifying week;
3   have been earning at least £44.50 per week;
4   must give at least 21 days' notice to her employer of her intended absence.

Benefits available.   A woman will be entitled to 18 weeks' maternity pay. This is payable from the eleventh week before the expected date of confinement. There are two rates:

1   the higher rate which is calculated at nine-tenths her weekly wage,
2   a lower rate payable for 12 weeks. This rate is set by the government.

A woman has the right to return to work at any time up to 29 weeks after the birth. This may be extended for four weeks with a doctor's certificate. The maximum allowed is 33 weeks.

An important change introduced in 1994 has been the extension of maternity rights to all women employees, irrespective of their length of service or whether they are full or part-time.

Statutory sick pay

An employer must pay sick pay to an employee who is away sick. No payment is due for the first three days of sickness but thereafter sick pay is payable on a wage of £52 or more. A scale of sick pay is laid down, which at present is:

Average weekly wage	Sick pay
£52–£184	£43.50
£185 or more	£52.50

An employee will be entitled to a maximum of 28 weeks SSP (Statutory Sick Pay) in any one period. Remember that, as with other aspects of employment law, these are minimum requirements and in many jobs full pay is available for quite long periods of sickness.

Employers can recover the amounts paid from government funds. Employers and employees contribute to the funds from national insurance contributions.

Data protection

The Data Protection Act 1984 was planned to regulate the use of personal data which can be processed by equipment operating automatically. A Data Protection Registrar is now in post and data users must register with him details of data held. From 1987 individuals have the right to be informed about personal data held on them. This right is available on request and must be provided within 40 days. Individuals may claim compensation if they suffer distress from disclosure of information to others.

This Act offers quite considerable protection to employees. There are a number of exceptions, particularly those relating to pay and so on. Also an employee can give his employer the right to disclose information.

Exercise 5

In the following examples advise the party in italics whether there exists a breach of condition.

1 Burlow Road Buildings Supplies Ltd decide to reduce the salary of their *office manager* from £250 to £215 a week.
2 *Michael Moore*, a development engineer, with Amalgamated Metals, is asked by the chief engineer to assist in painting the managing director's office. Michael refuses.
3 *Margaret Frances* is a confidential secretary to a solicitor and she is in the habit of discussing clients' legal problems with her friends.
4 *John Martin* is employed by a firm of motor engineers. He regularly takes home engine parts suitable for his own private car.
5 *Philip Hadfield* is a quantity surveyor with a large building contractor, and on three occasions he has made mistakes in working out estimates in jobs which have involved his firm in heavy losses.
6 *Richard Haigh* is a commercial traveller for Midlands Dairy Food but in the course of his work for one week he spends £123 on petrol and two nights' accommodation at a modest hotel. His firm refuse to pay out this expense.
7 *Fashion Textiles Ltd* cannot afford to provide protective guards and require all their employees to work on machinery which is unprotected and threaten them with redundancy if they complain.
8 *Reginald Pullen* has been with a TV rental firm for six years as an accounts clerk and has an excellent work record. He wishes to leave and applies for a post in London. His firm TV Rentals Ltd refuse to give him a reference for the post.

7.3   Unfair dismissal and redundancy

Notice

We have already seen that contracts of employment are just like any other contract, needing to contain the same essential elements. In this section we will be considering how contracts of employment may be brought to an end, what rights employees may have if they consider they have been unfairly dismissed, and the law in respect of redundancies.

> *Alan Phillips, aged 37, a married man with two young children, has been employed by Associated Engineering Co. in Newcastle-upon-Tyne for seven years as a storeman at a weekly wage of £250. Like many engineering companies, Associated Engineering are going through a very difficult trading phase and a decision is reached to trim the wages bill. In the stores where Alan works there are six employees and it is felt by the management that this section is overmanned. Alan, despite seven years' service, is the newest recruit and he is told that he will have to leave. Associated Engineering give Alan a week's notice and an* ex gratia *payment of £200. Alan feels he is entitled to more, but is not sure.*

Most contracts of employment end by means of one party or the other giving notice. How long this notice must be depends upon the particular contract between the employer and employee. Alan would check to see what it says in the particulars of employment which he should have been given (see page 110). These particulars should give details of the length of notice that needs to be given.

The Employment Protection (Consolidation) Act 1978 lays down minimum periods which must be given. An employer must give notice related to periods of continuous service on the following scale:

Length of service	*Period of notice*
4 weeks up to 2 years	1 week
2 years	2 weeks
3 years	3 weeks

and so on up to a maximum of 12 weeks for 12 years' service.

An employee needs to give one week after four weeks' service, and one week remains the legal minimum to be given by an employee.

It is important to remember that these are minimum periods and contracts of employment can stipulate any length of notice as long as they are at or above the minimum. In our example, Alan would be entitled to at least seven weeks' notice or, if Associated Engineering wished, seven weeks' pay 'in lieu' (instead) of notice, that is 7 × £250 = £1750.

Activity

If you are in employment, calculate the minimum period of notice your firm would have to give you as set out in the Employment Protection (Consolidation) Act 1978.

To qualify for those periods of minimum notice an employee must have been working at least 8 hours a week. What continuous employment means has been the subject of several cases which seem to give different opinions.

In *Ford* v. *Warwickshire County Council* (1983) a part-time teacher was held to have worked continuously for a number of years, even though she was given annual contracts. She argued that she always attended staff meetings even before the date of her annual contract. For the purposes of her notice period it was held that she had worked continuously.

However:

In the House of Lords in *Lewis* v. *Surrey County Council* (1987) the court came to a different decision and ruled that in similar circumstances Mrs Lewis could not argue continuous employment.

Exercise 6

Calculate the minimum amount of notice and the amount of money payable in lieu required by the Employment Protection (Consolidation) Act 1978 in the following examples.

1 Reg Pullin has been employed at Aston Containers Ltd for 14 years at a weekly wage of £300.
2 Carol Latham has been employed as a shorthand-typist with the local authority for 18 months at £120 per week.
3 Ken Gould has been a lathe operator with Trenchard Machinings Ltd for just three weeks at £162 per week.
4 Tracey Armstrong has been an office typist for two and a half years with Fisk, Mason and Wood, solicitors, at a salary of £120 per week.

Redundancy

Let us return to our example in respect of Alan Phillips – you will remember that, in addition to a week's notice, he was given an *ex gratia* payment of £200. *Ex gratia* means that it is a way for the company, Associated Engineering, to say thank you to Alan for his seven years' service. It is, however, likely that Alan is entitled to rather more than a £200 thank you. He may well be entitled to redundancy pay.

The Employment Protection (Consolidation) Act 1978 which incorporates the terms of the Redundancy Payments Act 1965 states that redundancy may arise where an employee is dismissed under one or other of the following circumstances:

1 the employer has ceased or intends to cease to carry on the business for the purposes for which the employee was employed by him; or
2 the employer has ceased or intends to cease to carry on that business in the place where the employee was so employed; or
3 the work needed to be done by the employee has either diminished or ceased to be necessary to the business of the employer (either generally or at the place where the employee worked) or is expected to diminish or cease.

It is important to remember that it is only the three reasons given above that can give rise to redundancy. It is possible for an employee to claim 'unfair redundancy' where he has been unfairly chosen. Employers must show that they have selected employees for redundancy in accordance with fair and objective procedures. They must show that they have provided proper consultation opportunities, using procedures laid down by ACAS (Advisory, Conciliation and Arbitration Service) and as indicated in decided cases such as, *Holden* v. *Bradwell* (1985).

The law also stipulates certain conditions whereby short-time working or temporary lay-offs can lead to redundancy.

Alan's situation would be similar to the third item. Alan has been dismissed because his work in the stores has diminished. There is no longer the need for so many storemen due to the fact that Associate Engineering have had a reduction in their business.

The Act also lays down the categories of employees who are not eligible for redundancy:

1 employees over retirement age, normally 65 for men and 60 for women;
2 part-time employees. For the purposes of the Act this means employees who work less than eight hours; [Until December 1994 to claim redundancy a part-time worker had to be working for 16 or more hours per week for two years. As a result of a House of Lords ruling following a European Directive in a case brought by the Equal Opportunities Commission the number of weekly hours has been reduced to 8.]
3 a woman employed by her husband or vice versa;

4   certain categories of employees, e.g. registered dock workers, government employees;
5   employees on fixed term contracts of two years or more who in the agreement establishing the contract or some time before expiry have agreed in writing to be excluded from redundancy payment at the end of their contract;
6   employees who have not reached their eighteenth birthday;
7   employees who have worked for the employer for less than two years.

Alan is a full-time employee, he has been with Associated Engineering for more than two years, he is not on a fixed term contract and he is not yet over retirement age. It would seem, therefore, that Alan would qualify for redundancy pay. The Employment Protection (Consolidation) Act 1978 lays down the following formula for calculating the amount of money that a person might claim for redundancy:

1   for whole years' service between the ages of 18 and 22 birthday, 1/2 week's pay for each year.
2   for whole year's service from the 22nd birthday to the 41st birthday 1 week's pay for each year.
3   from the 41st birthday until retirement age, one and a half weeks' pay for each whole year of completed service.

At present the maximum number of years service that can be taken into account is 20 years. The maximum salary to be taken into account is £205 per week. If the maximum salary is £205 and the maximum number of years is 20 then the maximum redundancy payment required by the state is $20 \times 1^1/_2 \times £205 = £6150$. Where a person's wage exceeds £205 then the amount by which the wage exceeds £205 is disregarded. This is the present position; the maximum wage allowed is revised from time to time.

The wage taken into account in the calculation is usually the wage earned in the last week of employment. Alan's wage was £250 but only £205 need be taken into account. Alan is 37 and all his 7 years' service is within the 22–41 band. He is entitled to a redundancy payment of $£205 \times 7 = £1435$.

In calculating redundancy pay, the employer must work back from the person's age so as to give him/her maximum benefit. If Janet Taylor (age 49) had been employed at a company for 20 years and her wages were £200 per week she would be entitled to:

$$8 \text{ years at } 1^1/_2 \times £200 = £2400$$
$$12 \text{ years at } 1 \times £200 = £2400$$

$$\text{Total} \qquad\qquad = £4800$$

A company is legally bound to give redundant employees full details of the way in which redundancy pay has been calculated.

Activity ─────────────────────────────────

The maximum wage which is used to calculate the statutory (laid down by Act of Parliament) redundancy entitlement is changed each year to reflect inflation and other economic changes. See if you can find out the maximum which is used at present.

Activity ─────────────────────────────────

If you are in employment, calculate the minimum amount of redundancy pay, if any, you would be entitled to under the law if you were made redundant.

Exercise 7 ─────────────────────────────────

In the following cases, for each (a) say whether the employee concerned would be entitled to redundancy under the Employment Protection (Consolidation) Act; (b) where appropriate, calculate the redundancy pay due.

1 Frederick Langton (58) has been a tax officer with the civil service for 20 years at a salary of £12 500 per annum. He is made redundant.
2 Bob Williams (24) has been with Associated Plant for eight years. His current wage is £140 per week. He is made redundant because of a serious fall-off in trade.
3 United Chemicals Ltd move from London to Manchester and Frank Brown (age 67), a cleaner, is made redundant. His wage is £75 and he has been with the firm for 30 years.
4 Rita Harrison (50) has been with United Foods Ltd as an accountant for 30 years at a wage of £210 per week. The company discontinue business and she claims redundancy.

Before we leave the subject of redundancy two further points need to be made. Firstly, what we have been considering is the minimum redundancy payment which firms must give. However, if a firm wishes to pay more than the legal minimum, this is in order. In fact many highly paid employees, particularly, receive quite lucrative 'golden handshakes' when they are made redundant: much more than the legal minimum. Secondly, when employees are made redundant they are sometimes offered alternative employment with the same firm and in some cases a refusal might jeopardise their entitlement to redundancy pay. To return to our original example:

Let us assume that Alan is offered the same job in Associated Engineering's London division. If, after considering this offer with his wife, Alan feels that a move from Newcastle-upon-Tyne, where he has lived all his life, is not really satisfactory and therefore turns down the offer, will he lose his redundancy entitlement of £1435?

Whether an alternative offer is suitable and therefore refusal is unreasonable will be judged on the facts of the particular case. Suitability is judged in terms of (a) status and (b) location. The following two cases will illustrate the position.

Taylor v. *Kent County Council* (1969)
A head teacher became redundant when his school was amalgamated with another. Kent County Council offered the head teacher alternative employment in a mobile pool of teachers to be used to cover staff shortages. His salary would be unaffected but he would have to move to another part of the county. It was held that the inconvenience and loss of status justified refusal and he was entitled to redundancy payments.

O'Brien v. *Associated Fire Alarms Ltd* (1969)
An electrician had lived and worked in Liverpool for many years. He was offered alternative employment in Barrow-in-Furness, which is 120 miles away, when the Liverpool branch closed. It was held he was entitled to redundancy payment.

It would seem that, in the light of these two decisions, Alan could justifiably refuse to move to London. It is likely that a man with family commitments such as Alan could more justifiably refuse a move than a single man.

It is, then, part of the law relating to redundancy that alternative offers of employment may be refused yet still redundancy pay may be claimed.

Exercise 8

Consider the following and say whether the alternative offer of employment is suitable.

1 Dr George Morris is a research chemist with Regency Chemicals Ltd. Owing to a downturn in trade, the company offer him the post of laboratory assistant at the same salary.
2 Deborah Harrison is an accountant with a firm in Wolverhampton. The firm closes its branch in Wolverhampton and she is offered the same post at Walsall, about ten miles away.
3 Fred Merrick is a head waiter at the Royal Oak Hotel, York. Fred, who is married with three children, is made redundant and is offered a post with the same firm in Torquay at the Regal Hotel. After a discussion with his wife he refuses this alternative offer.

Unfair dismissal

We have already learned that employees may be made redundant. There are, however, other reasons for which an employee may be dismissed. Since 1971 employees who have been dismissed for reasons other than redundancy may appeal against what they consider to be unfair dismissal. In this section we will be considering the question of unfair dismissal and the remedies available to employees if they consider they have been unfairly dismissed.

Activity _____

In the second section of this chapter we considered express and implied terms which related to employment contracts. Try to list the implied terms which bind (1) an employee, (2) an employer. If you cannot remember these then refer back.

The following examples might help to explain the law as it at present stands in relation to unfair dismissal.

1   Mrs Dorothy Armstrong has been employed as a coach driver for three years by United Coaches Ltd. In the last 21 weeks, however, she has been involved in no less than seven accidents. United Coaches Ltd decide to terminate her employment by giving her one week's notice.

2   Michael Hunter is an electrician with Adams Electrical (Contractors) Ltd. He has been employed by this firm for six months. The managing director, Paul Adams, is very much against trade unions and when he discovers Michael is a member of a trade union he warns him that continued membership will jeopardise his job. Michael refuses to leave the union and is given one week's notice.

3   Maureen Williams has been a cashier with a large food store for three years. Her employer discovers that over the past year Maureen has taken over £1000 of the firm's money. She is called into the manager's office and is dismissed without notice.

4   Philip Clapham has been with Northern Press for 20 years as a printer. He has been a most successful employee but on one occasion, even though he knows the firm's strict rule about outside work, he prints some cards for his local church. He is called into the manager's office and sacked without notice.

5   Sarah Thomas gets a job as an accountant with a large firm by saying she is a qualified accountant, having the qualification ACCA. Her firm finds that she has never gained such a qualification and she is dismissed after being with the firm for one year.

6   Frank Clements is a solicitor, having been employed by a small firm for three years. Over the last few months his work has deteriorated and he has made several quite serious errors. He is called in to see the senior partner of the firm and explains that he has had some domestic problems which may be affecting his work. The senior partner decides to dismiss him.

The Employment Protection (Consolidation) Act 1978 as amended by the Employment Acts 1980 and 1990 which consolidates the law on unfair dismissal since 1971 lays down that an employee can appeal to an industrial tribunal if he has been employed for 52 weeks or more. Since the Employment Act 1980, for firms employing 20 employees or less the qualifying period is 104 weeks (two years). In the light of this, let us examine the six cases outlined above. All employees commencing after June 1995 must complete 104 weeks before qualifying.

1 Dorothy could appeal against unfair dismissal because she has been with United Coaches for three years. It is unlikely that her appeal would be upheld because she is in breach of an implied term, the need to work competently and carefully, and seven accidents in 21 weeks does not seem consistent with this term.

2 The law lays down clearly that dismissal for trade union membership is inadmissible and therefore 'unfair'. In fact the two years qualifying period is not necessary for this situation and Michael could appeal despite having been with the firm for only six months.

   (Although a person cannot be dismissed for trade union membership, it would seem from the decision in *Carrington* v. *Therm-a-Star* (1983), that it may be possible to dismiss for union activity.) However, in *Marrison* v. *Kent County Council* 1995 the Employment Appeal Tribunal held that trade union activity or refusal of employment could not be grounds for dismissal.

3 Although normally notice is required by law, serious cases of misconduct, which this certainly is, will justify instant dismissal and there would seem little likelihood of Maureen's appeal against unfair dismissal being successful.

   A very high standard of conduct is demanded in certain jobs, especially those involving health and safety. In *Taylor* v. *Alidair* (1978), Lord Denning held that a 'first offence' of landing an aircraft heavily and damaging it justified immediate dismissal.

4 This is another case of misconduct, but less serious than in the previous situation. The law requires that an employee normally be given a warning before dismissal for misconduct and Philip would claim that he had been unfairly dismissed. Firms are expected to comply with codes of practice issued under the Employment Protection Act 1975 which are designed to promote good industrial relations. The industrial tribunal would consider that the failure to give a warning as recommended by the codes of practice was sufficient to justify a case of unfair dismissal.

   The question of misconduct is a difficult area and decisions of the courts in this respect must be looked at closely. In *Howe* v. *Tesco Stores* (1974) it was held that a till assistant was wrongfully dismissed for 'borrowing from the till' since company rules forbade her to carry her own money. However in *Brown* v. *SE Hampshire Health Authority* (1983) it was held that it was fair to dismiss a kitchen porter for stealing 50p worth of groceries. Then again, it was held to be unfair in *Rentokil* v. *Mackin* (1989) to dismiss an employee who helped himself to a milkshake on a customer's premises.

These cases show how difficult this subject of unfair dismissal is.

5   Sarah in this situation has certainly misrepresented the facts in applying for the post. There was between her and her employer no 'meeting of the minds'. There is little doubt that the industrial tribunal would not uphold any appeal against unfair dismissal.

6   Frank's work has deteriorated but, as explained earlier, it would be necessary for a warning to be given so that Frank could try to improve. If Frank appealed it is likely that the industrial tribunal would consider that the failure to give a warning constituted unfair dismissal.

If an employee who considers he has been unfairly dismissed wishes to complain of unfair dismissal he must do so by means of the procedure set out below.

1   A complaint of unfair dismissal must be presented to an industrial tribunal within three months of the termination of employment.

2   A copy of the complaint must be sent to the Advisory, Conciliation and Arbitration Service (ACAS) who will designate a conciliation officer to try to get a settlement which may involve re-engagement/reinstatement of the employee or compensation.

3   If the officer fails to get a settlement then the case will go to the industrial tribunal. The tribunal has the power to make a reinstatement order (the employee must be given his old job back) or a re-engagement order (the employee is given a comparable job). There are many circumstances under which it would be impractical for an employee to be reinstated or re-engaged. In some cases firms refuse to re-engage or reinstate.

Reinstatement and re-engagement orders made by the industrial tribunal are in fact very rare. It is quite obvious that, if a former employee brings a case to the tribunal, this could well cause resentment by the employer and, if the case should go in the employee's favour, it would be better to give a compensation award.

In these circumstances the industrial tribunal may award compensation. There is in the law provision for a basic award which is calculated in a similar way to redundancy awards, for a compensatory award, for an additional award and a special award. The maximum rate of pay for the calculation of the basic award is £205 and the maximum basic award is £5950.

The present compensation award is set at a maximum of £10 000, which takes into account loss of earnings, loss of pension rights and loss of benefits. This compensation is awarded if the employer fails to comply with a reinstatement or re-engagement order. The additional award is payable when the dismissal was an unlawful act of sex or racial discrimination. The present maximum is £10 000, which is payable in addition to the compensation award. A special award may be payable when the employee is dismissed for trade union membership.

In 1990 the Employment Act made it unlawful to *give or refuse* employment on union membership grounds. This represented a change in the law because hitherto the law only related to refusal if a person was in a trade union. Now an employer cannot insist on membership of a union and the new law therefore prevents what used to be called 'closed shop' agreements. Under this new law a trade union faces heavy penalties if it 'forces' an employer to 'dismiss' an employee because he is unwilling to join a union. Under the Trade Union and Labour Relations (Consolidation) Act 1992 all closed shop dismissals are automatically unfair, i.e. no qualifying period of service is required.

Exercise 9

1 What are the three possible stages in an appeal against unfair dismissal?
2 What four types of award may be given in compensation by an industrial tribunal in an unfair dismissal case?
3 What is the length of service to qualify an employee for an appeal to the industrial tribunal against unfair dismissal?
4 Examine the following three cases and say whether you think the employee concerned would be successful in an unfair dismissal appeal, giving reasons for your view.
   (a) Adam Crawford has been with Reliant Heating Supplies for five years. It has been discovered that he has been using his firm's materials, worth £2000, to do a number of private central heating jobs. He is dismissed without notice.
   (b) Jane Mason joins a trade union and is immediately given notice of dismissal. She has only been with her firm for two weeks.
   (c) Roy Bright has been employed as a salesman for two years. His sales record has been good but the last month has been a poor one for him. He is given two week's notice.
5 Roger Harrop is an engineer on a cross-Channel ferry. He will not join a union and his company is forced to sack him following pressure from the union to operate a 'closed shop'.

Exercise 10

1 All contracts of employment must be in writing: true or false?
2 Apprenticeship contracts must always be in writing: true or false?
3 Written particulars of employment must be provided within
   (a) one year of the start of employment;
   (b) two years of the start of employment;
   (c) 13 weeks of the start of employment;
   (d) four weeks of the start of employment.
4 An employer must provide an employee with a reference if he/she wishes to apply for another post: true or false?
5 How much minimum notice is an employee entitled to if he has worked for a firm for 15 years?
6 Calculate the redundancy payment entitlement for an employee 46 years old who has been with his firm for ten years. His salary is £150.

---

7 If an employee refuses an alternative offer of employment he may not claim redundancy: true or false?

8 How long must an employee have worked at a firm to be entitled to appeal against unfair dismissal?

9 Mary Jones is a teacher in a school in the Midlands. She tells the head teacher that she is expecting a child and will leave at the end of the term but would like to return. The head teacher refuses to re-employ her and Mary seeks advice.

10 Michael Bevan sees his employer and demands to see details of all personal data held on him in the firm's computer. The employer refuses.

It is interesting to examine what rights an employee has when his company or organisation is 'taken over'. This subject is particularly relevant in the light of privatisation of publicly run corporations. It seems that the UK has been very slow to harmonise its law in accordance with European Union articles and associated directives (see Chapter 3). The European Court of Justice in *Commission of the European Communities* v. *United Kingdom* (1994) held that the UK had failed to fulfil its obligations under the directives and article 5 of the treaty. The directive based upon article 100 provided that, in the event of a change in employer, the employee was protected against changes in his/her conditions. The Court felt that the UK regulation which intended to give the force of law to this directive provided insufficient protection. This provides another example of the status of European law and, as you may know, this judgement has caused some embarrassment to government ministers in the UK.

We have spent time discussing unfair dismissal and it is necessary to explain briefly what has been termed 'constructive dismissal'.

Dr Paul is head of research at a well known scientific company. A new managing director decides he no longer wants such a post and tells Paul that he will continue with the title but will lose his office and will not have any staff reporting to him. His main duties will be laboratory maintenance. Although Paul has not been dismissed, the change in his duties forces him to consider his position and he resigns.

Under certain circumstances an employee can claim 'unfair dismissal' even though he has not been technically dismissed. Paul, in our example, could argue that he was 'constructively dismissed'.

The whole question of employment law and unfair dismissal is very complex, and we have only been able to deal with it very briefly in this chapter. At the end of the book you will find a section which gives advice on further reading in this interesting area of the law.

8 Agency

Edward Burch runs a successful export business. He often has to make trips overseas in furtherance of his business. On one particular occasion he has to travel to West Africa and telephones a local travel agent to book him flights to Ghana, Nigeria and Ivory Coast, and hotel accommodation for the period of his ten day trip in various towns including Accra, Lagos, Kano and Abidjan. Edward gives precise details of his requirements and the travel agent, known as Ajax Tours, books flights with KLM and Swiss Air, and the hotels.

This is not a particularly unusual occurrence but it introduces an important aspect of law, the law of agency. In this case, the principal, as he is called, instructs his agent to make a contract on his behalf. Edward Burch is the principal and Ajax Tours is the agent. There are, of course, numerous examples where a person uses an agent to deal for him. Many people these days use estate agents to sell their houses. In these instances, the estate agent, as the name implies, is the agent and the seller is the principal. In our example, Edward Burch in his work as an exporter could well act himself as an agent for a company wishing to export goods abroad.

A manager of a company will act as the agent of his company when making decisions. A headmaster of a school may act as agent of the local education authority in offering employment to a teacher. In the case of schools which are grant-maintained, that is which get their funds directly from the government, the headmaster would be acting for the board of Governors. A principal of an FE college would be acting for his board of governors in the appointment of a lecturer or member of the non-teaching staff.

Exercise 1

In the following examples, identify the principal and the agent.

1 Alex Ferguson, manager of Manchester United Football Club, signs a player from another club for an agreed fee.
2 Janet Baker (Fashions) Ltd instructs Business Property Services to acquire property for her in Brighton.
3 Derek Butterfield, a wealthy businessman, phones his stockbroker to arrange for him to buy shares in a particular company.

8.1 Contract of agency

Contract of agency

Agency is really a contract whereby the principal contracts with his agents for particular services. Thus a client could ask an insurance broker to arrange insurance for him. The contract of insurance will be between the principal (the client) and the insurance company. The broker will receive his consideration, that is a commission for arranging the insurance, though, in practice, the commission is often paid by the insurance company.

There are, in agency arrangements, two contracts, as the following example shows.

Bev Merritt wants to sell a shop, and she instructs an estate agent to act on her behalf. The estate agent finds a buyer and when the sale goes through, she sends her account to Bev. There are two contracts:

1 Bev (the vendor) and the purchaser,
2 Bev (principal) and the estate agent (agent).

Agencies may be set up in a number of ways.

Express authorisation by the principal

This is where a principal, orally or in writing, instructs an agent to act on his behalf. You will remember that some contracts must be made by deed, for example, transfer of land. If a principal wants an agent to act for him in a transfer of land, then the agency must be made by deed. This is only where the agent (possibly a solicitor) signs the transfer deed when, for example, the vendor or purchaser is out of the country.

By implication

Often it is assumed that an agent has authority to act for his principal. A manager of a large shop will order goods on behalf of his company and it will be assumed that he has that authority. A principal becomes liable for any debts incurred because the law implies authority where such authority is usual in the position the agent is in.

In a decided case *Watteau* v. *Fenwick* (1893) the manager and licensee of a pub ordered cigars from a salesman. His principal tried to avoid payment, saying he had expressly forbidden such purchase. However the court held that the principal was liable because the manager had, despite the principal's instructions, made a contract on behalf of the principal. The salesman could not possibly have known that this was the case. You will appreciate that managers/licensees are usually assumed to have this authority.

By statute

The Partnership Act 1890 lays down quite clearly that partners in a partnership act as agents for each other. You will see from Chapter 14 that partners can bind each other by their actions.

By apparent authority

The following example will help to explain this.

> *John Harris has been an assistant solicitor with his firm for four years and he is asked if he would like to be a partner. John agrees and is given the task of sorting out the firm's computing and word processing requirements. He sees a number of salesmen and they have reason to believe he is able to act on behalf of the firm. He orders a computer for £2500 but the partners decide not to ratify John as a partner, and seek to avoid the contract with Computer Power plc. The court would find for the computer firm because agency, on the part of John, would be assumed by apparent authority. The rule is that a principal cannot hold out a person as his agent, then deny his authority to act as his agent.*

The situation is well summed up in *Freeman & Lockyer* v. *Buckhurst Park Properties Ltd* (1964) where BPP had allowed a director to act as managing director and then sought to avoid contracts made by him, saying he had not been expressly appointed.

In another, similar case, *Waugh* v. *Clifford & Sons* (1982), solicitors were acting for a building firm concerning a dispute over property. The other side suggested an independent valuation but the building firm did not accept this solution to the problem. However the message that the building firm would not agree to an independent valuation never reached the solicitor and he assumed agreement and went ahead in authorising the independent valuation.

The court held that the other side was right to assume that the solicitor had the power to act in this way: it was assumed that he was an agent of the builder and the valuation formed the basis of a settlement to the dispute.

By ratification

This applies where someone acts for another without authority but his action is then ratified and he becomes an agent. For example, Janet Davidson is a secretary to a managing director. She is visiting an exhibition of computers and associated equipment. She is offered a computer at a bargain price and she accepts on behalf of the company. The manager director could reject this and he would not be bound, or he could ratify, as it were, Janet's agency and the contract could be effective from the time the contract was made.

Ratification is possible where:

1   The agent acted as agent and not in his/her own name. Janet, in this situation, bought the equipment for her firm.
2   The principal must have had contractual capacity, that is, in the case of a company, to buy equipment must be within its powers.

By necessity

There are circumstances where an agent acts for his principal out of necessity. The following example will help to explain this.

Bob Dash works as a caretaker for a firm of civil engineers and lives above the offices. Fire damages one of the offices and, not able to contact any of the partners who were all abroad, Bob contacts a builder to do some necessary work to preserve the fabric of the building pending major reconstruction. It would be held that an agency of necessity had been established provided that it could be shown:

1   *Bob was in control of the property;*
2   *there was a genuine emergency;*
3   *Bob could not contact the principal/s;*
4   *he acted in good faith.*

___ **Exercise 2** _____

Name the five ways in which agency can be created.

8.2   Duties of principal and agent

Joyce Richards owns a number of properties in London which she lets out as flats, offices and for other uses. She decides to appoint a property manager, Philip Cheetham, to deal with these matters and, of course, in this situation Joyce is the principal and Philip is the agent. Let us take this example to identify the duties of principal and agent to each other.

It has of course now been established as a result of the Commercial Agents (Council Directive) Regulations (1993) that an agent whose contract has been terminated may still be entitled to any commission for his efforts before the termination. This change, as you will remember from Chapter 3, resulted from a European directive.

Duties of a principal to an agent

1   Joyce has a duty to pay Philip for his duties.

2 She will need to reimburse him for all expenses incurred, such as in any travelling involved.

Duties of an agent to a principal

1 Philip must obey Joyce's instructions; if she said she does not want 12 Green Park let as offices but only as residences, then Philip has to obey.
2 Philip must perform his services personally, not in any way subcontract his agency.
3 He must use reasonable care and skill; for example, if he let an expensive Chelsea flat for £2000 per year, this might not be an indication of his skill.
4 He must act in good faith to his principal; for example, he must never make any secret profit from his dealings.

In *Mahesan* v. *Malaysian Government Housing Society* (1974), Mahesan was engaged as an agent to find building land. He found a suitable piece of land and acquired it cheaply. He then sold it to a speculator, having accepted a bribe. The speculator sold the land to the Society at a very high price.

The court found for the Society and Mahesan, the agent, was required to pay to the Society both the bribe and the speculator's profit!

You will note that the list of the duties of an agent is not very different from the list of duties owed by an employee to his/her employer.

We must remember that, in an agency, arrangements such as the one we have described between Joyce and Philip – that the agent is merely the go-between – the contract is between the principal and the other party. In any contract entered into by Philip on behalf of Joyce, Joyce is liable, provided the agency is effective. If the agency is not effective then Philip will be liable.

8.3 How agency is terminated

There are basically two ways by which an agency may be terminated to an end:
1 *By law*
    (a) where either party dies, that is principal or agent;
    (b) the insanity of either party;
    (c) lapse of time, that is, where an agent has been appointed for a period of time;
    (d) performance where an agent has been appointed to do a particular job; for example, where a house agent is appointed to sell a house, his agency comes to an end when the house is sold.
2 *By agreement*
    (a) by agreement between the parties;
    (b) by the principal withdrawing his authority, that is terminating the agency. You see from time to time notices in the newspaper such as:

F. Davies Co Ltd wishes to point out that John Evans, formerly sales manager, is no longer employed by the company and therefore the company accepts no liability for any arrangement entered into by John Evans on its behalf.

This is really a protection to the company so that it is not liable for the former agent's actions.

(c) by the agent resigning his duties.

Exercise 3

1 List the four duties owed by an agent to his principal.
2 How might an agency be brought to an end?

Exercise 4

Answer the following questions, which are all based upon agency. Check your answers against those given and if you are unclear about any aspect of this topic, read the chapter again.

1 Advise the party in the following situation, identifying two separate contracts.
   Geoff Thomas, a wealthy antique dealer, employs Sheila Prince to go to Manchester to purchase regency furniture at a large antique sale. Sheila buys three pieces of furniture from NW Antiques plc for £19 000. When Geoff sees the furniture, he is angry and refuses to pay the balance outstanding of £17 000 (a deposit of £2000 has already been paid by Sheila).

2 Peter May is the manager of a sports shop owned by Kent Sports plc. Despite the managing director's instructions that they wanted to run down their stock of cricket gear, Peter buys 20 cricket bats carrying the name of Ian Botham from International Sports Equipment plc. Kent Sports plc refuse to pay the bill.
   Advise Sports Equipment plc.

3 Realising that the price of a particular share is likely to rise considerably, Greenfield (Stockbrokers) Ltd buy £500 000 of shares on behalf of one of their wealthy clients, Sir Roger Beckwith. Sir Roger refuses to accept these saying he had given no instructions and Greenfield could have easily contacted him.
   Advise Greenfield (Stockbrokers) Ltd.

4 Following the death of his principal, Sir Adrian Evans, John Martin agrees to sell a property for a good price, feeling it might benefit Adrian's beneficiaries.
   Advise John.

9 Consumer law

9.1 Sale of Goods Act 1979 and Supply of Goods and Services Act 1982

Rachel and Deborah both wish to purchase motor cars. Rachel buys a nearly new car from Associated Motor Sales Ltd for £6950. Deborah buys a similar model privately from a friend for £6250. Coincidentally within a month of their purchase both girls experience the same problems with their cars and are forced to have new gear-boxes fitted, at considerable cost.

In this case Rachel would be in a much better position because her contract to buy the car would be completely covered by the Sale of Goods Act 1979 because it would be considered to be a consumer sale. A consumer sale has been defined as such where the following criteria are satisfied:

1　The sale must be by a seller in the course of a business.
2　The goods must be of a type ordinarily supplied for private use or consumption.

If we apply these two criteria to the situation relating to Rachel then it is easy to see that this is a consumer sale. Associated Motor Sales Ltd are selling the car in the course of business; Rachel is buying it for her own private use and not in the course of business. Deborah's purchase, however, does not satisfy the first criterion. She buys the car from a friend, who is not selling in the course of business. This distinction is important because only consumer sales are completely protected by the Sale of Goods Act 1979, which we will be considering in this section.

Until 1982, the Sale of Goods Act 1979 provided some protection to the buyer of goods but did not assist a buyer of services such as holidays or insurance. The 1982 Supply of Goods and Services Act provided similar protection to buyers of services.

Exercise 1

Applying the two criteria we have just considered, which of the following would be regarded as a consumer sale?

1　Philip Latham buys a CD from Leisure Supplies Ltd for £450.
2　John Martindale, a furniture retailer, buys furniture from a furniture warehouse which he then resells in his shop.

> 3   United Food Ltd sell a consignment of biscuits to a grocery chain store,
>   Supersave Ltd.
> 4   Malcolm Trent sells his motorcycle to a motorcycle dealer for £650.

If you decide to buy goods or services privately, that is not from a person or organisation in business, then you take a risk. The principle which covers private sales is *caveat emptor*, which means 'let the buyer beware'. If the goods turn out to be faulty in some way and the seller has not misrepresented them in any way then there is nothing the buyer can do. In our situation, Deborah would have no legal claim against the friend from whom she bought the car unless she could prove that he had in some way misrepresented the facts about the car's condition, for instance if he had said, 'I have had trouble with the gear-box but the one in now is a new one.' If this was not the case then he has misrepresented and, as we have learned, one of the essential elements would be absent, that is there would have been no *consensus ad idem*. If the friend knew about the gear-box but said nothing, or honestly did not know, Deborah would have to bear the full cost of a replacement gear-box herself.

In Chapter 6 we learned that contracts may have within them implied (unexpressed) conditions. In any consumer sale the Sale of Goods Act 1979 implies certain conditions. If these conditions are breached then the buyer has the right to reject the goods and end the contract or sue for damages because of breach.

The following four examples will help to explain the implied conditions which exist in a consumer sale.

1 Barbara Dallow buys from London Road Motors Ltd a new Ford Escort GL. She trades in her present car which is a Ford Fiesta. London Road Motors sell the Ford Fiesta for £4250 to John Proctor. The Fiesta in fact had been stolen and belonged to David Beresford. The police trace the car and John is forced to hand it over to its rightful owner. John goes to see the manager of London Road Motors who explains that he had no idea the car was stolen and, although sympathetic to John, says he can do nothing.

There is no doubt that the contract between John and London Road Motors is a contract covered by the Sale of Goods Act, 1979. John is protected by an important implied condition of this act namely *that the seller has the right to sell the goods*. If the seller has no right to sell the goods then he is in breach of condition and must return the money. John therefore would be able to claim the return of his £4250 from London Road Motors Ltd.

Some of the cases which are quoted in this chapter are from before 1979. The 1979 Act replaced a similar act of 1893 which was also known as the Sale of Goods Act. The following case shows that a buyer is able to reclaim a full money refund on goods that he has bought which are stolen.

In *Rowland* v. *Divall* (1923), the buyer of a car used it for about three months, but then found that it was stolen and had to return it to the true owner. He was held entitled to recover from the seller the full price which he had paid even though, when he had to part with it, the car was probably worth rather less. He had paid to become owner, he had not become owner, and he was, therefore, entitled to the return of his money.

2 Margaret Hamilton buys a pair of trousers from Fashion Wear, a small shop in town. The trousers cost £34. When Margaret tries the trousers on at home she notices a serious flaw in them and takes them back to the shop. The shopkeeper is sympathetic and says he will send them back to the manufacturers and asks her to call again in about two weeks' time. Margaret is not happy about this and asks for her money back. The shopkeeper refuses, saying he will have to get in touch with the manufacturer before he refunds any money.

In this situation, which is similar to the one on page 22 in Chapter 2, Margaret could claim a full money refund. Fashion Wear is in breach of another implied condition of the Sale of Goods Act 1979, *that goods must be of merchantable quality*. Merchantable quality will vary with the price of the goods in question but for £34 for a pair of trousers you would not expect to find a serious fault in them. Incidentally the manufacturer is of no consequence to Margaret; she made the contract with Fashion Wear and, although shopkeepers often try to push the problem away from themselves and onto the manufacturers, in fact legally they are the supplier to the customer and it is they who must comply with the implied conditions. This is an important point to bear in mind when you have to return faulty goods to a shop. Remember the quality to be expected depends on the price paid and, in the case of second-hand goods, the age. In *Bartlett* v. *Sydney Marcus Ltd* (1965), a second-hand car was sold with a defective clutch. The seller had warned the buyer of the defect, and the price took account of this. The car was held to be of merchantable quality in the circumstances, even though repair cost more than the buyer expected.

However, in *Shine* v. *General Guarantee Corporation Ltd* (1988), the buyer of a car, Mr Shine, discovered that it had been submerged in water for 24 hours and was in fact a 'write-off'. The court held that the car was not of merchantable quality because, as the judge said, it was a car which 'no member of the public, knowing the facts, would have touched with a barge pole'.

3 Janet Beckford buys three pairs of cotton sheets in lilac from a large store in Oxford. The shop assistant gets the sheets from the shelf and they are already packed with a label indicating that they are 85 per cent cotton and are lilac. The full cost is £47.50. When Janet gets home she finds on unpacking them that the sheets are nylon and are yellow. She returns to the store with the sheets and demands a full money refund. The supervisor for the section is called and he apologises to Janet but says, since she has opened the parcels, she will not get a refund and suggests she should have checked before leaving the store.

In this case the supervisor is quite wrong because the store has breached an implied condition of the Sale of Goods Act 1979 which provides that where there is *a contract for sale of goods by description there is an implied condition that the goods shall correspond with the description.* The sheets in our example certainly did not and the shop would be wise to refund the money because the court would certainly find for Janet in this situation. The following case shows an example of the application of the rule 'goods bought by description must correspond with the description'. In *Beale* v. *Taylor* (1967), a car was advertised as a 'Herald convertible, white, 1961'. The buyer saw the vehicle before buying it, but only discovered some time later that, while the rear part had been accurately described, the front half had been part of an earlier model. The seller was held to be in breach of section 13 of the Sale of Goods Act.

Sometimes people will buy from a sample, for example a shopper may inspect goods on display and ask to buy them but in fact may be given goods from the shelves or from the storeroom. In this situation the shopper will be protected by section 15 of the Sale of Goods Act which states that, where goods are sold by sample, they ought to correspond with the sample. The rule relating to description will also apply where a customer buys goods by description from a newspaper or catalogue.

> 4 *James Frazier has just bought a large house with a large garden. He is a keen but rather inexperienced gardener and he decides to go along to the garden centre of a large department store. The store advertises regularly the fact that it has employed two staff in their garden centre who are expert gardeners and will give their advice to customers who ask for it. James is advised about a certain type of weedkiller to destroy weeds which are spoiling a very attractive rockery. James buys the weedkiller on the advice of the shop. Unfortunately he has been given the wrong advice and the weedkiller destroys all the plants on the rockery in addition to the weeds. James is upset and returns to the shop. The manager is sympathetic but reminds James that he did not need to accept the advice given him.*

James is fortunate because he can rely upon an implied term incorporated in the Sale of Goods Act 1979 which states: *Where the seller sells goods in the course of a business and the buyer expressly or by implication makes known . . . to the seller . . . any particular purpose for which the goods are being bought there is an implied condition that the goods supplied are reasonably fit for that purpose.*

James would have to show that he relied upon the skill or judgement of the seller. It would seem that James could show that the seller had indicated that he could give advice and certainly James relied upon it, being inexperienced himself. James could claim breach of a condition and could claim damages. To use this condition a buyer would need to show that he relied upon the judgement and that it was reasonable for him to do so. A conversation with a shop assistant in a supermarket over a brand of washing powder would not come into this category.

We have now examined the five implied conditions which can protect a consumer in a contract of sale.

The Sale of Goods Act applies to goods but not to services. The Supply of Goods and Services Act 1982, the first part of which became law on 4 January 1983, provides protection to purchasers of services. For example, motor car repairs and services must be of 'merchantable quality' and at 'reasonable rates'.

Weekend Breaks Ltd, a holiday firm, arranges weekend breaks in a number of tourist centres in the UK, namely London, Cambridge, Oxford, Canterbury, Bath, York, Edinburgh and Winchester. Each weekend has a fully inclusive price which includes first class rail fare and full board in one of the city's top hotels. It also includes three tours of the city. Hugh Lawler and his wife book a weekend in Canterbury which costs £350. When they arrive, they find that the hotel is fully booked up and are offered alternative accommodation at a small guest house. No tours have been arranged and Hugh and his wife return home thoroughly dissatisfied.

Fortunately, under the Supply of Goods and Services Act 1982, Hugh can take Weekend Breaks Ltd to court for breach of an implied condition that the service must be of merchantable quality, which clearly it was not.

Exercise 2

List the five implied conditions in the Sale of Goods Act 1979.

We have been concerned with consumer sales because a consumer is given complete protection under the Sale of Goods Act 1979 as far as the implied terms are concerned. As far as consumers are concerned, sellers cannot exclude liability from the implied conditions by means of an exclusion clause. The following example will illustrate this point.

Sheila buys a new television from Video Supplies Ltd for £350. On taking delivery she is given a manufacturer's warranty which she signs. The warranty guarantees the set for six months but contains the clause, 'The equipment is supplied subject to no implied condition nor to any statutory provision'. After seven months the set will not work and when Sheila returns it she is told the repair cost would be so great that she might as well buy a new one. Sheila, who knows something about the law, tries to use her rights under the Sale of Goods Act 1979, claiming the television set was not of merchantable quality. The manager of Video Supplies Ltd shows her the warranty she has signed which excluded her rights.

The Sale of Goods Act 1979 makes it impossible for suppliers to take away a consumer's statutory rights and Sheila could sue on the basis that after seven months the goods were not really of merchantable quality. Manufacturers' warranties or guarantees, as they are sometimes called, can only add to a consumer's rights under the Sale of Goods Act 1979. In fact often nowadays a warranty/guarantee will contain a clause such as: 'This statement does not restrict a customer's statutory rights under consumer legislation.' This really is a reminder to the buyer that the implied conditions for the Sale of Goods Act 1979 cannot be taken away.

In fact it is a criminal offence for manufacturers to omit to mention that their guarantee does not affect a customer's statutory rights. You will see this always printed with a guarantee which may be given when you buy goods.

However the rights of business buyers can be excluded by means of an exclusion clause, provided the exclusion clause is just and reasonable (see Chapter 6). This is a very important distinction as regards sales to ordinary buyers as opposed to business buyers.

Before 1982, the rights and protection afforded by the Sale of Goods Act 1979 was not available to purchasers of goods bought by hire-purchase or by means of trading stamps. The Law Commission, which is a group of lawyers set up to advise the government on legal matters, felt that goods bought by these two methods ought to have the same level of protection and this was introduced in part 1 of the 1982 Act.

Activity

Have a look at warranties/guarantees which you might have in connection with new goods you may have purchased recently. Try to find examples of clauses which remind you that your rights are not affected by the warranty/guarantee.

Exercise 3

Read the following examples and say whether you think the buyer in each example could sue for breach of contract under the Sale of Goods Act 1979.

1 David Harrison buys a tennis racquet from Sports Equipment Ltd for £63. After two games the racquet has to have new strings.
2 Brian Webb buys a new motor car from Unicorn Motors Ltd for £12 500 . It has a 12-month manufacturer's warranty. 14 months after the purchase, with only 8500 miles on the clock, such serious faults develop that the car needs a new engine, gear-box and clutch.
3 Muriel Wilshaw sees some delicious-looking English apples displayed at a greengrocers. She buys 2lb but is given some prepacked apples. When she arrives home she discovers they are French Golden Delicious.

4 Caroline Fletcher sees a car advertised by Union Motors Ltd: Vauxhall Astra, hatchback, H registration, 1300cc, £9350. She purchases the car but finds that it is not a hatchback and is 1200cc.

5 Philip Bagshaw is a professional photographer. Relying on the advice of the manager of a photographic supplier he buys a new type of colour film for £4.50 which will give, according to the advice, excellent results. Philip uses the film for some wedding photographs and the results are so bad that the disappointed newlyweds will not accept them.

6 David Knowles, a Citizen Band radio fanatic, buys some equipment from a local shop which he has to give to the police because it was in fact stolen property.

As we have shown, it is the retailer who will bear the main brunt of a claim from an aggrieved customer in respect of faulty goods, even though the fault may have been due to the manufacturer. It is of course possible for the retailer in turn to sue the manufacturer. The same principle applies to a travel agent who is sued by a customer who experiences problems with a holiday. For example:

Peter and Jenny Fairweather book a holiday with Spanish Leisure Tours in Costa Brava in a four star hotel overlooking the sea. In fact it is a small guest house about an hour's drive from the sea. The couple would have to sue Spanish Leisure Tours and not the operator, Costa Brava Holidays PLC.

Of course, in this case, Spanish Leisure Tours would sue Costa Brava Holidays PLC.

9.2 Trade Descriptions Act 1968 and 1972

Many buyers who may feel that they have been wronged in some way will often not do anything about it because they lack the knowledge of the Sale of Goods Act, or they lack the initiative or the energy. In some cases buyers are worried about the likely cost of proceedings. Consequently many sellers of defective goods or services get away with it. Consumers are given additional protection by the criminal law, however. Under the Trade Descriptions Act 1968 certain criminal offences were created in relation to false descriptions of goods or services. The Trade Descriptions Act, which only applies where the sale is in the course of business and therefore does not apply to private sales, attempts to protect the consumer from four main types of abuse. The following examples will help to illustrate how the Trade Descriptions Act tries to deal with these abuses.

1 Dream Kitchens Ltd advertise new kitchens in the following way: 'Free Formica worktops when you purchase an Eastham Kitchen from us. Offer applies August only.'

Mrs Sykes orders on 14 August a kitchen from Dream Kitchens but the firm does not supply the Formica worktops. When Mrs Sykes enquires into this she is told that supplies of the Formica have been used up and that Dream Kitchens Ltd can no longer afford to supply these.

Dream Kitchens have in fact committed a criminal offence because the Trade Descriptions Act lays down that it is an offence to apply a false description to goods. False descriptions may take many forms. This one falsely described what would be supplied with the kitchen, but such phrases as 'home-made', 'reconditioned', 'fitted with disc brakes', 'approved by AA', 'Staffordshire pottery', are all capable, if made falsely, of giving rise to the criminal offence of false description.

If trade description cases come to court the seller can try to show that they had genuinely made a mistake or had relied upon the information supplied by others. This defence is effective if disclaimer notices are used.

Activity

Look around a second-hand-car salesroom. Many dealers protect themselves from criminal action by placing a disclaimer notice over the milometer. See if you can find some examples of this. Look at the wording used.

---

2 Anxious to get rid of existing stock, Greenbanks (Men's Wear) Ltd offer a certain type of ready-made suit reduced from £100 to £50. A number of men, including Kevin Quinlan, take advantage of this apparently excellent offer. Kevin discusses his bargain with a friend who tells him that he bought the same suit from Greenbanks six months previously for £60. Kevin feels that Greenbanks have committed an offence but is not sure.

The Trade Descriptions Act 1968 makes it an offence to advertise price reductions of this sort unless the higher price had existed for a continuous period of 28 days within the last six months.

The difficulty with this section of the Act is in proving that the higher price did not exist for the stipulated period. The prosecution has to prove this. It has been suggested that the law be changed so that the onus of proof lies on the seller (that is, he/she has to prove that the higher price did prevail for 28 days) but the suggestion has not been implemented. In fact to date there have been very few successful prosecutions for this offence, which is called 'double pricing'.

3 Leisure and Pleasure Holidays Ltd is a firm specialising in holidays in historical towns in England and Wales. A holiday is advertised for 16 days which includes four days in each of the following towns – Bath, Oxford, London and Canterbury – at a cost of £350 per head, which includes transport and free entry into places of historical interest. The hotels arranged are high class hotels, each room having twin beds, private bath, w.c. and shower.

Mr and Mrs Edward Harris book this holiday but find that in two of the hotels there is no private bath, shower or w.c. Surcharges are made for the coach travel of £30 per head and in at least three of the visits entry fees have to be paid. Mr Harris decides to complain, but is told by the management that there is nothing they could do.

In fact Leisure and Pleasure Holidays could face prosecution under the Trade Descriptions Act 1968, which makes it an offence for a person in the course of business to make a statement which is false relating to services, accommodation and facilities. This section, section 14, states that the statement must be made 'knowingly or recklessly'. Therefore, Leisure and Pleasure could in their defence say that they honestly believed the facts in the advertisement to be true, and had received no information to the contrary. It would seem from recent decided cases that it is somewhat difficult to get a prosecution under this section.

In *Wings Ltd* v. *Ellis*, (1984) the company had advertised a holiday with accommodation in Sri Lanka in a hotel with air-conditioned bedrooms. The rooms were not in fact air-conditioned and Wings Ltd were prosecuted success-fully under the Trade Descriptions Act.

4 Because of his opposition to the South African government's policy of apartheid, Harold Gilman will never buy goods from this country. He buys some tins of fruit from a supermarket; the label on the tin states that the goods were from South Australia. Harold notices that on the tin itself it states Cape Town, S. Africa.

In this situation the supermarket could face prosecution because sections 16 and 17 of the Trade Descriptions Act 1968 state that it is an offence to import goods bearing a false indication of origin, and these tins certainly contravene this section because, although the fruit is from South Africa, it is labelled as a product of Australia.

Exercise 4

1　Contravention of the Trade Descriptions Act 1968 could lead to a civil action: true or false?
2　Name the four main criminal offences created by the Trade Descriptions Act.

Enforcement of the Trade Descriptions Act 1968

Prosecutions under this Act are brought by local authorities, usually by trading standards inspectors. Prosecution may lead to the normal penalties, such as fines, and sometimes imprisonment. Neither fines nor imprisonment of the offender is much consolation to a person who has, for example, had a holiday ruined as a result of a false description. Magistrates' Courts, however, have the power to award compensation to a person who has suffered. This compensation is limited to £2000, but it does provide some assistance to a consumer who may be reluctant for all sorts of reasons to pursue a civil claim in the courts.

The Consumer Protection Act 1987

This Act was passed as a result of a European directive of 1985. The Act applies to products for private and *not* business use. It provides for compensation to a purchaser from the producer or someone who holds himself out as the producer. As you know, a number of grocery chains, such as Tesco or Sainsbury's, will ask manufacturers to produce goods which are then sold under the grocery chain's name. In these cases it will be firms like Tesco or Sainsbury's which will pay the compensation if found to be liable. The remedies available only apply to certain types of loss, namely death, personal injury and damage to property exceeding £250.

Exercise 5

In the following examples say whether you think the seller in question has contravened the Trade Descriptions Act 1968.

1   Alan Harrison runs a small craft shop and he advertises crafts from the Third World. Most of the crafts are in fact made by a company in Western Germany, although all bear a stamp, 'Produced in the Third World'.
2   Torbay Holiday Flats Ltd advertise self-catering flats, each with a sea view and only five minutes' walk from the seafront. In fact most of the flats have no outlook over the sea and are situated at least 40 minutes' walk from the coast.
3   Sports Supplies Ltd advertise tennis racquets at half price.
4   Country Kitchen Bakery advertise home-made bread and cakes. The bakery in fact get all their supplies from a large bakery 20 miles away.

Exercise 6

Mecca TV PLC supplies televisions to a number of shops. One particular model has a fault which causes serious injury to a purchaser from one of the shops supplied. Does the customer, Michael Moss, have a claim against the supplier, Mecca TV PLC?

9.3 Consumer Credit

There are often occasions when individuals want to buy goods or services but have not got at that moment the money available to do so. It is possible to obtain from banks or finance houses credit to enable one to buy goods or services. There are a number of different types of credit arrangements which individuals can obtain and in recent years a number of Acts of Parliament have been passed to protect individuals from abuses and unfair terms. In this section we will deal with the law as it applies to consumer credit so that you will understand the main operation of the law in this respect.

The following examples will help to explain some of the main types of credit arrangements.

1 David Pritchard wishes to borrow some money for a number of purposes. For example, he wishes to take his family on holiday abroad and also to buy some furniture for his house. He decides that he wants £3000 spread over three years. David can go to his bank or he may go to one of the many finance houses willing to lend money, such as Mercantile Credit, Lloyds Bowmaker or United Dominion Trust. David will have to complete a form and, if satisfied, the finance house will make him an offer. For example, £3000 at 12.5 per cent per annum over 36 months will mean a repayment of £114.58 per month. If David accepts he will in due course receive a cheque for £3000 and he must repay the loan in 36 instalments of £114.58.

The company supplying the loan is known as the creditor because they supply credit. The person obtaining the loan is known as the debtor.

2 Tony Slack is very keen on boats and he sees a boat advertised for £2500. He decides he wishes to buy this but hasn't got the money. He decides to apply for credit from a finance house. He completes a form specifying exactly why he wants the £2500. After making its normal credit investigations, the finance company offer Tony £2500 over 24 months at 12 per cent per annum, making monthly instalments of £129.16. If Tony accepts this offer he will receive a cheque for £2500 which he will use to purchase the boat. This is known as a credit sale. As soon as Tony takes possession of the goods he becomes the owner and the finance company can only sue him for recovery of the money if he does not pay the instalments; under no circumstances can the company obtain the boat. In legal terms Tony's loan is really exactly the same as David's.

Both these loans are unsecured in the sense that the lender retains no interest in the borrower's property. Sometimes loans will be made by credit companies to houseowners and the house is mortgaged to the credit company so the company has certain rights in it, and if the instalments are not paid then there are rights of entry and of sale of the property. This type of loan is known as secured; that is, the lender has security in the house.

___ **Activity** _____

Newspapers frequently carry advertisements for credit companies anxious
to lend money to houseowners. See if you can find some examples of these.

An example of the sort of wording used in such advertisements is as follows:

> *Make your home provide a loan.*
> If you are a homeowner, you are probably sitting on quite a substantial sum
> of money – the increased value of your home since you bought it. You can
> use this increased value by raising a loan from £2000 to £40 000. The plan
> works just like a building society mortgage and our rates of interest are
> very competitive.
> Send for our free brochure today or phone us on Sternfield 666 666.

*3   Nicola Mallet wishes to buy a new car for £7500. She takes her old car
along to the dealer who offers her £4500 in part exchange, therefore leaving
a balance of £3000. Nicola wants to pay this by instalments and the dealer
arranges hire-purchase. The finance company requires that for the purchase
of a car the buyer must give a minimum deposit of one-third, which Nicola
has done by means of the £4500 trade-in, and payments must be over a
maximum period of 24 months. At 12 per cent per annum, this would mean
monthly instalments of £155.00.*

The common practice these days is for a triangular arrangement (see Figure 9.1)

Nicola will complete the hire-purchase forms at the garage and in effect the
finance company buys the car from the dealer and then hires it to Nicola.
When Nicola pays the final instalment ownership of the car passes to her. The
finance company is the owner of the car and this means that, unlike the credit
sale arrangement, if Nicola defaults in repayment then there are conditions
under which the car may be returned to the finance house.

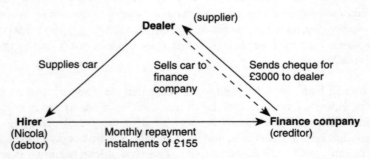

Figure 9.1   A hire purchase arrangement

4   *Philip Hargreaves decides to buy a suite of furniture for £550, using his Visa credit card. Philip is allowed a £1500 credit limit and, since he only has £200 outstanding, the £550 will present no problem. Philip buys his suite from Mammoth Furniture Stores plc. At the end of the month, he receives his statement from Visa which asks him for a minimum payment of £38.25. This is based upon £750 plus 21 per cent interest (or 1.75 per cent per month) which will be £763.12.*

A cardholder may pay back as much as he wishes but the minimum expected by the card company will be 5 per cent of the amount outstanding: if Frank Porter owed Access £1500 (inclusive of interest charges) then his bill from Access would show a minimum charge of £75, which is 5 per cent.

Some credit card arrangements require the full amount outstanding when the bill is presented. American Express operate in this way and so do a number of 'gold' and 'platinum' card arrangements.

Shops such as Marks & Spencers, Debenhams, Home Stores operate credit-card systems. They can be one of the two types.

(i) The customer is given a credit limit e.g. £1000. He/she must not exceed this limit. The customer pays back a monthly amount which is based upon a minimum of 5 per cent.

(ii) The customer agrees to pay a regular monthly payment and is allowed to spend 20 times that payment e.g. if he/she pays £20 than £400 credit is allowed.

Exercise 7

1   Explain the difference between a secured and an unsecured loan.
2   In a credit sale agreement, ownership of the goods remains with the company supplying the credit: true or false?
3   In a hire-purchase agreement, the person buying the goods becomes the owner immediately he/she pays the first instalment: true or false?

Consumer Credit Act 1974

An anonymous County Court judge between the wars once commented that much of his time was taken up with 'people who are persuaded by persons they do not know to enter into contracts they do not understand to purchase goods that they do not want with money they have not got'. While this may well be an exaggeration, abuses certainly have existed and the company supplying the credit, whether it be a credit sale or hire-purchase agreement, was in a position to use its stronger bargaining position to impose harsh terms on the debtor. It is because of this that various governments have passed legislation to protect debtors. The Consumer Credit Act 1974 attempted to bring together a good deal of the law as it applies to credit in various forms. The Consumer Credit Act was brought into force gradually by statutory instruments and was not fully operational until 1985, 11 years after the Act was passed. All three of our examples would come within the operation of the Act which defined consumer credit agreements as agreements

1   not exceeding £15 000 credit (that is, £15 000 is the actual amount loaned);
2   that are personal, and the borrower is an individual or partnership, not a company.

Agreements that come within the Act are known as regulated agreements. The borrowing of money to buy a house, even though it is £15 000 or less, does not come within the Act and is known as an exempt agreement.

Exercise 8

Which of the following agreements would come within the Consumer Credit Act and are, therefore, regulated agreements?

1   Fortrax Haulage Ltd buys two lorries by means of a credit sale agreement.
2   Martin Thomas buys a £50 000 house with the aid of a £35 000 building society loan.
3   Julie Prince buys a CD player for £430 by means of a hire-purchase agreement.
4   John Clements buys a new luxury car and borrows £18 000 to do so.

Protection under the Act.   The Consumer Credit Act is administered by the Director General of Fair Trading, whose duties under the Act include the following:

1   to administer and license under the Act;
2   to enforce the Act where necessary;
3   to supervise the workings of the Act;
4   to review the operation of the Act and to advise the Secretary of State from time to time.

Anyone wishing to engage in consumer credit business must first seek a licence from the Director General of Fair Trading. Licences will only be given when the Director is satisfied that the applicant is a fit person to engage in business of this sort. Engaging in consumer credit business without a licence is a criminal offence. Moreover an unlicensed creditor will have great difficulty in enforcing a loan against the borrower should the borrower, for example, default.

When someone applies for credit, the credit company will often check with a *credit reference agency* that keeps records relating to people who have poor credit records. For example, if a person has had a County Court judgement entered against him, then this will show up in the records and the credit company may refuse credit to the applicant. The Consumer Credit Act gives the right to anyone on payment of £1 to obtain the name and address of the agency and to receive a copy of their file. If the entry is wrong they can add a correction. Further protection to the public in this respect is given by the Data Protection Act 1984 (see Chapter 19).

Advertising of credit is subject to strict controls under the Act. False or misleading information is a criminal offence, as is canvassing by sending representatives to people's homes to persuade them to take credit.

The three advertisements shown below provide examples of the way in which finance companies advertise their services. Three types of advertisements are shown.

STOUR VALLEY LTD

Finance Company

15 North Lane
Maidbury
MD8 7XY

Telephone 01226 564456
Fax 01226 564488

A simple advertisement

CASH LOANS

£500–£10 000

FOR ANY PURPOSE

17.5% APR (variable)

STOUR VALLEY LTD
15 North Lane
Maidbury
MD8 7XY

Telephone 01226 564456
Fax 01226 564488

An intermediate advertisement

RAPID LOANS

£1000–£50 000

FOR ANY PURPOSE

Typical example

Borrow £4000 and pay back in 24 monthly instalments of £198.64.

Total amount repayable £4767.36 APR (variable) 18.8%

Written quotations on request

Loans may be secured against property

Warning: *Your home is at risk if you do not pay the mortgage or other loan secured on it.*

STOUR VALLEY LTD

15 North Lane

Maidbury

MD8 7XY

Telephone 01226 564456

Fax 01226 564488

A full advertisement

The following example will help to explain the other protection which the Consumer Credit Act 1974 gives to the borrower.

Michael Field wishes to borrow £3000 over a period of three years and makes application to Ready Credit Co. Ltd, a licensed finance company.

Ready Credit Co. Ltd must firstly send to Michael details of the loan; for example:

1   *loan £3000 over 36 months*
2   *interest £1125*
3   *total payments £4125*
4   *36 monthly instalments of £114.58*

If Michael is interested in the terms of this offer he will be sent an agreement form which must give particular details; for example:

'*I agree to borrow the sum of £3000 over a period of 36 months, repayable by 36 monthly instalments of £114.58. Signed . . .*

'*The loan of £3000 is made at an interest rate of 12.5 per cent per annum (which represents an actual rate of 24.6 per cent). The total credit charge is £1124.58, making a total repayable sum of £4124.88.*

'*You may at any time pay off the balance outstanding and you will be entitled to a rebate of interest at rates shown in the enclosed booklet.*

'*Ready Credit Co. Ltd, Commercial House, 119/122 High Street, Manchester MC1 3XX.*'

This example contains all the requirements of the Act, that is total interest charge, rate of interest, rights to termination. Usually there will be a bank mandate form attached, which Michael will sign, giving Ready Credit Co. Ltd the authority to debit his account by £114.58 each month for 36 months.

You will have noted the distinction in Michael's details between the rate of interest at 12.5 per cent and what is called the actual rate. This can be explained by the fact that, for example, when Michael has paid for 18 months he will owe £1500 of the original loan but still be paying 12.5 per cent of £3000. The actual rate over the life of the loan will be much greater, in this case 24.6 per cent, and credit companies must give this information.

The Act lays down that Michael must receive a copy of the form he has signed either immediately or, if it has to be processed in some way, within seven days of the signing. If finance companies do not comply with these regulations a court may refuse to enforce the agreement where (i) it is not in writing; (ii) a copy has not been given to the borrower.

Where the agreement is signed on the business premises of the creditor (the finance company) or on the business premises of the supplier of the goods, which is often the case, the agreement comes into effect immediately. Where, however, the agreement is signed elsewhere the Consumer Credit Act gives the debtor a period during which he can cancel the agreement – known as a 'cooling off period'. The right to such a period must be notified to the debtor in the credit agreement. The effect of the 'cooling off' period is that the debtor can, up to the end of the fifth day after receiving his copy of the agreement, terminate it. If he/she terminates the agreement within this period it is treated as though it never existed. If an agreement is ended in this way and it was for a money loan the debtor must return the money, but if goods are involved the creditor must collect the goods; the debtor must take reasonable care of them for a 21-day period. An agreement which can be cancelled in this way is known as a cancellable agreement.

Finally the Consumer Credit Act 1974 lays down that a court may interfere (the legal expression used is to 'reopen the agreement') and alter an agreement if it feels that interest rates are 'extortionate'. What constitutes extortionate will depend upon a number of circumstances, including the prevailing interest rates. Courts will use the ordinary principles of fair dealing when deciding whether interest rates are extortionate.

The following case shows how courts can deal with high rates of interest. In *Barcabe Ltd* v. *Edwards* (1983), a man on a very low income with four children had answered an advertisement and been persuaded to borrow £400 at interest totalling 100 per cent per year. There was no evidence that he had defaulted on earlier debts, or otherwise was a bad security risk. The court reduced the interest to 40 per cent. However, in *Ketley* v. *Scott* (1981), the court decided that an annual percentage rate (APR) of 57.35 per cent was not extortionate.

Exercise 9

Examine the following and explain the legal position of the person in italics in each exercise.

1 Jane Huxford borrows £1000 over 12 months from *Secure Finance Ltd* which is unlicensed. Jane makes only one payment of £96.89.
2 *John Hardy* borrows £1000 over 24 months from a licensed company but the agreement is made orally. John refuses to repay the loan.
3 *Ian Wood* signs a hire-purchase agreement at his home for a television set with West Derbyshire Financing Ltd. Three days later he changes his mind but the company refuse to release him, saying it is too late: he has already signed.
4 *John Lambert* borrows £500 for one year at a rate of interest of 50 per cent. He defaults on payment and asks the court to reopen the agreement.

Hire-purchase agreements. In addition to the rights outlined above the debtor (hirer) in a hire-purchase agreement has other rights, as the following example will show:

Richard Haigh decides to purchase a caravan for £5500. He pays a deposit of £2000 but obtains the additional £3500 by means of a hire-purchase agreement which he signs at the office of Luxury Caravans Ltd. The creditor, however, is United Finance Ltd. His repayments are over two years at 12 per cent, which amounts to £180.83 per month.

This agreement is based on the usual triangular system (Figure 9.2)

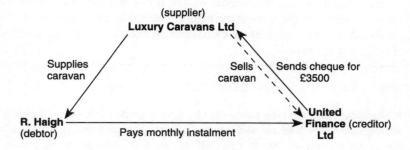

Figure 9.2   A hire purchase arrangement

The agreement which Richard has signed is likely to have included the following notice duly completed with details relating to Richard's agreement:

THE STATUTORY NOTICE BELOW IS APPLICABLE AND MUST BE COMPLETED ONLY WHEN THE HIRE PURCHASE PRICE DOES NOT EXCEED £5000

STATUTORY NOTICE
As Required by The Hire Purchase Acts 1938, 1954 and 1964/65

Right of Hirer to Terminate Agreement

1 The Hirer may put an end to this Agreement by giving notice of termination in writing to any person who is entitled to collect or receive the Hire-rent.

2 He must then pay any instalments which are in arrear at the time when he gives notice. If, when he has paid those instalments, the total amount which he has paid under the Agreement is less than £2170 he must also pay enough to make up that sum.

3 If the Goods have been damaged owing to the Hirer having failed to take reasonable care of them the Owner may sue him for the amount of damage unless that amount can be agreed between the Hirer and the Owner.

4 This agreement restricts the right of the owner to recover the goods as indicated below:

(a)   After £1446.66p has been paid, then, unless the Hirer has himself put an end to the Agreement, the Owners of the Goods cannot take them back from the Hirer without the Hirer's consent unless the Owners obtain an Order of the Court.

(b) If the Owners apply to the Court for such an Order the Court may, if the Court thinks it just to do so, allow the Hirer to keep either
   (i)   The whole of the Goods, on condition that the Hirer pays the balance of the price in the manner ordered by the Court: or
   (ii) A fair proportion of the Goods having regard to what the Hirer has already paid.

Certain conditions are part of a hire purchase agreement.

1   Richard can terminate the agreement by giving United Finance Ltd notice in writing. However Richard will have to pay any arrears to make up, if he has not already done so, up to one-half of the total hire-purchase price. In Richard's case this will be £4340 ÷ 2 = £2170. The Consumer Credit Act lays down that the limit on minimum payment clauses in this context is one-half (50 per cent).
2   If after termination the hirer receives the caravan he may sue for damage if it has been damaged owing to Richard's not having taken reasonable care of it.
3   If Richard did not pay his instalments regularly then, since the caravan belongs to the finance company, it has certain rights of recovery. However, Richard must be given seven days' notice of default. If Richard has not yet paid one-third of the total hire-purchase price, that is, £146.66, then the creditor can 'snatch back' the goods though the creditor is not entitled to enter the debtor's property to get goods back which are subject to a regulated agreement, as this is, without a court order. If the caravan was parked elsewhere then clearly it could be 'snatched back'. When, however, Richard has paid the third or more the goods become 'protected' and under no circumstances can they be 'snatched back'. A court order is necessary, and if the finance company took the matter to court the court might well give the hirer additional time to pay. Protected goods may only be recovered without a court order if they are abandoned by the hirer or returned voluntarily by him. The following case is an example of the effects of hire-purchase companies 'snatching back' unlawfully. In *Capital Finance Co Ltd* v. *Bray* (1964), a finance company took back, without a court order, a car which Bray had on hire-purchase. The car was protected goods and, when the company realised its mistake, it returned the car immediately. Bray used it for several months, refusing all requests for payment. Eventually the company sued for possession, and this was granted. The company could not, however, recover payment for Bray's use of the car after its return to him. Moreover Bray recovered everything which he had paid.

Finally a hirer has similar implied rights in respect of goods when he buys under a hire purchase agreement as given to a buyer under the Sale of Goods Act 1979 (and the Supply of Goods and Services Act 1982). These rights, relating to quality title and fitness description, will give the hirer a claim against the supplier or against the creditor. Thus if Richard's caravan was not of 'merchantable quality' he could sue United Finance Ltd.

__ **Exercise 10** _____

1 In a hire-purchase agreement the hirer is also the debtor: true or false?
2 A debtor under a hire-purchase agreement can terminate the agreement at any time provided he pays up to a maximum of:
   a one-quarter of the hire purchase price;
   b one-third of the hire purchase price;
   c one-half of the hire purchase price;
   d two-thirds of the hire purchase price.
Which of the above is correct?
3 David Harrison buys a car by means of a hire-purchase agreement. Having paid two-thirds of the hire-purchase price he decides he can no longer afford any further payments. The finance company send him notice of default and send a representative around, who drives the car away despite David's protests. Has the finance company the right to do this?

__ **Exercise 11** _____

Explain the legal position in each of the following examples. Check your answers against those at the end of the book and if you have not really understood any aspect of this chapter read it over again.

1 Bob White buys a one-year-old motorcycle from a friend for £850. A week after the purchase Bob finds serious mechanical flaws in the machine.
2 Deborah James buys a box of five bottles of French sweet wine from Spring Gardens Wines Ltd. When she opens the box she finds it is Yugoslav dry wine.
3 Wainwrights (Domestic) Ltd offer fridges at 20 per cent discount at £65. The old price had been £70 for the last two years.
4 Mr and Mrs Taylor go on holiday in Malta and, despite the advertisement which says that all rooms have sea views and that the hotel is close by the seafront, in fact the hotel is nine miles from the sea and the sea views are only possible with the aid of powerful binoculars. They feel they have wasted the £450 which the holiday cost.
5 Marlene Ward borrows £1000 from a finance company but never receives a copy of the agreement. She refuses to pay the instalments and the company sues her.
6 Audrey Worsley buys a vacuum cleaner from a travelling salesman. She signs a hire-purchase agreement. When her husband returns home from a business trip seven days later he is very angry, so she decides to cancel the agreement.

7 David Summerfield takes out a loan under a credit agreement which is for £7500 at an annual rate of interest of 150 per cent over 36 months.

8 Sure Credit PLC advertise loans which they indicate will be unsecured. Many unsuspecting customers sign agreements and find that they have agreed a charge on their houses to secure the loans.

⬡10 Insurance law

Keith Martin has, for the last ten years, managed a large shoe shop in the centre of a city. It has always been his ambition to run his own business but until recently he has never had sufficient money to be able to purchase a shoe shop. Keith is, however, left quite a large sum of money and by chance a shoe shop near his home is put up for sale. Keith decides to realise his ambition and purchases the shop.

In taking on his own business Keith, like any other businessman, is taking certain risks. For example, the demand for shoes may decline and he may make no profit or his shop, including stock, may be completely destroyed by fire. Although no insurance company would insure against the risk of making a loss, fortunately Keith could take out insurance against the risk of fire.

In this chapter we will be considering insurance contracts to see how they resemble any other business contract but also to examine some of their particular characteristics. In order to do this, let us return to Keith's business and concentrate upon his need to insure it against the risk of fire.

Keith has heard that Safesure Insurance Co has a very good reputation, so he decides to telephone the company to get a proposal form. A proposal form is really an application form on which Keith would need to give full details of the risk that he wishes the company to take on for him. It is on the basis of this information that the insurance company will calculate the premium, the amount of money which Keith needs to pay monthly, quarterly or annually to the insurance company. We will assume that Keith has calculated that, if his business was completely destroyed by fire, he would lose £400 000.

Safesure would assess the risk that they were taking on by pooling all similar risks together and estimating the amount of money they might have to pay out. These estimates will be based upon a number of criteria, including past experience. The 'pooling of risk' concept which allows insurance companies to take on risks at a modest charge is illustrated by Figure 10.1.

Assume that Safesure has 2000 similar risks on its books and that it estimates that £1 600 000 will be paid out in claims. The company has also estimated that each policy costs it about £80 per annum in administrative costs, including profit. The premium that Safesure would quote to insure Keith's business would therefore be:

> Total claims equal £1 600 000
> Number of similar businesses insured is 2000
> £1 600 000 divided by 2000 equals £800
> Administrative cost per policy is £80
> Total premium is £800 + £80 = £880

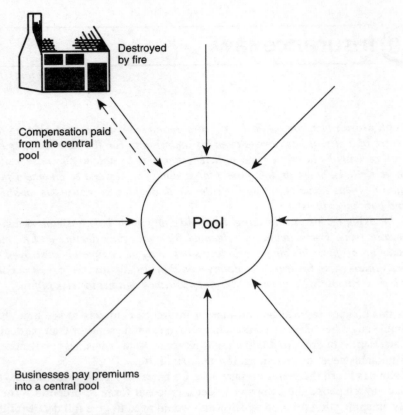

Figure 10.1   Pooling of risks

It is because the company can estimate with a reasonable degree of accuracy the likely number of claims that they can quote a premium. It would, however, be impossible for the company to calculate the number of claims for failure to make profit and therefore businesses cannot insure this risk because it is 'non-insurable', whereas, as we have seen, fire is estimable and therefore insurable. Some risks are also non-insurable because it is illegal to cover them. For example, it is unlawful for an insurance company to insure a person against imprisonment in the event of his committing an unlawful act.

Exercise 1

1   The form which is filled in by a person wishing to take out insurance is known as what?
2   Why is failure to make profits a non-insurable risk?
3   Insurance companies can keep their premiums low by putting all similar risks together. This is known as what?

Keith sends in his proposal form. Safesure Insurance will consider it in detail and will then make Keith an offer. Assuming that the detail he has put on the form does not suggest that his business is any different from the 2000 other similar businesses they are insuring, the offer will be that the company will take on the risk of fire at a cost to Keith of £880 per annum (the premium). If Keith accepts this offer – and remember that he must accept the offer unconditionally – then a contract is made; that is, the company makes an offer, Keith accepts the offer, consideration is supplied by Keith in the form of a premium of £880 per annum and is supplied by the company in that the company promises to compensate Keith in the event of loss resulting from fire. A legally binding contract has come into existence and Keith will receive in due course a policy. The policy is in fact the contractual document and will contain the terms of the insurance.

We can safely assume that the other four elements essential for a legally binding contract also exist. There is nothing illegal about fire insurance; both parties, that is Keith and the company, have the legal capacity; both parties intend that the agreement should be legally binding; and there was probably *consensus ad idem* (a meeting of the minds) as far as the agreement was concerned.

In addition to the seven essential elements which must exist in a contract, insurance contracts have other important characteristics. All insurance agreements must be based upon the principle of utmost good faith, the principle of insurable interest and the principle of indemnity.

10.1 Utmost good faith

When Keith completed his proposal form he would have been asked a number of questions about the premises in which the shoe business was conducted. If Keith had answered these falsely then he would have been misrepresenting the facts to the insurer, Safesure Insurance Co, and the agreement, as we have seen, because it would lack *consensus ad idem* would not be legally binding. In addition in an insurance agreement Keith is obliged to disclose information which might be relevant even though the proposal form did not ask for it. For example, if Keith's son Andrew was studying chemistry at university and used one of the rooms attached to the shop for his chemical experiments then it would be necessary for Keith to disclose this; or if the shop was next to a premises where inflammable liquids were stored then this would have to be disclosed.

This is an important principle because, if Keith did not disclose what, after all, is a fire risk, he has failed to disclose what is very relevant information. Then if fire did cause damage, the insurance company could treat the agreement as voidable and refuse to pay out.

If we think about the principle of utmost good faith, it is quite obvious that insurance companies, in order to assess a risk, must have all the relevant information. Conducting chemical experiments on the premises certainly changes the nature of the risk and would cause the insurance company to think rather carefully about the premium that it would charge.

All insurance contracts must be based upon the principle of utmost good faith, sometimes known by the Latin expression *uberrimae fidei*.

The principle of utmost good faith is well illustrated in *Arterial Caravans Ltd* v. *Yorkshire Insurance Co* (1973).

In this case the company seeking the insurance failed to reveal that another company managed by them had suffered a loss by fire. The court held that this failure was a 'non disclosure' of a material fact and therefore the insurance contract could be regarded as voidable.

Exercise 2

In the following examples say whether the insurance company in each case could refuse to pay out.

1 Roger Allen (44) takes out a £50 000 life insurance with Security Insurance Co but omits to mention on the proposal form that he spends a lot of time on his hobby of hang-gliding. He dies as a result of an accident in this activity and Security refuse to pay his widow.
2 Brian Webster keeps a small shop which sells sweets, tobacco and newspapers. It is a lock-up shop but Brian leaves a side window at the back open to let his cat get in. He has in fact been burgled five times in two years. Brian decides to take out insurance but forgets to mention either of these two facts. When he tries to claim for yet another burglary the insurance company refuses to pay out.

10.2   Insurable interest

The following two examples will help to illustrate the meaning of this principle.

John Smith decides to insure his next-door neighbour Philip Green's life for £40 000. Most insurance companies refuse to accept such insurance but one company, Fidelity Co Ltd, decides that, for a monthly premium of £60, John can arrange this. Philip dies a year later and John seeks to collect £40 000. Fidelity refuses to pay.

In fact, Fidelity need not pay because this contract is void by illegality. The Life Assurance Act 1774 lays down that:

No Insurance shall be made by any person or persons ... Wherein the person or persons for whose use, benefit or on whose account such policy or policies shall be made shall have no interest.

John has no 'insurable interest' in Philip Green's life. It is illegal for such insurance to be taken out and clearly if such practices were allowed there could be considerable encouragement to crime; for example, life insurance could be taken out on a person and that person could be disposed of and the insurance collected. Generally speaking, you can only insure your own life or another person's in whom you have a financial interest. It is, of course, possible for a wife to insure her husband's life and vice versa. It is also possible for one partner in a business to insure another partner. In both these cases the death of husband/wife or partner would represent a loss to the person taking out the insurance.

In *Harse* v. *Pearl Assurance Co Ltd* (1904) it was held that the plaintiff had no insurable interest in the life of his mother. The policy was judged therefore to be illegal and the plaintiff was not entitled to recover any money under it. It is, however, possible to take out a small life insurance for a son or daughter because, if they were to die, the parents would need to meet the costs of a funeral and so on.

Carol and Florence both own teashops in a small town. They are firm friends and, in addition to insurance on their own shops, they decide to insure each other's shops. Following a fire which completely destroys Carol's shop, the insurance company pay her £80 000, the sum insured, but refuse to pay Florence.

Although what Florence has done is not illegal, that is she can insure someone else's business, in practice it would be a waste of money because insurance principles lay down that you can only collect insurance if you have suffered a loss. Florence certainly has suffered no financial loss as a result of Carol's situation and therefore could not collect. Insurance companies will not normally make agreements with persons who have no insurable interest in the risk they wish to insure.

The object of a contract of insurance is to protect the interest of the insured, therefore the insured must have an interest in the subject matter of the policy.

Exercise 3

In the following cases say whether you think the person taking out the insurance has an interest in the subject matter of the policy.

1 Michael borrows his friend's boat occasionally and therefore decides to insure it for £1000.
2 Mrs Yeomans insures her husband's life for £35 000.
3 Victor Wood insures his car by taking out a comprehensive insurance policy.
4 Sheila Pullin insures her best friend's life for £20 000.

10.3   Indemnity

Adam Cranston owns a house valued at £80 000. Being a cautious and careful man, he decides to insure the house for £140 000. Shortly after he has taken out the insurance, Adam's house is completely gutted by fire and he can either have the house rebuilt for £60 000 or buy a comparable property. Adam decides to buy another, superior property and claims the full £140 000 from the insurance company.

The insurance company pays out £80 000, which it claims is the value of Adam's loss. Adam feels cheated and decides to sue the company.

In this situation Adam would not be successful because one important principle of insurance is that of 'indemnity', which means the insurance company have a duty to compensate the insured for his loss but no more. It is an important fact of insurance that it is not intended that an insured person *gains* from insurance. The intention is that the insured person be put back in as near as possible the position which existed before the accident. The £140 000 represents the maximum sum payable under the insurance, not what the company will actually pay. Since the value of Adam's property was only £80 000 the additional £60 000 cover represented for Adam a waste of money.

This, however, does not work in reverse: if Adam had only insured his property for £60 000 then in the event of a fire he could only get £60 000. The principle of indemnity states that an insured be compensated for his loss. The insured can only obtain, however, the maximum sum payable under the policy, that is £60 000.

This example perhaps illustrates the folly of being underinsured and the waste in being overinsured.

For obvious reasons the principle of indemnity can never be applied to life policies because the loss resulting from the death of a husband, for example, is not really assessable.

Exercise 4

1   What do you understand by the term 'indemnity' in respect of insurance?
2   Why can indemnity never apply to a life policy?
3   Explain the terms 'overinsurance' and 'underinsurance' in relation to property.

Linked to the principle of indemnity are two other principles of insurance contracts, 'contribution' and 'subrogation'. The following examples will help to explain them.

Contribution

Thelma Sheldon owns and runs a business offering secretarial services to local firms. She estimates that the total value of her equipment in the business is £65 000. Being a careful woman, Thelma insures her business with two separate insurance firms, Security Co Ltd and Northern Union Insurance. Unfortunately her business is completely lost by fire, but Thelma is not really worried because she claims two lots of £65 000, that is £130 000.

If we think about this example we can see it goes against the principle of indemnity because Thelma has gained from the fire. In this situation the principle of contribution is applied. Each company would pay a 50 per cent contribution to Thelma's loss. This example illustrates that double insurance is really a waste of money. Again, however, the principle of contribution does not apply to life insurance and in this respect a person may have as many life policies as he wishes and can afford.

Subrogation

David Ekin has insured his toy shop against fire with the Sapphire Insurance Co for £80 000. As a result of fire and following an inspection of the premises, David gets the full £80 000. However David decides that he can advertise some of the toys as fire-damaged and he holds a sale which realises £5500.

It is easy to see that David has gained an extra £5500 and of course this is against the principle of indemnity. The principle of subrogation states that the £5500 belongs to Sapphire and, if the company discovers that David has made an additional £5500, it can sue him for recovery.

Exercise 5

1 If Carole Newsome insures her house with two companies and it is damaged why can she not get double compensation?
2 After an insurance company has paid out for a loss in full any additional money obtained by the insured belongs to the company. Is the fact based upon the principle of: (a) utmost good faith, (b) subrogation, (c) contribution or (d) insurable interest?

It follows that, whilst it is a waste of money to overinsure a risk since the insurance companies will only compensate for a loss and will never exceed the value of the loss, it is most unwise to underinsure a risk, as the following example shows.

Lenny Lyons-Mucksiep has just bought a house for £120 000 and has over-reached himself. He cannot really afford a large insurance premium and insures the house for £60 000. A fire causes considerable damage and the repair and rebuilding costs £60 000. Lenny claims from his insurance and receives just £30 000.

Lenny is underinsured; in fact his insurance covers only 50 per cent of the risk. Quite legally the insurance company will use the 'average' principle and pay only 50 per cent of the repairs. Lenny's situation serves as a reminder that to be underinsured is very risky.

Exercise 6

In the following examples explain the legal position involved. Check your answers with those at the end of the book and, if you have not understood any of the points, read over this chapter again.

1 John Phillips forgets to disclose in an application for motor insurance that he suffers from epilepsy.
2 In a proposal for fire insurance for his business, Bob Brown forgets to mention that his wife has had several convictions for arson, all in relation to his business property.
3 Cyril Ruback's carpet warehouse is completely gutted. His insurance compensates him in full but Cyril sells of a large number of fire- and water-damaged carpets.
4 Pat Browett insures her cottage for £100 000; its value, however, is only £65 000.
5 Ann Bishop insures her neighbour's life for £4500.
6 Bob Dash insures his new car with two companies. Following an accident his car is a write-off and he uses the money from both companies to buy a car for himself and one for his wife.

11 Torts (I): negligence

11.1 The tort of negligence

Mrs Fiona Sykes owns a grocery shop which is situated in the suburbs of a large town. During the last two years she has run her shop as a self-service store. Customers select the goods they wish to purchase, placing them in wire baskets, and then pay at the cash desk. On one occasion a customer, Sheila Hayward, is reaching to get some tins when the shelf on which the tins are placed comes away from the wall and Sheila sustains quite a serious arm injury as a result of the shelf and its contents falling on her. Sheila's injuries cause her considerable discomfort and necessitate hospital treatment. She is also forced, because of her incapacity, to give up some typing she was doing at home for a local firm. Sheila decides to take the matter to court.

Incidents like this happen frequently, and lawyers and courts spend a lot of time dealing with claims for compensation such as Sheila is attempting to make in this example. In fact, Sheila will be suing for the tort of negligence. Negligence is just one of a number of torts which we will be examining in this chapter and the next. The word 'tort' is from a French word which means 'wrong'. As well as negligence there are torts of nuisance, trespass and defamation of character. As with contract, which we have already met, it will be the civil courts which deal with torts. In this chapter we will look at the tort of negligence. Using the example of Fiona and Sheila will help you to understand the main aspects of negligence and help you see how this important branch of law can be applied to business situations.

You will no doubt remember from Chapter 1 that in civil cases there are two parties involved; in our example, Sheila will be the plaintiff and Fiona will be the defendant. If she is going to be successful in getting compensation, Sheila, as the plaintiff, will need to prove negligence; to do this she will have to prove three things. (It is important to note that in negligence it is for the plaintiff to prove and therefore we say that the 'burden of proof' in negligence is on the plaintiff.)

Exercise 1

1 What does the word 'tort' mean?
2 In the situation relating to Fiona and Sheila, who must do the proving?
3 The tort of negligence is criminal: true or false?

What then are the three things which Sheila will need to prove to be successful in negligence and therefore in getting compensation?

Duty of care

First, Sheila must prove that the defendant, Fiona, owed her a duty of care: English law imposes upon people a duty to be careful in their dealings with others. In an extremely important case, *Donogue* v. *Stevenson* (1932), the principle of the duty of care was established. Mrs Donogue attempted to sue the supplier of a ginger beer drink, which she had drunk and which contained the remnants of a decomposed snail. In *Home Office* v. *Dorset Yacht Co* (1970), the neighbourhood principle relating to duty of care was used in this decision when the Home Office was held to be liable for damage to yachts when boys from a Borstal escaped and damaged property.

The judge, Lord Atkin, in *Donogue* v. *Stevenson* defined the duty of care as being that owed to one's neighbour and then went on to define a neighbour as anyone who you might reasonably foresee could be affected by your acts or omissions, in other words by something you did or failed to do. In our example it is quite clear that Fiona had not adequately checked the shelving or had overloaded it and that she (Fiona) 'might reasonably have foreseen that anyone coming into her shop might have been injured as a result of this omission [failure to check] or act [overloading]', to quote from Lord Atkin.

There are many examples in a shop situation which could give rise to negligence actions, and shopkeepers have a duty towards any customer coming into the shop. Not only can people be liable for careless deeds or omissions but it is possible for them to be liable for careless statements. Thus it might be said that a professional person, such as a bank manager, solicitor or accountant, owes a duty of care to his customers or clients and can be held liable for negligent (careless) statements. So, for example, where a credit company takes up a reference from a bank manager in respect of an applicant for a loan, the bank manager must be particularly careful in supplying information – the bank could be liable, should the person receiving the loan default. *Hedley Byrne* v. *Heller & Partners* (1963) illustrates the principle well that a bank, for example, may be held liable for a negligent mis-statement: a firm of advertising agents gave credit to a client in reliance upon a banker's reference, and suffered loss when the client became insolvent. The reference had been given carelessly but, since the bank had expressly disclaimed liability when giving it, the action failed. Nevertheless the House of Lords stated that, contrary to what had previously been believed, liability for negligence may extend to careless words as well as to careless deeds and that damages may be awarded for financial loss as well as for physical injury to persons and property.

In another case, *Smith* v. *Eric Bush* (1989), a surveyor employed by a building society to value a house knew that his report would be relied upon by the buyer. The House of Lords held that the surveyor had been negligent to the buyer, even though the buyer was not his client.

The question of negligence relating to financial loss is well summed up in the Lloyds so-called 'names' cases.

In *Deeny and others* v. *Gooda Walker Ltd and others* (1994), the Queen's Bench Division judge determined that the underwriters had been negligent in the manner in which they conducted their business and as a result losses were made. The judge held that all 70 defendants had breached their duty of care to their clients and awarded damages to the plaintiffs. The judgement meant that 3095 plaintiffs shared £630 million.

Activity

To help you understand the concept of duty of care, you might think for a moment about all those people to whom you have owed a duty of care today.

You may be surprised at the large number of people covered by the term 'neighbour'.

Certain people have been exempted by law from owing a duty of care. For example, a barrister will never be liable in negligence for his careless handling of a case because he does not owe a duty of care to his clients; but clearly barristers will not get many clients if they gain a reputation for careless dealings. This was well summed up in the House of Lords judgement, *Rondel* v. *Worsley* (1969). The law also says that occupiers of premises do not owe a duty of care to certain people. An occupier of premises owes a duty of care to all lawful visitors but he does not owe a duty of care to trespassers. A trespasser must take the premises as he finds them. So if Sheila had broken into Fiona's shop and had injured herself on the shelving while helping herself to goods then Fiona would not be liable because she would not have owed Sheila a duty of care.

There are two circumstances where an occupier might owe a duty of care to trespassers.

1 The law requires that a duty of care is owed to children who trespass onto property. The case of *British Railways Board* v. *Herrington* (1972) illustrates this. A young boy aged six wandered onto railway property through a hole in the fence and was injured on an electrified section of rail. The Board was held to be liable in negligence even though the boy was a trespasser.

2 There are some circumstances where people become so used to walking across property where the occupier has done nothing to prevent them that they could be forgiven for not realising they are trespassers. If one of these people had an accident then the occupier would be held to be liable because the courts would assume the existence of a duty of care. Acts of Parliament,

Occupier's Liability Acts 1957 and 1984, go a long way to clarifying the law relating to trespassers and other visitors. The 1984 Act makes it clear that an occupier has a duty of care to children and to other trespassers such as hitch-hikers who might be lost on someone's property.

Breach of duty of care

Having established the existence of a duty of care, and we have seen that a duty of care does exist towards Sheila, it is necessary to show that the duty of care has been broken or, to use the legal term, breached. In our example, Sheila would need to show that the standard of care exercised by Fiona was not that of a reasonable person. In other words, Sheila would need to show that regular checks should have been made on the shelving and care should have been taken that the shelves were not overloaded. If Fiona could show that she had maintained regular checks or that she had recently employed the services of a competent joiner to look at the shelving then she might be able to show that she had not broken her duty of care towards Sheila. We will assume that this was not the case and that the duty of care had been breached.

Exercise 2

Read the following example:

Richard Huyton is a company secretary for a large company and is in a hurry to attend a meeting. He is driving far too fast and skids on an icy stretch of road, injuring a pedestrian, David Pritchard.

1 Name the defendant and plaintiff.
2 Does a duty of care exist from the defendant to the plaintiff?
3 Do you think the duty of care has been broken?

Whether a duty of care has been breached will depend upon the circumstances. The courts use the concept of a reasonable man – one definition describes it as 'doing what a reasonable man would not do or failing to do what a reasonable man would do'. You don't, in other words, have to be perfect, just reasonably careful.

In some circumstances an accident occurs where the only possible cause is negligence. In *Richley* v. *Faull* (1965), the defendant's car skidded violently, turned round and collided with the plaintiff's car on the wrong side of the road. It was held that this, of itself, was sufficient evidence of negligent driving. Since the defendant was unable to give a satisfactory explanation of his skid, he was held liable. In this case it was up to the defendant to prove he was not negligent. The court has applied the rule 'the facts speak for themselves' or, to use the Latin phrase often used by lawyers, '*Res ipsa loquitur*'.

Loss arising

We have seen, therefore, that to prove negligence it is necessary to show (1) the existence of a duty of care and (2) that this duty has been broken. We have seen that Sheila could easily prove the existence of these two elements. However it is also necessary for the plaintiff to prove a third element and that is that he/she suffered some loss as a result of the defendant's breach of the duty of care. The loss can include damage to property, personal injury and in some cases financial loss. There is little doubt that Sheila had suffered personal injury as a result of Fiona's breach of duty. Her injury also made it impossible for Sheila to continue with her typing work and therefore she suffered financial loss.

It would seem, then, that Sheila can prove the existence of these three essential elements: a duty of care, a breach and a loss. She would be successful in an action for negligence and the court would award her damages. The damages awarded would be calculated to try to compensate her for the pain she suffered and also to compensate her for the financial loss she suffered as a result of her inability to engage in typing.

The question of resulting damage is well summed up in *Barnett* v. *Chelsea and Kensington Hospital Management Committee* (1969). The details of the case are as follows. Mr Barnett went to the casualty department late at night, complaining of vomiting having drunk tea. The duty doctor did not examine him but sent him home and advised him to call his own doctor. Three hours later Mr Barnett died of arsenic poisoning. The hospital doctor, and therefore the hospital committee, owed Mr Barnett a duty of care and had breached it by not examining him. However, since there is no cure for poisoning of this sort, the damage did not result from the breach and Mr Barnett's widow was unsuccessful.

It should be noted that purely financial losses are more likely to be recoverable through breach of contract. In *DF Estates Ltd* v. *The Church Commissioners* (1988) it was held by the House of Lords that the tenants could not claim damages for bad workmanship through a negligence action, although in *Targett* v. *Torfaen BC* (1991), the landlord was held to be liable to a plaintiff who fell down the stairs of a council house which had no lighting or handrail. However, as we have seen in *Deeny and others* v. *Gooda Walker Ltd and others* (1994), there are circumstances where damages will be awarded for only financial loss.

Exercise 3

1 What are the three elements which a plaintiff must prove to be successful in an action for negligence?
2 George Shaw breaks a leg while shopping. Negligence is proved; George claims £400 loss of earnings. How would the court assess the amount of compensation (damages) paid?

Exercise 4

Examine the following cases carefully and say whether you think the person or organisation in italics would be successful in suing for negligence. In each case apply the three elements (a) duty of care, (b) breach and (c) loss. If you feel that there is no case, give the reason for your view. Spend some time on these examples making sure you get them correct before you continue.

1 *Michael Street* has broken into the offices of Buxted Engineering Co. While switching on a light Michael is injured by an electric shock caused by a faulty electric fitting.
2 *Mary Goodwin* has been interviewed for a post as secretary with Low Peak District Council. Coming down that steps from the office, Mary slips, and reaches for the stair rail, which gives way. Mary sustains a broken leg.
3 Alan Harrison is managing director of Sparkes & Co Ltd (Electrical Suppliers). He has always been a most careful driver and is driving down the main street of a country town at about 14 mph. A child runs onto the road and Alan brakes, but he skids on some oil on the road. His car collides with a pedestrian, *Rachel Martin*, who is injured. Alan is able to explain why the skid occurred when he gets out of the car and sees the patch of oil.
4 Margaret Brown is suffering from an incurable disease and is likely to die at any time. While walking in the hospital ward she slips on some loose floor covering. A day later she dies. *John Brown* her husband, sues the hospital board for negligence.
5 An explosion due to a faulty process occurs in the laboratory of Filton Chemical Co. *Michael Pullin*, a laboratory technician, although nearby, miraculously escapes injury.
6 Andrew Knowles, aged five, wanders onto a building site and ignores the sign, 'trespassers will be prosecuted'. He falls down a hole and is badly injured. His father, *David Knowles*, decides to sue the builders, Easibuild Co Ltd.

If you have answered these 6 questions correctly, go on to the next part, which deals with defences which might be used in a negligence action. If you are still unsure then read the section again and then attempt the questions again.

11.2 Possible defences against a negligence action

We have seen that for a plaintiff to be successful in negligence he must prove (i) the existence of a duty of care, (ii) the breach of that duty and (iii) loss or damage arising from the breach. Clearly it is for the defendant if he wishes to try to show that in fact one or other of these elements did not exist. If he can do this then he can show that there was no negligence. The defendant may claim, for example:

1 that he owed no duty of care to the plaintiff; or
2 that although he owed a duty of care he had acted reasonably and had not been in any way careless and therefore had not breached the duty of care which he owed; or
3 even though he owed a duty of care and he had been careless, his negligence did not cause the plaintiff's loss.

In these instances the defendant is countering the plaintiff's claim that negligence existed by denying the existence of one or other of the 3 elements.

There are however situations where a defendant may offer as a defence the fact that the plaintiff consented to take part in the event which led to the plaintiff's loss. This is known as consent and is explained below.

Consent

Dove Dale Engineering Ltd have built a sports and social club for their employees and families. At the entrance of the club there is a cloak room where members and guests can leave their coats under the charge of a cloakroom attendant. Clearly displayed at the entrance to the cloakroom is a notice which reads:

Dove Dale Engineering Ltd cannot be held liable for loss or damage to any property which is left in the cloakroom. Persons leaving their belongings in the cloakroom do so at their own risk.

Brian Hamilton and his wife Margaret have spent an evening at the club. When they return for their coats Margaret finds that hers is missing and Brian discovers the loss of a cigarette lighter, car keys, cheque book and various credit cards from the pockets of his coat. When Brian makes further inquiries he discovers that the cloakroom attendant had been in the bar for 15 minutes and had left the coats unattended. Brian is very angry and decides to sue Dove Dale Engineering Ltd.

Although all the three elements necessary to prove negligence exist here, the defendant, Dove Dale Engineering Ltd, would use the defence of consent and would draw that court's attention to the notice which disclaimed liability which is displayed at the entrance of the cloakroom. If a person consents to suffer damage, or consents to run the risk of it, he cannot then claim compensation. This consent is sometimes expressed by the Latin phrase, *volenti non fit injuria*, 'to one who is willing no harm is done'. It is important to remember that the notice which disclaims liability must be brought to the attention of the plaintiff before the event; thus in our example Mr and Mrs Hamilton saw the notice before they deposited their coats. You will remember that, although it is possible for firms or individuals to disclaim liability for loss, they can no longer use as a defence a notice which disclaims liability for personal injury or death (Unfair Contract Terms Act 1977; see Chapter 6).

The principle of consent is well illustrated in *Morris* v. *Murray* (1991) in which the plaintiff was severely injured in a plane crash in which his colleague, the pilot died. The two had consumed considerable amounts of alcohol before the flight. The court held that the plaintiff had consented to the take the risk and was not entitled to damages.

The defence of consent is rarely allowed to employers seeking to avoid liability by saying the employee consented.

It is possible in some circumstances for the defendant to argue that the plaintiff contributed in part to the situation which resulted in the loss. This is known as contributory negligence and is explained below.

Contributory negligence

It is also possible for a defendant to attempt to show that the plaintiff was partly responsible for loss or injuries sustained. The next example will help to explain this.

Mrs Fraser is a secretary with Westshire County Council. On one cold and icy morning, she is rushing to get to her office on time and slips on a frozen section of a pathway in the grounds of County Hall leading to her office building. Mrs Fraser is injured and damages her coat in the fall. Despite the cold conditions Mrs Fraser is wearing boots with extremely high heels. Mrs Fraser decides to sue Westshire County Council in negligence, claiming that no attempt had been made to clear the pathway even though it was the only way to the office.

If we apply the three elements to this case it can easily be seen that the county council was negligent. The county council may argue, however, that the fall was partly caused by the wearing of inappropriate footwear. If the court hearing the case accept this it may well reduce the level of damages that would have been awarded to Mrs Fraser. This is known as contributory negligence; that is, the plaintiff has contributed to the loss or damage sustained. The principle of contributory negligence is well illustrated by the fact that courts are becoming increasingly reluctant to award car drivers claiming negligence full compensation, arguing that they have contributed to their injuries by not using their seat belts.

A well-known case also illustrates the principle of contributory negligence: *Sayers* v. *Harlow UDC* (1958). Mrs Sayers found that she was locked in a public lavatory. Unable to get help she decided to climb over the door. To aid her climb she used the toilet-roll holder as a foot rest. The toilet roll rotated under her weight and she fell, injuring herself. The court held that Harlow UDC had been negligent in allowing a faulty lock to be on the door but that 25 per cent of the blame was Mrs Sayers' for attempting this climb. The damages awarded were thus 75 per cent of the total.

In recent cases drivers or passengers injured in accidents but not wearing seat belts have had damages reduced. In *Froom* v. *Butcher* (1976) a front-seat passenger injured in a car accident had his damages reduced by 25 per cent because he had not worn a seat belt.

Exercise 5

1 List the five defences which a defendant may use in an action for negligence.
2 Disclaiming liability for death or personal injury is possible provided it is brought to the attention of the plaintiff: true or false?

Activity

Within the next few days look for disclaimer notices. See if you can recognise those which could be used as a defence in a negligence action and those that could not.

Remoteness of damage

It is possible for a negligent act to give rise to a succession of events and the courts have to decide where to draw the limit in deciding whether or not the damage is too remote. The following example may help to illustrate.

> *Anton Bendrey runs a small engineering works in Kent. One of his employees, Jack Gardiner, is badly injured using a lathe which was faulty. Jack's wife is informed and she tells her mother, who lives in Bristol. The mother tells a friend the details and circumstances of the accident and the friend, on hearing the news, becomes quite ill. The friend, Mrs Lillian Jones, decides to sue the owner, Anton.*

It is most likely that the case would fail because the court would apply the principle of what was reasonably foreseeable. It is fair to assume that Anton could not reasonably foresee that his omission in allowing a faulty lathe to be used would affect someone remote from the event.

A number of decided cases illustrate the principle of 'remoteness of damage' well:

In *Bourhill* v. *Young* (1943), a claim was made against a motor cyclist who was involved in an accident. The plaintiff was getting off a tram 50 yards away from the scene when she heard the sound of the collision. Later she saw the blood on the road and suffered nervous shock and had a miscarriage. The House of Lords held that, although the motor cyclist owed a duty of care to other road users including pedestrians, he could not reasonably foresee the effect upon a person 50 yards from the scene.

In a more recent case, *Alcock* v. *Chief Constable of South Yorkshire* (1991), which concerned the Hillsborough football disaster, it was held by the House of Lords that illness caused by witnessing scenes of the accident on television which the plaintiffs claimed caused psychiatric disorder was too remote from the situation to give rise to an action for negligence.

Exercise 6

Read the following and say whether you think that Alan would have a good case in negligence.

Alan Pilkington is staying at the Hotel Regal on the south coast. He books in at the reception desk and a porter is called to assist him with his luggage. When the porter and Alan arrive at Alan's room, the porter draws Alan's attention to a notice which reads:

The Management cannot accept any liability for the loss of any guest's property while the guest is staying at the Hotel Regal; guests are advised to deposit valuable property in the safe at reception.

Alan is in a rush to get a meal and leaves some valuable property, worth £1000, in the room. While he is in the restaurant a member of staff with a known police record uses his pass key to get into the room and steals the £1000 worth of equipment, which is never recovered.

Occupier's liability

We have already seen that generally one is not liable for negligent acts towards trespassers. The Occupier's Liability Act of 1957 lays down that a duty of care is owed by an occupier to all lawful visitors, and goes on to establish three categories of lawful visitors:

1 Persons with an express permission to be on the occupier's premises (for example, friends invited for a meal, a person invited for an interview for a job).
2 Persons with implied permission (for example, customers in a shop, a door-to-door salesman).
3 Persons with a statutory right to enter (police to enforce the law with a search warrant, officials reading gas or electricity meters).

As we have already seen, the Occupier's Liability Act makes it very clear that an occupier owes a duty of care to certain trespassers, especially children, and those who perhaps have regularly walked through property and have assumed that this was not unlawful.

Activity

In this section we have examined in some detail the law relating to negligence. You may care to think of your own experiences and think whether you have been negligent recently or have suffered from the negligence of others. Relating this section to your own experiences will help you understand better the important tort of negligence.

Liability for defective goods

Manufacturers of defective goods can, as we have seen, be liable for negligence; that is, they can be sued by a person injured while using the defective goods, even if they were not the direct supplier. Often, of course, it is a retailer who supplies the goods and of course retailers are subject to the Sale of Goods Act which we considered in Chapter 9. We have already seen in the present chapter that the manufacturer was liable in the famous case of *Donogue* v. *Stevenson* (1932). The rules relating to the liability of a manufacturer have been supplemented by the Consumer Protection Act which we also looked at in Chapter 9.

The law relating to defective goods does give the customer protection against defective goods but, as we have seen, to prove negligence the onus is on the plaintiff and this is sometimes difficult for an ordinary buyer of goods. The courts have been inclined to apply the rule of 'the facts speak for themselves' or *res ipsa loquitur* to quote the Latin (see page 174). In *Steer* v. *Durable Rubber Co Ltd* (1958) a girl of six was scalded when a hot water bottle split. The Court of Appeal in this case held that it was for the defendant to prove that he had not been negligent. Durable Rubber Co Ltd could not prove this and thus the little girl got damages.

It is worth emphasising that normally the burden of proof in negligence lies with the plaintiff, but where the courts apply the *res ipsa loquitur* principle then the burden of proof passes to the defendant.

A customer is also given protection in respect of services provided, as the following example illustrates:

Len Lyon owns a small catering business and runs a Ford van. The van is taken to a local garage for a full service and for the brakes to be relined. When the work is completed, Len loans his van to a colleague, Maurice Worgan, who needs to complete some important delivery work, but while he is driving the van the brakes fail and he is injured. Clearly Maurice could not sue under breach of contract but he could sue under negligence since the garage owes him a duty of care.

The following case illustrates this well. In *Stennett* v. *Hancock* (1939) Mrs Stennett, a pedestrian, was injured when a wheel from a badly serviced lorry broke away. She was able to claim damages under negligence.

Liability of builders

A builder has a duty to ensure that what he does is safe and, although his main duty is towards the person who engages him, he may also be liable to any other person who may be affected by his errors or omissions. The following example may assist.

Robin Todd is a local builder who is contracted by Harrop's Health Foods Ltd to repair the front of its shop. Owing to carelessness on the part of Mr Todd, one of the walls collapses and a passer-by, David Summerfield, sustains injuries. There is no doubt that Mr Todd owes David a duty of care and David could sue him in negligence.

This principle is illustrated in *Billings (A.C.) & Sons Ltd* v. *Riden* (1958) where a builder was held to be liable to an elderly visitor to a house which he was repairing when, owing to the builder's negligence, the visitor fell and was injured.

Of course, often, defects due to poor workmanship may not become apparent for some years after the work has been completed and the victim may be debarred from claiming under the Limitation Act of 1980. This Act means that the plaintiff must bring the action within six years of his/her knowing that there was cause for action. The Latent Damage Act 1986 has introduced a 15-year 'long stop' time in respect of damage to property.

Liability of vendors of property

Jon Hartley is a keen do-it-yourself man who has made a number of 'improvements' to his house. Some of them, particularly those involving electrical work, leave a little to be desired. He sells his property to Christopher Field who buys it according to the general principle relating to house purchases, 'let the buyer beware', or caveat emptor. Christopher is badly injured as a result of an electrical fault attributable to Jon's work. Under the Defective Premises Act 1972 a seller who has done unsafe work on his property before the sale becomes liable to the new owners or the new owner's visitors.

Thus, in this case, Jon would be liable to Christopher in negligence.

Vicarious liability

It is possible for one person to be responsible for the negligence of another, as the example below illustrates.

Medway Motors, owned by Andrew Perkins, employs a number of young persons as youth trainees on motor vehicle repair work. The mechanics are under strict instructions not to allow these young workers to raise the hydraulic lift. One boy does this unsupervised with the express approval of the senior mechanic, Nick Bater, and another trainee is badly injured. The injured boy, Wayne Young, sues Medway Motors in negligence. In fact, because Andrew Perkins is the sole owner, it is he who will be sued vicariously; that is, he was not personally negligent but is responsible for the tort, in this case negligence of his employees.

A decided case illustrates the principle well. In *Rose* v. *Plenty* (1976) a milkman was under strict instructions not to allow youngsters to assist him. However he allowed a 13-year-old to ride with him and the boy was injured as the result of the milkman's negligence. The employer was vicariously liable.

You can understand that a plaintiff, given the option, would rather sue an employer than the employee.

Exercise 7

1 Name the three elements necessary to prove negligence.
2 What principle did the case *Alcock* v. *Chief Constable of South Yorkshire* (1991) illustrate?
3 Only the person making the contract can sue for injuries resulting from faulty workmanship. True or false?
4 If an employer is sued for the negligence of an employee, as what is this known?
5 A good defence of an employer in a negligence action is to say that he/she strictly forbade the activities which caused the injuries: true or false?

Torts II: trespass, nuisance, defamation and passing off

In addition to the tort of negligence which we considered in the last chapter, there are a number of other torts which relate very much to business and commerce. In this chapter we will be looking at the torts of trespass, nuisance, defamation and passing off.

12.1 Trespass

Trespass to land

The following example will help to explain the law relating to trespass to land.

> *Associated Timber Supplies Ltd own a large store which is situated near a housing estate. The timber yard which forms part of the store provides a very good short-cut to local shops. Despite the presence of a large sign, 'trespassers will be prosecuted', two women, Mrs Rachel White and Mrs Doreen Saunders, persist in climbing over the wall so that they can get to the shops more quickly. The person in charge of the store, Syd Lambert, is concerned about the two women's presence on company property and on one occasion asks them politely to leave the company's premises and not to use the yard as a short-cut. The women refuse to leave and are abusive to Syd, who attempts to use force to eject them. He reports the matter to the company secretary, who decides to start legal proceedings against the two women. When they hear this, the women decide to sue Syd for assault and battery.*

There is no doubt that Rachel and Doreen have committed the tort of trespass to land which is defined as 'direct interference with the land of another'. Rachel and Doreen are unlawful visitors since they have never received any invitation to be on the property of Associated Timber Supplies Ltd. Thus, because this is a tort, the women in question can be sued in the civil courts. Despite the notice, 'trespassers will be prosecuted', which one often sees, trespass is a civil offence and prosecution relates to criminal offences. Only occasionally is trespass a crime: for example, when trespass takes place on military or railway property.

Recently more and more trespass to land situations have been brought under criminal law by legislation. Because of concern at the problems caused by trespassing on school property, trespass has become, in these situations, a criminal offence, which makes the warning 'Trespassers will be Prosecuted' perfectly relevant.

It is likely that Rachel and Doreen would first receive a letter from the company's solicitors explaining that they are trespassing and warning them of legal action. If the women still persisted in trespassing then court action would be taken and the company might get damages, but more likely an injunction would be awarded against the two women. An injunction, as you have learned, is an order forbidding someone to do something. In this case it is forbidding Mrs White and Mrs Saunders from trespassing.

Exercise 1

With reference to Rachel and Doreen, explain what you understand by the term 'injunction'.

When talking about Rachel and Doreen we used the term 'unlawful visitors'. It is important that you understand exactly what this means. There is little doubt that Rachel and Doreen are unlawful visitors, but the definition is not so straightforward. In some instances someone may enter premises quite lawfully but then by their behaviour they become an unlawful visitor. For example:

Michael Moore is in the habit of going to the public house during the lunch hour and then returning to his factory where he is a toolsetter. On one particular occasion he returns to work and begins to act quite aggressively towards the supervisor and he is clearly the worse for drink. The works manager is called and Michael is asked to leave the factory. Michael refuses and becomes by his refusal an unlawful visitor and therefore a trespasser.

It is also important to understand the distinction between unwelcome visitors and unlawful visitors. The police have certain powers of arrest and powers to search property. They may not be welcome in a suspected criminal's house but they would not be unlawful visitors. Health and Safety inspectors, as we shall learn in the next chapter, can enter a factory to inspect it without the permission of the owners.

In addition to the legal remedies against trespassers in the courts, that is injunction and damages, the owner of premises has the right to eject a trespasser using minimum force, provided he has asked the trespasser to leave. It is thus likely that Rachel and Doreen would not be successful if they sued Associated Timber Ltd because, as you will remember, the supervisor asked them to leave and then tried to force them to leave. Provided the use of force was reasonable, this would be a defence.

Trespass to land also includes dumping rubbish on someone else's property. An owner of property has the right, for example, to retain a vehicle which has crashed (trespassed) onto his property until the vehicle owner agrees to fix any damage caused by the crash.

Battle of the leyland cypresses

TWO elderly neighbours embroiled in a costly and bitter 15-year feud over a fast growing leyland cypress hedge were urged by a Court of Appeal judge yesterday to bring their "unhappy dispute" to an end.

Lady Justice Butler-Sloss, who said she grew the conifers in her own garden, made her plea at the end of the latest round of a battle that could cost Charles Stanton, 86, and Michael Jones, 66, more than £50,000 in legal costs and damages.

Both admit their lives have been made a misery by the *cupressus leylandii* hedge which runs between their properties in Bournville, Birmingham. Publicity about the case has sparked questions on *Gardeners' Question Time*.

Mr Stanton, a widower, is claiming £32,000 compensation for trespass and damage to the hedge after Mr Jones pruned it in 1990. The *leylandii* trees in the hedge had grown to 35ft before Mr Stanton agreed to trim them to 25ft. Then Mr Jones, tired of the "absolutely depressing winter gloom" caused by the trees, said he reduced them by a further 9ft. Mr Stanton alleges he lopped them back to only 7 ft.

Mr Stanton's legal campaign suffered a setback at Birmingham County Court in February when the Recorder, Harry Wolton, QC, declared in a preliminary hearing that Mr Jones had a right to trim the trees as they constituted a party hedge between the properties. Yesterday the legal costs mounted as Lady Justice Butler-Sloss, sitting with Mr Justice Millett, rejected an appeal by Mr Stanton against that ruling.

Mr Justice Millett said that it would be for the county court at the full hearing of Mr Stanton's compensation claim to decide whether or not his neighbour had exceeded his legal rights to "maintain and repair" the hedge and was therefore liable for damages.

Robert Willer, for Mr Jones, told the court that the feud had become heated: saying: "There has been violence in the past and a conviction." Lady Justice Butler-Sloss said she would be grateful if the damages claim could be heard by the County Court within a reasonable time.

She said: "These two elderly gentlemen should really bring their unhappy dispute to an end as quickly as possible."

Afterwards Mr Stanton refused to comment, but Mr Jones said he was delighted with the decision. "I have extracted myself at last from the unreasonableness of my neighbour," he said. "There is still a court case to fight and any damages will have to be assessed, but there is no apparent damage. I am confident that the next stage of the action will be in my favour.

"It is absolutely ridiculous. I tried to reason [with Mr Stanton]. I only wanted to trim it to a reasonable height. That is all I wanted to do, but he would not accept it."

Trespass onto someone else's property is legal if it is to 'prevent a greater evil'. For example, if a cat was trapped in a tree on land belonging to someone else then it would not amount to trespass if you went onto the property to rescue it.

From the extract above, taken from an account of the case *Stanton* v *Jones* (1994), it would seem that trespass is legal where a person is trying to deal with what might be regarded as an unreasonable situation. It would seem that Mr Jones had a right to trim the offending trees and to do this he needed to 'trespass' on his neighbour's property.

Exercise 2

Examine the following examples and advise the parties concerned of the legal position.

1 Burlow Motors Ltd threaten to prosecute two youths who persist in wandering through their showrooms.
2 Marc Holburn, security guard at Weaving Brake Linings Ltd, asks a man who is acting suspiciously to leave the factory premises. He refuses and Marc forces him to leave. The man in question threatens Weavings with legal action.
3 Complaints have been made about health standards at a food factory. Health inspectors go to the factory to investigate and they are sued for trespass.
4 Bill Usher goes to his firm's dance. He has rather too much to drink and is asked to leave. He leaves under protest, saying he will sue the firm because he has paid for his ticket.

Trespass to person

Frank Brown is manager of a supermarket near the centre of town. He is a man with a fairly short temper. In recent weeks he has been concerned about youths who are unemployed hanging around outside the store and generally being troublesome. There has also been a spate of shoplifting in the store. One morning Frank is called outside to deal with two 17-year-olds, Bob and John. Frank is very angry and punches Bob, injuring him; Frank threatens John in such a way as to make him very frightened. When Frank goes back into the shop, one of his assistants reports that they suspect a woman of shoplifting. Frank, in haste, asks the wrong woman, Mrs Green, to go into his office. He locks her in to attend to the problems outside and then calls the police, who arrive an hour later; unfortunately for Frank, the woman who has been locked in for over an hour is able to prove her innocence.

In this situation we have three examples of trespass to person for which Frank could well be sued. Trespass to person can take one of three forms:

1 Assault – which means threatening someone in such a way that they genuinely believe they are going to be physically hurt.
2 Battery – the actual application of force.
3 False imprisonment.

It is easy to see that John has been assaulted (note the word 'assault' has a different meaning from when it is used in criminal law): he really feared the threat. Bob has suffered a battery, and Mrs Green has been falsely imprisoned.

Assault and battery are civil offences which often occur together: the threat followed by the force.

There are several offences which a defendant might use if he is being sued for trespass to person:

1 He could say he was acting in self-defence; that is, he was being attacked.
2 He could say he was preventing a 'greater' evil; that is, someone else was being attacked and he was assisting them.
3 A parent who punishes his child could say he has the right to do this – the defence is parent authority – though the law protects children against excessive and unreasonable punishment.
4 In some instances the defendant may have consented: it is hardly likely that a boxer could sue his opponent for battery. (There are instances where rugby players or footballers have been sued in the civil courts for 'trespass to person' where they have caused injury to an opponent.)

> In a case *Elliott* v. *Saunders* (1994), Paul Elliott, a footballer with Chelsea, received injuries which finished his career. He sued Dean Saunders, who, at the time of the tackle which caused the injury, was with Liverpool. Elliott was unsuccessful. At the time of writing, Elliott had lodged an appeal against the decision in the Court of Appeal.

5 Finally there are instances where it is legal to arrest someone, and even though the person in question subsequently proves his/her innocence, provided the defendant had reasonable grounds for his/her suspicion then it is unlikely that he/she would pay damages. An offence must, however, have been committed. This is known as a citizen's arrest. The police have wider powers of arrest than an ordinary citizen.

Exercise 3

1 List the three types of trespass to person.
2 Study the following and say, with reasons, whether you think the plaintiff in italics might be successful in suing for trespass to person.
   (a) Ray Ellis goes to the aid of an old woman who is being mugged and injures *Mike Edwards*, the assailant, in giving this aid.
   (b) *Mrs Smythe* beats her 13-year-old son with a strap because he comes in after 10.30 one night.
   (c) Fearing for his own safety, John Duffy, site foreman, punches *one of his employees* who is threatening him.
   (d) *Nick Smart* is acting suspiciously outside the premises of Peak Engineering Ltd. The security man, Phil Goodwin, arrests him and locks him in a storeroom and calls the police.
   (e) Having asked him to leave the shop because he has been causing a disturbance, the manager punches *Michael* and pushes him out.

(f)   *Jack Phillips* plays rugby for his local club and after one game threatens to sue one of his opponents for a painful injury he received after a tackle.

Trespass to goods

Plant Hire Ltd hires out heavy earth-moving equipment. As part of this business it hires to a local builder, Westons & Co (Builders), a large earth remover for one week. The hire charge is paid in advance but Westons refuse to return the equipment or pay for a further week's hire.

Plant Hire could sue Westons either for the return of the equipment or, if it was damaged beyond repair, for damages to cover the loss. Plant Hire would sue for trespass to goods and because Westons & Co are denying Plant Hire their goods this is known as conversion. (Conversion could arise also where a person buying goods on hire-purchase tried to sell them without permission of the owner – see Chapter 9.)

Trespass to goods can also arise where goods are removed from someone's premises or damaged in some way. If, for example, someone's car was wilfully damaged by a neighbour, he could sue for trespass to goods. You will note that the word 'wilfully' has been used, because if it was an accident then the action would be one for negligence, as we saw in the previous chapter.

The law relating to trespass to goods and the related tort of conversion is contained in the Torts (Interference with Goods) Act 1977. It is really the tort of conversion which is important. Conversion means denying the owner his right of possession to the goods.

In *Perry (Howard) & Co Ltd* v. *British Railways Board (1980),* BR held some steel belonging to the plaintiff. The plaintiff tried to collect its steel but BR refused, thinking the collection might cause further industrial trouble. The court held that BR's refusal amounted to conversion.

Banks can also be sued for conversion if they pay out on a cheque to a person who has not title to it. If a cheque is stolen and the thief presents it for payment, the bank could be liable for the loss if it honours the cheque. This fact is confirmed in *International Factors* v. *Rodriguez* (1979).

___ **Exercise 4** _____

Read the following, explaining the legal situation involved.

1   While Graham is reversing out of his drive he accidentally collides with his neighbour's car. The neighbour decides to sue Graham for trespass to goods.
2   Mary borrows some very expensive books from her firm's library. Being short of money, she decides to sell them for £100.

12.2   Nuisance

In the last section when we considered trespass to land we defined it as unlawful direct interference with the land of another. In this section we will be considering indirect interference which may result in an action for nuisance. The following example will help to explain this.

Western Printing Supplies Ltd is a fairly small company which specialises in the production of inks and dyestuffs for the printing industry. The managing director, Simon Beckford, has discovered a new process which involves loud banging every hour and the emission of quite a distasteful smell. Mr and Mrs Ogden who have lived next door to the factory for the last ten years complain about this but the company does nothing, so they decide to sue.

As we can see, this involves indirect interference with Mr and Mrs Ogden's enjoyment of their property and would be termed private nuisance. Private nuisance, which is a tort, can take many forms, such as noise, smoke, smells, vibration, fumes or the blocking of a right of way.

In Mr and Mrs Ogden's case, they would argue that the noise and the smells were unreasonable. In coming to a decision the court would try to balance the company's need to produce at lower cost and Mr and Mrs Ogden's convenience. In nuisance cases it is this delicate balance which the court tries to find: an owner of land can do what he wishes provided this does not interfere unduly with others. The court would take into account such factors as frequency and duration of the alleged nuisance. If in our situation Western Printing Supplies Ltd allowed the bang and the smell to occur only once a week then this might be allowed; or if the hour-interval bangs and smell only lasted one week in a year this might be allowed. The court will also take into account the locality: for example, you may have to put up with more in an industrial area than in a residential area.

Two points need to be stressed in nuisance:

1   It is no defence for a defendant to say that the plaintiff came to the nuisance. If the Ogdens moved and other people bought their house, the fact that they came to a nuisance will not carry any weight in the court. The new occupants could still sue for nuisance.
2   A defendant may not plead a necessity. In some cases doctors who have to make night emergency calls have been sued successfully for nuisance by neighbours disturbed by their departure. A plea of necessity is not acceptable by the court.

Having taken all these matters into account, if the court held that the Ogdens were in fact suffering a nuisance then it could award damages; however, the most likely possibility is the granting of an injunction ordering Western Printing Supplies to refrain from this process.

A case which illustrated the law of nuisance very well is *Halsey* v. *Esso Petroleum Co Ltd* (1961).

The defendant, Esso, operated an oil distribution centre near the plaintiff's house. In the court it was alleged that:

- (i) acid smuts affected the plaintiff's washing,
- (ii) acid smuts caused damage to the plaintiff's washing,
- (iii) a regular nauseating smell came regularly from the depot,
- (iv) there was a noise at night from depot machinery, and
- (v) there was a noise at night from the arrival and departure of delivery vehicles.

The plaintiff obtained from Esso both damages and an injunction because the court accepted that this constituted a nuisance.

Generally nuisance is a tort and action is taken in the civil court, usually the County Court, but where large sections of the public are affected it can be termed a public nuisance and therefore a crime. In this case action is taken in the criminal courts; for example:

Eastern Haulage Ltd have a large depot in Ashford. Lorry drivers awaiting check-in often park the lorries on a road leading to the depot, and residents and other vehicle users are subject to long delays because of this.

This would be an example of Eastern Haulage committing a public nuisance. A Magistrates' Court, if it found the company guilty, could order it to refrain from parking lorries in this way.

The law of nuisance has been reinforced by the Environmental Protection Act 1990. Section 80 of this act allows a local authority to visit the area of an alleged nuisance and if the inspector is satisfied that a nuisance exists he can issue an abatement notice, which means the person(s) causing the nuisance must prevent it. These abatement notices can apply to a range of activities, from noisy parties to dust from construction works. If a person chooses to ignore the notice then he will face legal action.

Exercise 5

1 What is the difference between a public and a private nuisance?
2 Study the following examples and say whether you think the party in italics would have a case in nuisance.
  (a) Michael lives next door to *two old-age pensioners*. Michael is very quiet but he always has a birthday party each year with music and so on. The two pensioners threaten to sue him.
  (b) *Frances* has just come to live near a restaurant. The smell and noise from the restaurant are, she feels, excessive. The restaurant

> owner argues that it has always been like this and that Frances' predecessors had never complained.
>
> (c) *John* lives next door to a vet who sometimes has to make emergency calls. John claims he is disturbed by the noise of the vet going out late at night. The vet claims that his visits are essential.

A person can acquire the right to continue a nuisance by what is called 'prescription'. The nuisance must have continued for 20 years or more. Acquiring a prescriptive right means that the person causing the nuisance may use it as a defence in any action based upon nuisance.

Nuisance is a difficult area for the courts for they need to steer some sort of middle road between the concept of a 'man's house being his castle' and the needs and concerns of his neighbours.

12.3   Defamation

Timeright Ltd produces a range of watches. One of its sections specialises in the production of expensive ladies' quartz watches. Despite what the company had regarded as very good security systems, it appears that a member of the workforce is taking watches out. The management order a close investigation and suspicion falls on one of the supervisors, Mrs Patricia Pryce. The personnel manager decides to take immediate action and pins a notice to the staff noticeboard which reads:

> We have reason to believe that Mrs Patricia Pryce has abused her position of trust with the company and is responsible for the spate of thefts recently. I should be grateful if Mrs Pryce could report to my office immediately.
>
> J. Jackson,
> Personnel Manager
> Timeright Ltd

Mrs Pryce, who is in fact quite innocent, is very angry and decides to take the company to court, saying she believes this is a defamation of her character. (In any event most people would agree that pinning up a notice of this sort was not a very sensible thing to do.)

In order to be successful in a defamation action it is necessary for the plaintiff, Pat in this instance, to prove these things:

1   Did the statement refer to Pat by name or innuendo? In this instance she was named, though it is possible for a person to be referred to by a nickname or described in such a way that no one is in any doubt that the statement referred to him or her.
2   Was the statement communicated to a third party or parties? There is no doubt it was communicated; in fact all the workforce had the opportunity to see it.

3   Was the statement capable of lowering a person's reputation in the eyes of right-thinking members of society? In other words, was it likely that the person about whom the statement was made might be regarded with ridicule, contempt or even hatred? It would seem that dishonesty of the sort alleged against Pat is something which causes her reputation to be lowered.

Because the answer is 'yes' to all three questions as far as Pat is concerned she would have a case in defamation. Defamation is in two forms: *libel*, permanent and usually the written form; and *slander*, temporary and usually the spoken form. Statements made on television or the radio would be termed libel because, although spoken, they are more permanent. Pat would sue for libel. The case would come before the High Court because the tort of defamation can never be heard in the County Court. The reason for this rule is so that frivolous actions are discouraged. High Court actions are of course very expensive.

An interesting case is *Pyke* v. *Hybernian Bank* (1950).

The bank returned a cheque to the presenter (the payee) with the words marked on it, 'refer to drawer'. In other words, the cheque appeared to have 'bounced'. This could give the impression that the drawer had insufficient funds in his account. The plaintiff, who was the drawer, sued for libel and was able to show the three elements necessary to prove libel existed.

The law relating to banking will be dealt with in greater detail in Chapter 17.

Exercise 6

1   Defamation may be in two forms: (a) which is the written form and (b) which is the spoken form?
2   Name the three things which must be proved in an action for defamation.
3   Study the following case and say whether the person italicised has a case in defamation, and if not why not.

Paddy Byrne works for a firm manufacturing cigarettes. He and six friends have organised a system whereby they are stealing from the company to the tune of about £50 per week. The management decide to tighten up security and it becomes impossible to do this any longer. The friends think Paddy has informed management, which in fact is not the case. One friend pins a notice to the staff noticeboard which contains the lines:

'He who gave the game away let him *byrne* in hell and rue the day.'

Defences in defamation

There are a number of defences a defendant might use in a defamation action. If a defendant who is being sued for defamation can prove the truth of a statement then there can be no defamation, because if we think about it there is no reputation to spoil. If, in our first example, Pat Pryce had been stealing watches and the defendant could prove it then Pat would not be successful. However it is important to note that a defendant would only use this defence if he was absolutely sure he could prove the truth of the statement. If he was not sure then his attempt might cost him additional damages because a court would take the view that a plaintiff who has been defamed is suffering greater indignity as a result of an unsuccessful attempt at proof in the court.

On some occasions statements are given absolute protection or privilege from defamation action. Statements made in Parliament or in court proceedings are given this protection. This means that, for example, a judge can say anything he likes without fear of any legal action.

Some statements are given what is called qualified protection or privilege, which means that action can only be taken if it can be shown that the statement was made maliciously. The best example is in references – if an employer is asked to give a reference to another employer. Generally the employer giving the reference is protected from defamation actions unless it can be shown that he maliciously made the statement about his employee.

If a newspaper unintentionally publishes a defamatory article, for example if in reporting a case it gets the defendant's name wrong, then it can offer as a defence that (a) a statement was made unintentionally, (b) an offer of amends is made to the person named, (c) an offer of a printed apology is made. For example:

Michael Street picks up his local newspaper and reads that Michael John Street of 14 Winchester Way, Basingstoke has been convicted in the Crown Court of rape. He is surprised and annoyed because this is his address. The convicted person was Martin James Street of 14 Warwick Street, Basingstoke. Michael rings the Hampshire Gazette *and the editor offers him £250 and prints an apology which reads: 'We wish to point out that Michael John Street of 14 Winchester Way, Basingstoke, was not the person convicted of rape on 14 March 1981 and we apologise for any inconvenience or embarrassment caused by our error.'*

If Michael refused the £250 and decided to sue then the Hampshire Gazette could use this as a defence.

This particular defence is quite a complex one and a newspaper could still be sued successfully, even if it did make an offer of amends.

Finally certain people in public life, or perhaps sportsmen, can expect that they will be criticised. If, therefore, a newspaper writes of a footballer, following a poor performance, that 'he must have been burning the candle at both ends recently', he would not be successful in an action of defamation though, if the newspaper went on to comment on his private life, this might be different. This defence is sometimes known as fair comment.

There is a related tort which is known as 'injurious falsehood' and can be used by businesses against those who make injurious statements relating to services or goods provided by the business

Westfield Glass are a new firm in the double glazing, conservatory trade. They are anxious to capture a share of the market and decide to place a large advertisement in the local paper which, as well as making claims about its own products, makes several very injurious remarks about a competitor's product, saying that a number of conservatories built and fitted by Eastshires Glass have collapsed in moderately windy conditions. Eastshires Glass are incensed and sue for injurious falsehood.

Eastshires would have to prove three elements: (i) the defendant's statement was untrue; (ii) it was made maliciously; (iii) it caused economic loss. In the latter case, since the Defamation Act 1952, actual loss need not be proved: that the statement could result in loss is now good enough.

If the alleged collapses of conservatories had not taken place, it would appear to be easy to show the other two and it would seem that Eastshires would be successful.

It is important to note that advertising which compares a company's goods favourably with those of competitors is not actionable, as an old case, *Hubbock* v. *Wilkinson* (1899) shows.

Activity

See if you can find examples of advertising which do suggest a product of a company is superior to those of its competitors.

The motor car industry provides some good examples.

Of course, as you have seen, the Trade Descriptions Act of 1968 and 1972 does provide a remedy against advertising false information. The remedy is in the criminal courts.

Defamation can only be used against actual persons, whereas the tort of 'injurious falsehood' is available to businesses against unfair competition.

Exercise 7

Examine the following and say whether you think the defendant might have a defence in a defamation action.

1 Mary Moore, an accountant with Associated Metal Products, applies for a post as chief accountant with a firm of TV rentals. In the reference which Associated Metal Products writes to the TV rental firm Mary is

described as incompetent and disloyal. Mary sees the reference and threatens to sue her firm.

2   Mr Green MP in a speech in Parliament makes a serious allegation against the chairman of one of the nationalised industries.

3   Roger Lewis is a reporter with the *Bristol Times*. He has always had a grudge against his neighbour, Phil Brayshaw, and, following a conviction for theft against a Philip Bagshaw, Roger maliciously reports that it was Philip Brayshaw and this is printed. When his neighbour complains to the editor, the editor offers amends of £300 and a printed apology.

4   Jennie Rogers, who has been convicted of shoplifting, decides to sue the *Kent Times* for printing details of the case.

12.4   Passing off

This is a very important tort for business and commerce because it helps businesses to keep their customers' goodwill. The following example may help to explain.

The Cathedral Close Hotel in a famous cathedral city in England enjoys an international reputation because of its closeness to the world famous cathedral. City Hotels, a hotel chain, sees great potential in the area and builds a hotel nearby, calling it the Cathedral Hotel. In its advertising it indicates that it can now offer attractive rates and that it is ideally situated near the cathedral close. THS, the owners of the first hotel, notice that their trade goes into decline and decide to sue City Hotels in the tort of passing off.

To be successful in this tort it is necessary to show the following, as stated in *Warninck* v. *Townend* (1979): a misrepresentation; made by the defendant in the course of trade; made to customers or potential customers of the plaintiff; calculated to injure the business or goodwill of the plaintiff; which does actually damage or threaten to damage the plaintiff's business.

— **Activity** —————————————————————————————

Applying the five elements above, do you think that THS would be successful?

Firms have often sued successfully because of what is called 'get up'. This is where, for example, a firm packages its product in such a way as to lead the public to believe that the product was that from another company. Thus, if a company marketed cornflakes in a very similar box to 'Kelloggs' but called them 'Kellock's Bran Flakes' then it is likely that the public would be confused and no doubt Kelloggs, if they wished, could win a case against the company marketing the product.

A very interesting case was Bollinger v. Costa Brava Wine Co Ltd (1961) in which Costa Brava Co marketed Spanish champagne. J. Bollinger, a champagne manufacturer from the Champagne region in France, successfully sued the Spanish firm for passing off. It was held that the defendants had passed off their products as being that of the plaintiffs.

Exercise 8

1 In what way has the Environmental Protection Act (1990) assisted those wishing to take action against a nuisance?
2 What are the three elements necessary to prove defamation?
3 Name one situation where a statement is protected absolutely and one where a statement is given qualified protection.
4 Name the three types of trespass.
5 Why is the notice 'trespassers will be prosecuted' usually misleading?
6 Making 'unfair' comparisons in an advertisement makes a company liable to action in the tort of 'injurious falsehood': true or false?
7 What are the five elements which must be proved to be successful in the tort of 'passing off'?

13 Safety at work

Bert Ogden is an apprentice electrician employed at a large paper mill in the South of England, International Paper Products Ltd. Bert has nearly finished his apprenticeship and in fact has just come back from his last block release course at the local technical college. Part of the electrical equipment to do with one of the pulp machines has developed a slight fault and Bert is asked by his foreman, Mick Mason, to examine the problem. Company rules lay down quite clearly that all electrical equipment must be isolated before it is examined. However the managing director has issued a statement to his employees that they must in all circumstances make every effort to keep production going.

Accordingly Bert, encouraged by Mick, looks at the equipment while it is still operational. While examining the equipment Bert receives an electric shock which causes him to fall against the pulp-making machinery and he is very badly injured.

When the trade union hears about the accident the steward, Eric Disdale, decides to notify the Health and Safety Executive and urges a full inspection. Four Health and Safety inspectors visit the mill and they are not happy with what they find. Their report makes a number of recommendations to the management, including a prohibition order and an improvement order. The inspectors promise that they will make another visit in 14 days' time. At the same time they decide to charge International Paper Products Ltd with having committed a criminal offence under the Health and Safety at Work Act.

13.1 Health and Safety at Work Act 1974

It seems that International Paper Products Ltd are running a mill which is not very safe. Health and safety at work questions are regulated by the Health and Safety at Work Act 1974, and in this chapter we will be dealing with the operation of this Act and also the remedies available to an injured employee following injuries at work.

The Health and Safety at Work Act 1974 was passed with a view to bringing under one Act the various health and safety legislations which had been passed.

198

It does not replace the Factories Act 1961, but gradually the Factories Act will be replaced by regulations under the Health and Safety at Work Act. The Health and Safety at Work Act is what is known as an enabling Act; that is, it allows a Minister of State to issue regulations which have the force of law. You will remember that in Chapter 2 we gave an example of a regulation issued in 1981 regarding of first aid.

The Health and Safety at Work Act imposes certain duties on the employer:

1   To provide and maintain plant and systems of work which are as far as practicable safe and without risk to health.
2   To make arrangements for the safe use, handling, storage and transport of articles and substances.
3   To provide information, training and supervision to ensure as far as is practicable the health and safety at work of the employees.
4   To provide a safe place of work, including safe means of access and egress (entry and exit).
5   To provide a working environment that is as far as practicable safe and consistent with the welfare of the employees.

These duties to employees are supplemented by a general duty to non-employees who may be at the particular place of work. This means that visitors are protected by the Act.

If we examine for a moment Bert Ogden's case then it is quite clear that International Paper Products are at fault. It is obviously unsafe to work on electrical equipment which is live; although a company rule was that electrical equipment had to be isolated, this was rather confused by their request that production must go on. You will remember that Bert was encouraged by the foreman to work on the equipment without turning it off. Another question we might ask ourselves is, was Bert aware of the company rules concerning isolation of electrical equipment? Under the Health and Safety at Work Act, companies must issue for their employees a statement outlining the company's safety policy.

Activity

If you are employed, see if you can find the statement of your firm's safety policy. It may be on a noticeboard or may have been given to you personally.

Because International Paper Products are in breach of the Health and Safety at Work Act they are liable to a fine of up to £5000. The case would be laid before a Magistrates' Court. Health and Safety inspectors have a right to inspect places of work and normally make recommendations. In serious situations, as clearly found at International Paper Products, they can issue:

1   a Prohibition Order which prohibits (stops) the use of a particular part of a process. It is possible for a prohibition order to stop the whole factory; and/or
2   an Improvement Order which requires the situation to be improved within a certain time.

It is important to note that inspectors are more anxious to establish by persuasion safe practices in places of work, and usually reports which they issue are persuasive rather than mandatory; in other words, they recommend rather than order. It is possible in more serious breaches for cases to come to the Crown Court, and of course heavier fines are possible.

Exercise 1

1   The Health and Safety at Work Act 1974 introduced a new range of civil offences: true or false?
2   Explain the term 'enabling Act' as it applies to the Health and Safety Act.
3   Explain the meaning of an Improvement Order.
4   What is the maximum fine for an offence under the Health and Safety Act?

The Health and Safety at Work Act also imposes duties on any employee. Employees have a duty while at work:

1   to take reasonable care for the health and safety of themselves and other persons who may be affected by their acts or omissions;
2   to cooperate with the employer in matters of health and safety;
3   not to intentionally or recklessly interfere with anything provided in the interest, safety or welfare of employees.

It does seem that the foreman, Mick Mason, in our example has breached the first of these duties in allowing Bert to do this job. The Act provides that not only the employer (International Paper Products) but also the employee (Mick Mason) can be fined for breaches of the Act.

The following examples will help to explain the duties of employees.

Dave Stewart, a foreman at a heavy engineering works, encourages his men to engage in heavy lifting without using the regulation lifting gear. One of the employees suffers a severe back injury.

Jackie Redstone works in a busy insurance office. She is aware that the electrical connection for some office machinery is faulty but she decides it is none of her business. She does not make a report and one of her colleagues is seri-

ously injured. She admits to the manager that she had known for a long time that this fault existed.

Terence Clapham is a waiter in a busy hotel, with a reputation as a practical joker. He decides to change the signs on the IN/OUT doors. One of his colleagues carrying hot food is badly burned as a result.

In all three cases the employee in question could be fined under the Health and Safety at Work Act: Dave Stewart for 'not taking reasonable care of other persons who may be affected by his acts or omissions', Jackie for 'not cooperating with the employer', and Terence for 'recklessly interfering with something provided for health and safety'.

Exercise 2

In the following examples say what might be the legal position under the Health and Safety at Work Act 1974.

1   Ten employees have suffered serious accidents in the last five weeks while operating a piece of machinery at London Road Engineering Co.
2   An injury of a chef at the Hotel Regal reveals that he has never been instructed in the use of new infra-red ovens.
3   Two apprentices at a firm of electrical engineers have been warned about skylarking while at work. As a result of another incident of this kind one of them, John Hartley, is badly injured.
4   Because of extreme humidity the environment at Victoria Laundry is very unhealthy and the floors have become like ice rinks. A complaint is made to the Health and Safety Executive.

There has been a good deal of discussion recently in relation to the Health and Safety at Work Act and some would argue that it puts an unnecessary burden on businesses. The government is at present (1994) considering dismantling some of the elements of this legislation.

13.2   Civil action available to employees injured at work

Although the Health and Safety at Work Act 1974 has done a great deal to improve health and safety in workplaces, as we have seen breaches result in criminal action. In our example relating to Bert Ogden and International Paper Products, Bert would not be compensated as a result of criminal action. We have, however (in Chapter 11), seen that it is possible for persons to sue for negligence, and in fact Bert could do this as long as he was able to show the existence of three elements.

___ **Exercise 3** _____

See if you can remember the three elements necessary to prove negligence.

___

It would, then, be necessary for the plaintiff (Bert Ogden) to prove the existence of these three elements. There is no doubt that International Paper Products owed Bert a duty of care. This duty of care had been breached by allowing Bert to work on electrical equipment which had not been isolated. Bert suffered injuries as a result of the breach and thus he could claim damages. The duty of care is sometimes known as a common law duty of care. International Paper Products could point to the existence of their rules that no electrical equipment should be worked upon unless it was isolated, and indeed it was Bert's foreman, Mick Mason, who had authorized the work. However this would be no defence because the law provides that employers can be vicariously (indirectly) liable for the torts of their employees. International Paper Products would therefore be liable for Mick Mason's action. In fact, even where a company forbids a course of action, the company still could be held liable if an employee engages in it.

For example, in *Hudson* v. *Ridge Manufacturing Co Ltd* (1957), a plaintiff's wrist was broken when he was tripped by a fellow worker who was skylarking. The firm was held to be liable vicariously for the tort of its employee, even though the company had expressly forbidden this sort of behaviour.

International Paper Products could argue in their defence that the fault in the electrical appliance was not their concern since it had been supplied by another firm, Associated Electrical Products Ltd; therefore it was to this firm that Bert's claim ought to lie. If this sort of defence was possible then plaintiffs would have considerable trouble in ever making a successful claim because companies would blame suppliers, who in turn might blame other suppliers. The Employers' Liability (Defective Equipment) Act 1969 now enables a worker to sue the employer in these circumstances and the employer may then claim from the supplier. Thus Bert would sue International Paper Products, who might in turn sue Associated Electrical Products.

___ **Exercise 4** _____

Read the following cases and say whether you think the plaintiff in italics would have a case in negligence.

1   *Ben Bennett* is a lathe operator with Peakdale Engineering Co. The lathe has developed a fault which has been reported. Ben is injured while using the lathe.

2   *Fred Wingfield* is a bricklayer working on a large office block. His firm is very strict about safety regulations, especially the standards of scaffolding. The site foreman is less careful and, in an effort to keep in front of the schedule, he orders scaffolding to be erected which is not up to

standard. Fred, who is working on the third floor, falls following a collapse of the scaffolding and is very badly injured. The firm, North West Builders Ltd, claim that the foreman was not acting under instructions and refuse to pay out any compensation to Fred.

3 The Hotel Sceptre has just installed new infra-red ovens. One of these ovens is faulty, and a chef, *Adam Cranston*, is injured quite badly. The hotel disclaim responsibility, saying Adam has a claim against the supplier, Midland Catering Equipment Ltd.

We have seen, then, that employees injured in accidents may sue their employers in negligence. It is necessary for them to prove the existence of the three necessary elements. In addition to suing for a breach of common law duty it is also possible for an injured employee to sue for a breach of statutory duty. (We learned in Chapter 1 that Acts of Parliament are called statutes and this gives rise to the term 'statutory'.) In practice, workers will often be advised to sue for both negligence and breach of statutory duty in the hope of succeeding in one or the other. If he succeeds in both he will of course not obtain double damages, but only damages sufficient to cover his loss or compensate him for injury.

The following example will help to explain how breaches of statutory duty will apply.

David Stanley has just completed his apprenticeship as a craft engineer. He is employed by Burlow Engineering Co. While operating a grinding wheel which has not been properly guarded he so badly injures his thumb that it has to be amputated.

David goes to his lawyer who advises him to sue Burlow Engineering for a breach of statutory duty. In order to do this, David would have to show that the Factories Act applied to this situation. This would clearly be the case because the Factories Act 1961 applies to workshops of this kind, and there is a definite duty to fence such machinery. David would have to show that the duty to fence the machinery applied to his employer and was owed to him. Neither of these two elements would be difficult. David would then have to show that the statutory duty had been broken, and Burlow Engineering Co's failure to fence machinery indicates this clearly. Finally David would have to show that he was injured as a result of the breach of the statutory duty, and again this was the case.

As you can see, proving a breach of a statutory duty is not very different from proving negligence – the difference in this case is that the statute applies to workers, whereas negligence can apply to any situation.

A plaintiff wishing to sue under the Factories Act must therefore show, as David Stanley needed to show:

1 that the Act applied to the situation;
2 that the defendant owed a duty of care;
3 that the defendant was entitled to benefit from that duty.

The following case sums up the situation in respect of the Factory Act very well. In *John Summers & Sons Ltd* v. *Frost* (1955), the respondent injured his thumb on a revolving grinding wheel which had only been partly guarded. It was held that the duty to fence dangerous machinery was strict and that it was no defence that fencing would make it impossible or impracticable to operate the machine.

Employers have a common law duty to provide their employee with:

1   a safe place of work,
2   a safe system of work,
3   safe fellow employees,
4   safe equipment.

It is easy to see that Mr Frost could show that his employer had breached both his common law duty and any statutory duty.

Many workers who are injured at work will not go to court to prove negligence or breach of statutory duty. It is sometimes difficult to prove negligence or breach of statutory duty and often workers do not have sufficient knowledge of the law, or perhaps they lack any initiative to take action; even if they do, the possible cost of a lost case proves to be a powerful deterrent. The Social Security Act 1975 provides that an injured employee can gain industrial benefit irrespective of whether his injuries arose from negligence or breach of statutory duty. Benefits are payable by the state provided that:

1   personal injury was caused by an accident which arose out of and in the course of employment; or
2   the employee has suffered an illness not as a result of an accident but as a result of working on a process. The regulations which govern claims for industrial illnesses are the Social Security (Industrial Injuries) (Prescribed Diseases) Regulations 1980.

If, for example, an employee claims that he has suffered from a skin disease as a result of working with particular materials he may be able to claim industrial benefit.

The present regulations for industrial benefit include provisions for a disablement pension, a dependant's allowance and a death benefit.

Exercise 5

1   If an injured employee decided to sue his employer for breach of statutory duty, under which Act of Parliament would he sue?
2   If an injured employee cannot prove his employer was at fault he will get no compensation for his injuries: true or false?

3 Linda Brazier, who works in an office, is injured in the works canteen when she slips on a patch of grease on the floor. The company proves it has done everything reasonable to keep the floor clean. Can Linda obtain any compensation?

4 The duty of care in negligence is sometimes known as a what?

Exercise 6

In the following examples explain the legal principles involved. If after checking your answers you find that you do not understand a particular aspect of the law as it relates to safety at work, read this chapter again, paying particular attention to that aspect.

1 David Hogg, a supervisor in a chemical plant, fails to do the safety checks which the company has laid down; as a result a serious explosion occurs.

2 John Adams, one of her Majesty's Health and Safety inspectors, is refused permission to enter a factory premises, but he decides, despite this refusal, to go in and make an inspection. He orders one particular process to be discontinued. John is threatened with civil action for trespass.

3 Philip Brown is a fork-loft driver. As a result of a serious fault in a new fork-lift truck he is driving, Philip sustains a serious head injury. The company say that the supplier of the truck is to blame.

4 Maureen Williams is an operative at a firm using a process involving asbestos. She finds as a result of a hospital examination that she is suffering from cancer, which she claims is due to the process she works on. Her company employ a leading lawyer to prove that the process is not responsible.

5 John Harris injures his back carrying heavy loads for his company, who claim that he was not acting under the company's instructions for handling heavy equipment.

6 Despite company rules to the contrary, Bob Bown the foreman orders one of his apprentices to work on an unfenced machine. The apprentice is injured. The company deny liability, blaming the foreman.

14 Business organisation (I): sole traders, partnerships and companies

14.1 Sole trader and partnership

Rino Rinaldi is an Italian waiter working in a large restaurant in London. It has always been his ambition to run his own restaurant and he feels that a restaurant concentrating on relatively cheap meals but with emphasis upon good quality service will do well. As a result of a lucky pools win of £160 000, Rino is able to achieve his ambition and he buys a restaurant in Maidstone which he names Italiano, *specialising in steak and wine. The business does well and Rino decides to expand his business to other towns in Kent, but unfortunately he lacks the capital. He decides on a partnership and his wife Wendy uses £60 000 of her savings, and two ex-colleagues, Stuart Conway and John Drew, decide to provide £120 000. This, together with money from Rino's present business, allows the partnership to buy another two restaurants, one in Ashford and the other in Sittingbourne. The emphasis upon good service, Italian wine and well-chosen steaks is obviously very effective and the three restaurants do very well indeed. Rino and his partners decide to form a company and Rino, John, Stuart and Wendy are each given shares in the company. A number of other shareholders are interested and their money buys additional restaurants in Horsham, Hastings, Tunbridge Wells, Brighton, Canterbury and Broadstairs.* Italiano Steak & Wine Co. Ltd, *as the new company is called, clearly is a success story; Rino and Stuart Conway, the two directors, decide that they must expand and 'go public', that is, form a public company: £1 million ordinary shares are offered to the public. This allows branches all over the South of England to be opened.* Italiano, *from such small beginnings, has become a prosperous and well-known company.*

This very successful venture has resulted in four different types of business organisation being formed, and in this chapter we will use this example to explain the legal difference existing between the various types of business.

Sole trader

Rino started his business as a sole trader, which means that he was the only owner. He may have employed people full-time or part-time to work at the restaurant but he was the only person who had money in the business. There are of course many one-man businesses in this country, perhaps more than any other kind. Just like any individual, Rino can be sued, can sue and can be prosecuted for anything he might do in the course of his business. Thus, for example, if customers in the restaurant were injured as a result of Rino's or his staff's negligence then Rino could face action in the civil courts.

One of the problems of running a business in this way is that the owner has what is called unlimited liability. To explain what this means, remember that Rino started his business with £160 000. In fact the business flourished but let us assume for a moment that the venture was a complete failure and after a year Rino was faced with debts amounting to £180 000. Rino's liability for debts is not confined to the original £160 000 but is unlimited and in court action by creditors to recover the money Rino could find that he could lose his own personal property, such as his house or car, which the court could order to be sold to pay his debts. This is what is meant by unlimited liability: sole traders' liability is not limited to the amount of their initial investment.

To lose one's home is of course a considerable loss but, since it is often the sole trader's main asset, the creditors (those to whom the sole trader owes money) will be keen to realise money to pay their outstanding bills. However Rino's wife, Wendy, will have her own rights in respect of the matrimonial home. She may be a joint owner, in which case she would need to give her permission for the house to be sold. If not a joint owner, she may have registered an interest in the property at the land registry (see Chapter 18). Rino's two children, Michael and Simon, are both under 18 and a court would not force a sale on the property in these circumstances (see Chapter 16). The important point to note, however, is that a sole trader who falls on difficult times risks losing his personal property.

___ **Exercise 1** _____

John Hartley invests £50 000 in a small lock-up shop which he runs himself. John is not really cut out for shop work and the business runs heavily into debt. John finds to his horror that his creditors are asking the court to order him to sell his own private house to meet his debts. Is this a risk which John might face?

You will also have noticed that Rino has decided to call his restaurant *Italiano*. The law relating to business names is regulated by the Business Names Act 1985 is that a business operating under a name other than its owner(s) must:

1   display the name(s) and address(es) of the owner(s);
2   show this information on business letters, written orders, invoices, receipts and written demands for payment of debts.

┌─ **Activity** ───┐
Have a look for examples of this. You will find examples of names displayed in any business or shop which is trading under a name which is not the name of the owner(s). You may still find certificates relating to the old regulations under the Registration of Business Names Act 1916, which has now been replaced.

Failure to comply with the regulations regarding business names can lead to a fine but, perhaps what is more serious, contracts entered into by Rino using the name *Italiano* cannot be enforced against another party.

If, for example, Rino gave credit to a company for senior executives to have meals at his restaurant, then if he had not complied with the registration requirements as far as the business name was concerned he would not be able to enforce the contract against the company if it refused to pay the bills in respect of their staff.

A sole trader who buys a business will often want to continue under the name of the former business. It is obvious that this might allow him to retain the goodwill of existing customers. However, in choosing a name for the business which is not his own, the sole trader must comply with the Business Names Act 1985. Certain names will not be allowed, such as (i) names suggesting an international connection: for example, it is unlikely that the name 'International Stores' would be allowed; (ii) names giving the suggestion of a national or royal connection: for example, it is unlikely that the name 'Royal Village Stores' would be allowed. It should be noted that a business not complying with the 1985 Act would be guilty of a criminal offence.

You will remember from Chapter 12 that any business can be sued for 'passing off'. A sole trader who sells goods persuading his customers that they are from a well-known company could be sued.

Partnership

Rino's business flourished and after some time he decided to expand to buy two additional restaurants, but to do this he formed a partnership with four partners, namely himself, Wendy Rinaldi, John Drew and Stuart Conway. A partnership is defined by the Partnership Act 1890 as 'the relation which subsists between persons carrying on business in common with a view to profit'. The Companies Act 1985 lays down that there should be a maximum of 20 in a partnership. Rino's partnership seems to satisfy both rules:

1   It has been set up with a view to profit.
2   It has four partners and therefore has not exceeded the legal maximum of 20 partners.

A decided case shows that there must be a business element in a partnership.

In *Spicer Keith Ltd* v. *Mansell* (1970) the Court of Appeal decided that the two persons were not partners until they had actually started business and one could not bind the other by his actions until they commenced business. A supplier who had supplied gouds to Bishop, knowing he had gone bankrupt, tried unsuccessfully to sue Mansell. The Appeal Court held that this was not possible.

As with a sole owner, the partners will not enjoy limited liability, which means that Wendy, Stuart and John could risk losing much more than their original investment of £60 000, £120 000 and £120 000, respectively. Also it would be necessary for the partnership to comply with the business name requirements of the Companies Act 1981.

It is most likely that before entering into partnership with each other the four persons involved would have drawn up an agreement which defined clearly their rights and obligations. It is likely that such an agreement, sometimes known as a partnership deed, would include such matters as:

1   The involvement of the partners in the business: it may be that Rino's wife is designated a 'sleeping' partner, which means that, although she has invested £60 000 and will receive a percentage share of the profits, she will not take any part in the running of the business. If Wendy starts to take part in the running of the business she becomes a general partner. The agreement may also lay down the duties of the other three partners.
2   The agreement will probably lay down how the profit is to be shared and define clearly the precise amount of money Rino has invested, because you will remember Rino formed the partnership from an existing business.
3   Each partner will have agreed not to start any competing business and to give the other partners full information about any dealings in respect of *Italiano*.

It is possible for partnerships to be formed without an agreement and in this case the Partnership Act 1890 lays down clearly the relationship between the partners. It is important for partners to trust each other because each partner can make the other liable for his acts. If, therefore, one of the partners ordered expensive equipment for the firm's use then the other partners would equally be liable in contract. If as a result of John's negligence a customer is hurt then all the partners will be sued. It is possible for a partner who has retired from the partnership to remain liable for debts. Thus if John retires from the partnership and the partnership incurs a debt with a company then he could be liable unless he has expressly told the company in question that he has retires or he publishes the fact that he has retired in the *London Gazette*.

In addition to 'dormant' or 'sleeping' partners, there is a category known as 'salaried' partners. This category is often found in firms of solicitors or accountants. The following example may explain this.

Ian May has been working for a firm of solicitors, known as Beddoe and Beddoe, for five years and he is asked to become a salaried partner. Ian is pleased and accepts the offer. His name appears on the firm's letterhead. His terms and conditions of employment remain the same. After a period of five years, the firm suffers some losses and Ian finds that he is faced by having to contribute with the two general partners, Eric Beddoe and his brother Rodney Beddoe.

This is a problem facing salaried partners and Ian would have been advised to take out a full indemnity from the two general partners to 'indemnify' him (protect him) from having to pay any contribution to the firm's debts.

The case of *Stekel* v. *Ellice* (1973) is a very good reminder that a person allowing his name to be on the letterhead could find himself liable for debts of the firm should the firm get into financial difficulties.

Unlike a company, a partnership is not a legal entity. That means it cannot technically sue or be sued in its own name. In other words, Rino, John, Stuart and Wendy are all liable individually for debts incurred by the company and certainly there is unlimited liability. However in practice a partnership does make contracts in its own name, that is, *Italiano*, and can be sued in this name. This is a convenience, however, and the four partners in a civil case would effectively be sued separately.

Partners such as Rino, John and Stuart (remember Wendy was a sleeping partner) have two sorts of authority.

Actual authority.   This means that, if Rino decides to take out a lease for a new restaurant in Bromley, he binds his colleague partners by this as though they had together made the agreement.

Apparent authority.   If the partnership agreement forbade one partner from purchasing equipment for more than £5000 without the express permission of the others, if Rino saw an expensive item for £10 000 which he agreed to buy, the partnership is likely to be liable if the supplying firm assumed, as they probably would, that Rino had the authority.

The rule re apparent authority is neatly summed up in *Mercantile Credit Co Ltd* v. *Garrod* (1962).

In this case the partnership agreement between a Mr Parkin and Mr Garrod to run a garage hire and repair business expressly forbade the purchase of cars. Parkin bought a car without the permission of Garrod and the finance company sued Mr Garrod. The court held that Mr Parkin was using his apparent authority. Mercantile could not have known about the agreement and Mr Garrod was liable as if he had made the agreement with Mercantile himself.

___ **Exercise 2** _____

1 Define the expression 'sleeping partner'.
2 Explain the expression 'unlimited liability'.
3 Name two acts which regulate partnerships.
4 If a partner wishes to retire he can avoid being liable for partnership debts by taking two possible courses of action. What are these?
5 Linda Brasier and Christine Benton form a partnership and open a shop known as Canterbury Fashions, selling women's fashion clothes. Unknown to Linda, Christine orders very large stocks from SE Clothing Products Ltd and the partnership falls heavily into debt. SE Clothing Products Ltd have not been paid and sue the partnership, Canterbury Fashions, but Linda refuses to be held liable, saying she did not agree to the order from SE Clothing Products. Is Linda liable?
6 What is a salaried partner, and in what type of business is this type of partnership often found?

Dissolution of the partnership. There are two main ways by which a partnership may be brought to an end or dissolved and we will use the *Italiano* example to explain these two ways.

First, *Italiano* could be brought to an end without any legal necessities and in fact this is the most usual situation.

1 It could have been that the four partners agreed that the partnership would last for just five years and when the five years were up the partnership would be automatically ended.
2 If a partnership is entered into for a specific purpose then when that purpose is ended so does the partnership. In *Winsor* v. *Schroeder* (1979) two partners agreed to enter into a partnership to buy, renovate and sell a house. When the house was finally sold at a profit the contract came to an end. If *Italiano* was formed to open a restaurant and then sell it when it was under way, then when the restaurant was sold this would end the partnership.
3 Our partnership could come to an end if, for example, Stuart gave notice to this effect. However if mutual consent is required in the agreement then all partners must agree to end the partnership.
4 If one of the partners died then this would bring it to an end. However most partnership agreements have a clause to prevent the partnership coming to an end at death and if John died then whoever he designated in his will would become the new partner, provided the other partners agreed.
5 If Rino became bankrupt (see Chapter 16) the partnership would end. The other partners could agree to continue.
6 If the purposes of the partnership are or become illegal then the partnership ends. Thus, if *Italiano*'s main purpose was the import of illegal drugs from Italy, the partnership would end by illegality. In *Stevenson & Sons* v. *AG für Cartoggen Industrie* (1918), the court held that the partnership ended

because it was illegal from 1914 to trade with the enemy. Also, in a very different situation, in *Hudgell Yeates & Co* v. *Watson* (1978) a solicitors' partnership was held to be illegal because one of the partners did not have a certificate to practise.

7   If Stuart owed money to a creditor separately from the partnership, the creditor could charge his partnership share and this could bring the partnership to an end.

Second, the partnership may be brought to an end by the court under the following circumstances:

1   a partner's mental incapacity;
2   a partner's physical incapacity where this is permanent, though of course the agreement may provide for temporary incapacity;
3   conduct by one partner prejudicial to the business: thus if John, who manages one of the restaurants, uses it for immoral purposes then the court may order a dissolution;
4   when the business can only be carried on at a loss: this seems reasonable when we think of the basis on which a partnership is formed;
5   where one partner constantly breaches the agreement: for example, if Rino failed to turn up at any of the partnership's monthly meetings;
6   the court may decide for other reasons which it thinks are sound; that is, if none of the five reasons above is applicable the courts are given quite wide powers to decide what is just.

Any of the partners can petition the court to end the partnership, though a petition by a partner who was the reason for the required dissolution would not be acceptable on its own.

Limited partnership

The law does allow limited partnership whereby partners have limited liability; that is, they are only liable for the amount they have invested. They cannot have any say in the running of the partnership. There must be at least one general partner. These partnerships are allowed under the Limited Partnership Act 1907 and a limited partnership must register just as a company must with the Registrar of Companies.

In our example, *Italiano* was not a limited partnership but a general partnership.

Exercise 3

1   Explain the meaning of the phrase 'dissolution of a partnership'.
2   Explain the two main ways partnerships may be dissolved.

14.2 Formation of a company

We have now considered two types of business organisation, namely the sole trader type and the partnership. You will remember, however, that Rino, because he wanted to obtain further finance, decided to form a company and the existing partners were given shares in the new company, Italiano Steak & Wine Co. Ltd. Also shares were sold to several new investors. At first a private company was formed and, as you will remember, later this became a public company. The major differences between a public and a private company are:

1   A private company may not offer or advertise shares to the public but a public company may do so. In fact, this is the reason for the word 'public'; that is, the company's shares are available to the public. A private company's shares, however, are only available privately.
2   In its memorandum of association, which is one of the legal documents setting it up, a public company must state that it is a public company.
3   A public company must have a minimum share capital of £50 000. (This amount can be altered by the Secretary of State.)

___ Activity _____

In many newspapers you can find examples of companies advertising their shares. Look out for some examples. All these companies will be public companies because they are selling their shares to the public.

A company, whether public or private, is quite different legally from a partnership. In order for a company to be formed, certain important requirements have to be met. These requirements are laid down by the Companies Acts 1985 and they are therefore called statutory requirements.

___ Exercise 4 _____

What does 'statutory' mean?

To illustrate the method by which companies are formed, let us return to the restaurant business, *Italiano*. You will remember that it was decided to form a private company to be called Italiano Steak & Wine Co. Ltd. It would be necessary for the promoters, Rino, Stuart and John, to deposit with the Registrar of Companies two documents: the memorandum of association and the articles of association.

Memorandum of association

This document must contain certain information and we will illustrate this by reference to *Italiano*'s application:

1   The name of the company with the word 'Limited'; that is, Italiano Steak & Wine Co. Ltd.
2   The address of the registered office, which in this case is 14 Canterbury Road, Maidstone, UK; this in fact is an office over the very first restaurant which Rino bought.
3   The objects of the company or, in other words, why the company is being set up. Italiano Steak & Wine Co. Ltd is being set up 'with the object of providing food and drink in restaurants to the public'. It is important that the promoters get the objects correct and the document contains exactly what they wish to do because, as we will see, there are difficulties when a company tries to engage in activities outside the range of its objects. There are provisions to vary the objects within certain laid-down guidelines.
4   The promoters would have to make a statement under this clause that the shareholders of the new company would have limited liability. This means that they could only lose what they put in. For example, if Christine Benton decided to buy 500 £1 shares from the newly formed company Italiano Steak & Wine Co. Ltd, then this is all she could lose. This then explains the word 'limited'. Each shareholder is limited in liability to the amount of his shareholding.
5   The promoters have to state the nominal amount of capital the company will start trading with and it is likely that Italiano Steak & Wine Co. Ltd would start with about £600 000. The promoters also have to state how this is to be divided: 600 000 £1 ordinary shares is a possible and likely division.
6   Finally, for a company at least two people must sign the association clause. We will assume that Stuart, Rino and John are the three signatories in this case and they also have to indicate their own shareholding. Thus John may indicate 140 000 £1 shares. This document, known as the memorandum of association, is really a document setting out the relationship of the company Italiano Wine & Steak Co. Ltd to the outside world.

Until 1992 it was necessary for at least two people to form a company. In 1992 the UK adopted a European directive and the UK regulation adopting the directive allowed one person to form a company; also, where the two founder members become one, this does not affect the legality of the company. It is possible now in the UK for single member companies to exist. In practice most companies have more than one member.

Exercise 5

1   Name two differences between a public and a private company.
2   When you see 'Motor Supplies Company Limited', what does the term 'limited' mean?
---

3 In addition to the memorandum of association, name the other document which must be provided to the Registrar of Companies before a company can be formed.
4 In the memorandum of association what do you understand by the 'objects' of a company?

Articles of association

Just as the memorandum of association regulates the external affairs of a company, the articles of association are concerned with the internal running of the company. It is likely that Italiano Steak & Wine Co. Ltd would have included in their articles of association such matters as:

1 how shares would be transferred;
2 the powers of the company to borrow money;
3 how meetings are to be arranged and their frequency;
4 voting rights of shareholders.

The articles must be signed by the same people who signed the memorandum; in the case of Italiano Steak & Wine Co. Ltd, it would have been Rino, Stuart and John.

The two documents, the memorandum and the articles, are sent to the Registrar; one of the directors and the company secretary must sign what is called a statutory declaration. This is merely a form which states that all the requirements of the Companies Acts have been complied with. Once the Registrar is satisfied he will issue the applicant company with a 'certificate of incorporation' and this means, in the case of a private company, that it can begin trading right away.

It is important to understand what incorporation means. You will remember that in the first section of this chapter we pointed out that partners in partnerships could be sued or prosecuted for matters relating to the partnership. In a company the shareholders will not be sued or prosecuted for illegal acts of the company. This is because by incorporation the company takes on a legal status and becomes, as far as the law is concerned, a 'legal person'. Thus a company has a legal existence quite separate from its shareholders; if Italiano Steak & Wine Co. Ltd were in breach of contract for non-payment of orders they had made, the company would be taken to court. This is a very important legal principle and it is what distinguishes companies from the other two types of business organisation. A company, just like an individual person, can sue, be sued, prosecute or be prosecuted.

A famous case, *Saloman* v. *Saloman Co Ltd* (1897) laid down that 'a limited company is an artificial legal person with a separate and distinct existence apart from its members'.

You will remember that when explaining the memorandum of association mention was made of nominal capital. This is the amount of money that the company thinks it may raise. The sum of £600 000 was mentioned for Italiano Steak & Wine Co. Ltd. A separate statement of this amount must be given, for companies are taxed on this amount. A company need not issue the full amount and so Italiano might issue £500 000 and keep £100 000 aside. Thus a distinction is made between nominal capital of £600 000, that amount which the company is authorised to raise, and the issued capital of £500 000, which it has actually raised.

Another clause of the memorandum which needs to be explained more fully is the objects clause. This sets out the purpose for which the company is operating. For Italiano Steak & Wine Co. Ltd the object was to provide food and drink in restaurants to the public.

It is quite apparent that Rino has a good business head on his shoulders and it has not escaped his notice that a restaurant which they have acquired on the outskirts of Canterbury has quite extensive grounds with some very large outbuildings. Rino persuades his fellow directors and the shareholders that for a modest outlay these buildings can be converted into large vehicle repair shops and he hits on the idea of advertising MOT and servicing 'while you eat'. This proves very successful but, unfortunately for the company, the repair, servicing and testing of vehicles is not part of the company's objects.

Italiano Steak & Wine Co. Ltd runs a serious risk because, if several of its customers refused to pay the servicing or repair bills, that money could not be recovered because the contract between the company and the customers would be *ultra vires*, beyond the company's powers as laid down in the memorandum. Any agreement entered into by a company which is beyond its powers is void and cannot be enforced against the other party.

Ashbury Railway Carriage Co, v. *Riche* (1875) is a case which illustrates that any act outside the objects is *ultra vires* and therefore void. The company in its object was authorised to make railway carriages, but entered into an arrangement to finance a railway line. This was adjudged to be *ultra vires*.

If, however, Italiano Steak & Wine Co. Ltd had ordered £5000 worth of spares for its motor trade, could it avoid payment saying it was *ultra vires*, beyond the powers of the company? This would be very unfair on the firm supplying the spares, but until the UK became a member of the EEC this very unfair rule applied. The following example was, as you can see, before the time when the UK became a member of the EEC. In *Introductions Ltd* v. *National Provincial Bank Ltd* (1969), a company formed in 1951 with the object of promoting tourism was not bound by contracts made when it went into pig farming many years later. However, because it is necessary for our commercial rules to coincide with those of our partners in Europe, the law now is that, if a company deals with another in good faith, that is not knowing that the other was acting beyond its powers, then a contract can be enforced against the other company. Thus, provided the £5000 of spares was supplied by a company which did not know that

Italiano was acting *ultra vires*, the £5000 could be enforced despite what is technically a void contract. Section 9 of the European Communities Act 1972 would allow the supplier to enforce the contract against Italiano Steak & Wine Co. Ltd.

Company name

The 1985 Companies Act set up a system to control names. A name will never be registered:

1   if it conflicts with another company name on the Registrar's list;
2   if it includes 'Ltd' or 'PLC' at a place other than at the end;
3   if the name is offensive: the Registrar refused names such as 'Prostitutes Ltd' or 'Hooker Ltd' when a prostitute applied to register a name (*Attorney General* v. *Lindi St Claire Personal Services* (1989));
4   if it is a name claiming an international, European or national connection: for example, it is unlikely that 'European Union PLC' or 'Royal Cereals Plc' would be allowed;
5   if it is a sensitive area; for example, it is unlikely that 'Apartheid Services Plc' would be allowed.

The rules re company names outlined above also apply to a changed name which also needs to be registered.

Exercise 6

1   A company in its memorandum states that it will raise £1 m but only decides to sell 500 000 £1 shares. What is the company's (a) nominal capital, (b) issued capital?
2   Explain the legal positions in each of the following.
   (a)   Unicorn Motor Supplies Co Ltd owe Ford plc £500 000. Ford plc decide to take the managing director, Bill Boyle, to court for breach of contract.
   (b)   SE Touring Co Ltd was set up to provide tours of the South East of England to foreign visitors. The managing director decides to develop a road haulage sideline and orders two wagons for £60 000 from Heavy Vehicle Supplies Ltd. The vehicles are delivered but the £60 000 is never paid. SE Touring Co Ltd claim the contract is void because it is *ultra vires*.
   (c)   Palatine Publishing Co Ltd decide to extend their business into sports shops and open up three shops in the North of England. A football club orders £2000 of equipment from them but does not settle the bill. The football club chairman is a solicitor and he knows that supply of sports equipment is not included in Palatine Publishing Co Ltd's objects.

We have already explained the differences between a private and a public company. A public company, unlike a private company, cannot begin trading when it gets a certificate of incorporation; it must await the issue of a certificate of trading. Thus, when Italiano Steak & Wine Co. Ltd decided to go public it needed to apply to the Registrar with details of its proposals for issuing shares. Public companies must include 'Public Limited Company' in their title, or the abbreviation 'plc'.

Exercise 7

Try to answer the following questions which all relate to types of business organisation. Check your answers and if there is anything you do not understand then refer to the chapter again.

1 John Hartley decides to set up business as a market gardener; he calls his business *Garden Produce*. He contracts to sell £1000 of produce to a local restaurant, who refuse to pay the bill, claiming that John has not complied with the need to display the name *Garden Produce*. Would John be able to claim his money?
2 Name the Act which regulates partnerships in this country.
3 What is the minimum and maximum number of partners allowed in a partnership?
4 David Stuart, managing director of Smalldale Engineering Co Ltd, is sued in the courts for recovery of debts incurred by the company. Advise David as to whether he would need to pay.
5 Name the certificate which brings a company into existence.
6 What change has been made in the *ultra vires* rule by European Community law?

---

15 Business organisation (II): privatisation, merger and monopoly control

15.1 Public corporations and privatisation

Dean Simmonds has just retired as a professional footballer and wishes to use the gratuity and benefit money he has obtained to invest in shares. He decides it would be safer if he invested his money in a large company and decides to buy shares in Southern Water PLC and the Post Office. He consults a broker who informs him that, while he may be able to purchase shares in Southern Water if they are available, it is impossible at the moment to buy shares in the Post Office.

Southern Water is a public company and therefore its shares are sold on the stock exchange. In fact Southern Water is one of the companies which was privatised when the water industry was privatised in 1992. Before 1992 water was controlled in the main by public corporations, which means it had a legal status just like a company (see Chapter 14) but it was owned by the state. The government at that time decided that it would be more efficient if water was run by the private sector and Southern Water, along with a number of other regional water authorities, ceased to be a public corporation and became a public company. The use of the word 'public' is somewhat misleading in both contexts. When it is used in the term *'Public Corporation'* it means a legal body ('corporation') owned by the public. When it is used in the term *'Public Company'* it means a privately owned company whose shares are available to the public.

The Post Office is a public corporation; that is, it is owned by the state. In 1994 the government started the process of privatising British Rail and, as you know, have created a number of public companies such as Great Western and Midland, known initially as shadows franchises. The process whereby a public corporation becomes a public company is known as privatisation. The company or companies are created by Act of Parliament, and the shares are sold to the public. Often an existing company will purchase sufficient shares to control the company and it will then operate as any other public company operates subject to the legal rules and regulations as described in Chapter 14.

Because these new companies, such as the water, electricity and gas companies, supply products which are essential, the government has appointed a regulator for these industries to ensure that there is balance between the interests of the consumers and the needs of the shareholders. The regulator can fix prices to attempt to balance these interests and needs. Recent publicity has suggested that the balance seems to be in favour of the shareholders as news of windfall profits for the chairman and chief executives of these privatised companies are announced.

The Post Office, however, is a public corporation which was established by various Acts of Parliament to supply a range of postal services. Its powers are laid out in those Acts of Parliament and it is possible for anyone to challenge the corporation if there is a feeling that it is exceeding its powers, that is acting *ultra vires*. The following example may assist:

Queensdown Haulage PLC has been running a very successful heavy goods delivery service from its Bristol depot. The general manager, Lynne Lyndley discovers that the Post Office is taking on extra staff and buying lorries to extend their delivery service to include heavy articles. Mrs Lyndley, fearful of the impact on her own business, decides to challenge this in the courts and claims that the Post Office are exceeding the powers allowed them under the Act.

It is likely that the court would find in favour of Queensdown Haulage PLC, for it is likely that the carrying of heavy freight is not part of the Post Office's objectives as laid down by Parliament.

There are other examples of public corporations, such as the British Broadcasting Corporation and British Rail, though the latter is in the process of being privatised.

Exercise 1

1 What is the main difference between a public corporation and a public company?
2 Explain the term '*ultra vires*' as it applies to a public corporation.

In addition to public corporations such as the BBC and the Post Office, there are local authorities which were set up by the Local Government Act of 1974. By this Act county councils such as Kent County Council and district authorities such as Canterbury were established. Although counties had existed before, they were given different powers by the 1974 Act and districts were created. Some changes in local government are to be implemented in 1995.

The 1974 Act gave certain powers to the two authorities, county and district, and at the same time gave them a legal status, just like a company or public corporation. These authorities cannot exceed their powers as allowed under the Act and if they do they could be taken to court for acting *ultra vires*.

Activity

In your own area try to identify the two local bodies set up to administer local government (the county and the district)

Try to find out the name of the regulator in respect of electricity, gas, water and the telephone services.

Try to find out the procedure by which the rail system in the UK was privatised.

15.2 Competition law

The British economy is an example of a market economy, like most of the economies in Europe and many other parts of the world. However it is generally felt that it is government's duty to protect individuals from some of the excesses of a market economy. Three examples may help to explain the way in which the law seeks to provide protection.

1 Two large supermarket chains in the UK decide, rather than engage in price competition, it would be better to merge the two businesses. The merger would result in the merged company having 45 per cent control of the food retail business in the UK. This would in English law create a monopoly, and therefore would be subject to control.

2 Ashton Packaging PLC of Bristol and Medway Corrugated PLC of Maidstone decide they are both losing out by trying to compete with each other. The two chief executives, Mr Reg Pulleyne and Mr Robert Bown, meet in a Reading hotel and agree a series of terms, including charging the same prices for their identical products and also agreeing the same rules regarding the settlement of accounts and discounts. They also agree to split the country into two parts, with one firm supplying the one and the other firm the other part. A written agreement is drawn up and customers find prices rise by 15 per cent in both companies. This is known as a restrictive trade practice and is likely to be regarded as illegal.

3 Anxious to maintain their prices, GRM (Sports) PLC, a well-known producer of famous football teams' kits, refuse to supply several of its customers because they have sold the kits at less than the recommended price. This example of resale price maintenance might well be judged to be illegal.

Let us look at each of the examples in turn.

1 The Fair Trading Act 1973 lays down that a monopoly arises when a company controls 25 per cent or more of the supply of a product. The situation described above is where two companies decide to merge. Special arrangements apply to mergers. When two companies decide to merge, it is sensible to refer

the matter to the Director General of Fair Trade and he will recommend to the Secretary of State for Industry whether the proposed merger should be referred to the Monopolies and Mergers Commission (MMC). Companies are not obliged to refer the matter to the Director but he, acting on the advice of an inter-departmental mergers panel, may decide to recommend referral to the MMC. Once a matter is referred to the MMC no further progress in the merger must be made. The MMC, using criteria related to the question whether it will be in or against the public interest, will make a decision and the Secretary of State then may take the necessary action which might prevent this merger going ahead, for example by issuing an order prohibiting the merger taking place.

You may remember that, in 1993, the proposed merger of Midland Bank PLC and Lloyds Bank PLC was adjudged to be against the public interest and did not take place.

Of course it is not only mergers that may be referred to the MMC, but also existing monopolies. A company having a large share of the market, that is more than 25 per cent, whose activities are felt to be against the public interest may be required by the Secretary of State, following a report from the MMC, to take the appropriate action voluntarily and, if it does not, an order may be issued.

Remember that the 1973 Monopolies and Mergers Act is often complied with by companies taking their own remedial action.

2 The sort of agreement described in (2) is termed a restrictive practice. The 1976 Restrictive Trade Practices Act lays down that four categories of agreement must be registered with the Director General :

1   restrictive agreements as to goods,
2   information agreements as to goods,
3   restrictive agreements as to services,
4   information agreements as to services.

The Director then takes the agreement before the Restrictive Practices Court and the Court and the parties to the agreement then have to show why the agreement is in the public interest. There are a number of 'gateways' and if the parties can convince the court that their agreement can get through one of the 'gateways' it will be declared in the public interest and thus allowed. Thus it would be necessary in our example for the agreement to be registered and then for the two companies to argue the case.

An example of one of the eight 'gateways' is that: *'The restriction or information provision does not directly or indirectly restrict or discourage competition to any material degree in any relevant trade or industry and is not likely to do so.'* Two agreements to successfully negotiate this gateway were Re Scottish Newspaper Society's Agreements (1972) and the Building Employers Confederation Application (1985).

It is necessary under the law to register an agreement and failure to do so can result in penalties. If an agreement is not registered within a prescribed period then it becomes void. In 1986 leading bookmakers Corals, Ladbrookes, Mecca and William Hill failed to register an agreement about opening and closing times and this meant that it could not be enforced; nor could an agreement relating to support in objecting to new licences to competitors be granted.

If an agreement is not allowed by the court it must be discontinued. Not many agreements getting to the court have been allowed and therefore the practice has been for agreements to be discontinued. It would be necessary for the agreement in our example to be registered and it is unlikely that it would be allowed. It would be difficult for Mr Pulleyne or Mr Robert Bown to show that it was in the public interest.

3 The agreement in (3) comes under the Resale Prices Act 1976, whereby such agreements, as with (2), must be registered and the company concerned, in our case GRM (Sports) PLC, must attempt before the Restrictive Practices Court to show that this 'resale price maintenance' is in the public interest and, as with restrictive practices, GRM will use one of the gateways under this Act. There are 5 gateways relating to resale price maintenance.

Very few references have been made to the court, either under this Act or its predecessor, the Resale Price Maintenance Act of 1964. Most agreements are withdrawn. It is, however, illegal, as shown in *Comet Radiovision Services* v. *Farnell Tanberg Ltd* (1971), for a company to withhold supplies to a customer who has sold goods below the recommended price. Two agreements relating to pharmaceutical products and books have been upheld by the court on the grounds that to exempt them would lead to a reduction in the number of chemist shops and small bookshops.

Activity

Why do you think that the Restrictive Practices Court allowed the appeal by the pharmaceutical companies and by the publishers?

Exercise 2

1 Name the three types of competition control possible under the Fair Trading Act 1973.
2 What is regarded as a monopoly under the Fair Trading Act 1973?
3 What is resale price maintenance?
4 Give one example of a 'gateway' re restrictive practices.
5 If a merger is against the public interest, how is it stopped?

15.3 Competition and the European Union

The rules described above are designed to protect the consumer in what sometimes is called the domestic market, that is the home market. The UK is of course a member of the European Union and as such is subject, as we pointed out in Chapter 3, to European directives. The Treaty of Rome, which of course is an important source of European Union (EU) law, sets out the rules relating to competition and has by and large adopted the German model. The rules are laid out in article 85 and article 86.

Article 85 deals with restrictive practice agreements between organisations independent of each other and cartels, which are types of trade organisations.

Article 86 deals with monopolies which are described as situations where an organisation or groups of organisations reach a position of strength which makes the normal constraints of competition no longer applicable. The article calls this a 'dominant position'.

Article 87 deals with the way the rules are incorporated into the law and basically this is the same as described in Chapter 3 – Commission-Parliament-Council – and then a directive is introduced. This directive then becomes part of English law following a regulation issued by a minister or maybe, if necessary, an Act of Parliament.

If, however, there is a conflict between the national law of a member state and EU law then EU law prevails as the case *Wilhelm v Bundeskartellamt 1969*. Here *German* law re cartels conflicted with EU law or EC law as it was then called and the case showed that German law had to give way.

Article 85

The law relating to article 85 is broadly similar to the UK law on restrictive practices, in that it prohibits, amongst other things', price fixing, agreements to limit or control production and share markets or sources of supply. However, if the offending undertaking can show that the agreement contributes to technical or economic efficiency and to increasing production while allowing customers a fair share of the resulting benefits, it may be allowed to continue.

The law may be best explained by means of an example:

Five companies, Ferrado PLC (UK), F. L. Mercier SA (France), B. F. Reinart AG (Germany), Automatica SA (Spain) and J. Cruyff BV (Netherlands) all produce certain components for the motor industry. The respective chief executives decide it would be a good idea if they met to discuss areas of mutual interest. Meetings are held at Banbury (UK), Metz (France), Ludwigshafen (Germany), Gerona (Spain) and Breda (Netherlands). As a result a complicated agreement is drawn up which relates to prices to be charged, prices to be paid to suppliers of essential raw materials and to share technical and commercial expertise. The agreement also involves splitting Europe into zones and these zones are allocated to one of the companies. A German motor manufacturer finds that it can only trade with Reinart AG as a result of the agreement.

This agreement would seem to be contrary to article 85, unless the companies concerned could show that the benefits of such an agreement went to consumers. The Commission in Brussels could declare it to be void and if necessary could ask for a ruling from the European Court of Justice. It would be for the court to determine whether the agreement fell within the scope of article 85.

An example of a case brought by the Commission is *IAZ International Belgium NV* v. *Commission* (1983) which ruled that an agreement between water undertakings in Belgium only to fix to the mains supply dish-washing machines carrying a conformity label from a Belgian association of manufacturers of this equipment was illegal because it restricted competition against other suppliers in the European Union.

However in *Publishers' Association* v. *Commission* (1992) British publishers argued before the European Court of Justice, sitting as an appeal court, that their agreement, which had been ruled illegal by the court of first instance, was in the interests of purchasers of books.

Article 86

This article seeks to protect consumers from the abuse of monopoly power where a company in a dominant position might seek to use this to charge higher prices for its goods or service or pay lower prices for the goods or services it buys. For example,

Europa PLC is a British firm which specialises in the production of specialist medical equipment. It has bought out a number of suppliers throughout Europe and has obtained a 45 per cent share of the market. It charges very high prices and enters into an agreement with one of its suppliers to reduce the prices of the raw materials supplied to it. As a result of these changes, its profits soar and its share prices reach a very high level. It also conducts a very vicious price war against a small producer of the same product in Spain by focusing very low prices in the area of Andalusia supplied by the small company.

This is just the sort of case which might be referred by the Commission to the European Court of Justice. It will be up to Europa to argue that their arrangements are in the interest of their customers. The dominant position is not in itself illegal but only if it is abused. If the court finds against Europa then the Commission will require it to change its policies to avoid the abuse.

There have been a number of decided cases; two examples are given below:

AKZO Chemiw v. Commission (1985)
AKZO is the union's largest supplier of benzoyl peroxide, which is used in the manufacture of plastics and blanching flour. The Commission discovered that AKZO conducted a price war against a small firm which supplied flour additives and wished to break into the plastic trade. Very big price reductions

were offered to the potential customers of the small firm. The European Court of Justice, to which the matter was referred, held that this represented an abuse of power as defined under article 86.

British Leyland Plc v. *Commission (1987)*
Leyland, concerned at the effect on the home market of the reimportation of cars, especially from Belgium, which were sold in the UK at substantially reduced prices, increased substantially the price of certificates to its agents in Europe. This had the effect of reducing imports of BL cars from the continent. The Court of European Justice condemned this practice as being contrary to article 86.

The Treaty of Rome made no provision for dealing with mergers, but the court had to rely on articles 85 and 86. In 1990 a regulation (4064/89) was passed which allowed the commission to intervene when the following thresholds were exceeded:

1   where the total world turnover of the merger would exceed 500 million ECU;
2   where the aggregate turnover of two of the merging companies exceed 250 million ECU;
3   where less than 66.66 per cent of each merging company's turnover is within one member state.

In this short survey of European competition law, only a little of this complex topic could be covered. If you wish to know more, there are many books written on the law relating to the European Union.

__ Activity _____

The Times, *Guardian* and *Independent* often print details of cases relating to European competition law. Try to find examples, for this will help you to keep up to date and give you a better understanding of this aspect of the law.

__ Exercise 3 _____

1   Name the three main articles regulating competition in Europe.
2   Give an example of circumstances under which restrictive practice might be allowed by the European Court of Justice and the Commission.
3   What was the purpose of regulation 4064/89 and when did it become law?

4 A 100 per cent increase in prices is announced by Allied Chemicals, a company with a 75 per cent control of the EU market for two chemicals much in use in printing. Is there any action which the European Commission could take?

5 Four leading banks in Spain, the UK, France and Germany announce an intention to merge their activities. Does the Commission have the power to stop such a merger?

16 Insolvency law: bankruptcy and liquidation

16.1 Bankruptcy

John Smith has been employed as a garage mechanic for about ten years with a large motor company in Exeter. He has always wanted to go into business and an opportunity presents itself when a small garage with showroom and petrol pumps becomes available on the outskirts of Exeter. John sets up business operating under the name of Merton (Motors). He has no real experience in running his own business and after about a year of trading he finds that he is quite heavily in debt. With trade particularly poor in all aspects of his business, that is in petrol sales, servicing and second-hand cars, he cannot see any prospect of settling the following outstanding debts:

(1) £ 1 059   to the local authority for business rates
(2) £ 4 900   to Associated Motors for spares
(3) £25 500   to Quality Cars Ltd for three second-hand cars
(4) £ 9 000   to United Motor Equipment Ltd for garage equipment, tools, testing gear, etc.
(5) £15 900   to a leading petrol company for petrol
(6) £   360   to Allcock & Sons Ltd, a local builder, for building repairs

John is very anxious about these debts and would like an opportunity to get rid of the embarrassment and to make a fresh start. The creditors, that is the firms and so on which John owes money, are anxious that they get some payment. Obviously whatever is available ought to be shared out by some fair method.

Dealing with such problems is the object of bankruptcy. In Chapter 14 we considered the various types of business organisation. Sole traders and partnerships can go bankrupt, but companies can only be liquidated. In this section we will be considering the law of bankruptcy and liquidation.

John Smith is a sole trader and therefore can be made bankrupt. We will use this example to explain the law of bankruptcy. The law relating to bankruptcy is laid down in the Insolvency Act 1986. Let us for a moment consider John's position. It is quite clear that he is 'unable to pay' and it seems likely that he has 'no reasonable prospect of paying'. These phrases are taken from the Insolvency Act of 1985. It would seem that there are a number of possibilities for John, which we will now examine.

Individual voluntary arrangement (IVA)

John could go to an insolvency practitioner and ask his advice. Insolvency practitioners are qualified accountants who specialise in this subject. It is possible that the practitioner would advise John to seek an individual voluntary arrangement (IVA). This sort of arrangement is possible under the insolvency law introduced by the Insolvency Act 1985 and 1986. It is available to debtors who have not been fraudulent and have some assets to distribute.

John is in fact in this position, having some garage equipment and some second-hand cars and vans. An insolvency practitioner will only assist if he knows he will get a fee and that is why there need to be some assets available.

John and the insolvency practitioner will prepare a statement of affairs, which will contain details of debts and assets, and an application is made to the court for an 'interim order', which gives a breathing space as it were for the debtor, assisted by the insolvency practitioner, to come up with an arrangement. There can be no petition for bankruptcy during the life of an interim order. The application to the court for an interim order must be accompanied by an 'affidavit', which is a statement sworn before a solicitor saying in effect that the details in the statement are true. Interim orders may be granted for a period of 14 days and are renewable. However courts have shown in recent cases, such as *re Gilmartin, a debtor* (1989) that they are not willing to go on extending the period if there is no reasonable chance of an agreement.

The courts have shown impatience with poor insolvency practitioners and in *Re Jackson a debtor* (1990) the judge, Mr Harman, required the practitioner to pay 50 per cent of the costs of a creditor seeking to have an arrangement annulled because of a faulty procedure. When an arrangement is agreed in addition to a notice being lodged in the court, a copy is sent to the Secretary of State for Industry, with whom all IVAs are recorded.

The practitioner is usually appointed as supervisor to ensure that the terms of the agreement are implemented. If an IVA is approved as set out above then the debtor is not bankrupt. This procedure is often used since creditors recognise this is an inexpensive way of getting some of their debts paid off.

The sequence for an IVA is as follows: (i) statement of affairs, (ii) interim order, (iii) proposal, (iv) order to attend meeting, (v) approval. It is possible to 'short circuit' the sequence by combining the first four stages into one.

John, of course, is a sole trader; partners can also get a voluntary arrangement, although, as the term 'individual' suggests, it is better if partners obtain the agreements individually. Doing it this way is much simpler and avoids the considerable difficulty of trying to reach a partnership arrangement.

The debtor and his practitioner will prepare a plan which sets out a proposal of how John intends to deal with the debts and the court sets a venue (i.e. time and place) for a meeting of creditors. The creditors will meet to consider the proposal. In order for the proposal to be accepted by the creditors, it must be agreed by those creditors present at the meeting together with voting by proxy (i.e. authorising someone else to vote for them). The agreement must have a seventy five percent majority. This seventy five percent is based upon the total debt owed to those present at the meeting and those able to vote by 'proxy'. If creditors do not attend and do not arrange to vote by proxy then they are not included in the calculation of seventy five percent. Creditors have a right to challenge the proposal for up to 28 days. This is possible for example if a creditor could argue that he/she had not been properly notified of the meeting.

Exercise 1

1 What is the function of a supervisor in an IVA ?
2 Look back to the list of debts of John Smith and say whether, if creditor 3 and 5 agreed to the arrangement, this would ensure approval.
3 What is the function of the 'interim order'?

Deed of arrangement

John could utilise the 1914 Deed of Arrangement Act to settle his affairs privately. This method is not often used because, by drawing up a deed, John would be admitting that he could not pay his debts and there were no reasonable grounds to suppose he could in the future. This could invite a petition from one or more of his creditors for him to be declared bankrupt. However if a petition is made the court could dismiss it if the debtor could show that the arrangement was being unreasonably refused by the petitioning creditor. The advantage of the method is that it is cheaper than the voluntary arrangement (IVA).

This method involves drawing up a deed which will benefit his creditors and will involve either:

1 John's assigning some of his property to his creditors: for example, if John owned several houses in Devon he could assign them to his creditors who could use the proceeds to meet some if not all of the debts;

or

2 John's drawing up what is called a composition, setting out how he would pay the debts or some of them.

Under either method a trustee is appointed to supervise the arrangement. Unlike the IVA it needs a majority of approval from the creditors in number and in value. In our example, at least four creditors would need to approve, but it would not be sufficient if creditors 1, 2, 4 and 6 were those approving.

Exercise 2

Can you say why, if only creditors 1, 2, 4 and 6 approved, there would be no arrangement?

The deed, if approved, is usually similar to a normal contract and the creditors can deal with the matter under the law relating to contract (see Chapters 5 and 6).

Bankruptcy

There are a number of stages.

Petition. It is possible that one of John's creditors, United Motor Equipment Ltd, petitions for bankruptcy. To make a petition to the court, certain conditions must be fulfilled:

1 John was carrying on a business individually or in partnership (the Insolvency Act defines business).
2 He is living in England and Wales (there are a number of rules relating to what the Insolvency Act says about this question of where the debtor was living).
3 The petitioner must be either a creditor or John himself.
4 The grounds for the petition are:
  (i) the debtor appears unable to pay his debt;
  (ii) there appears to be no reasonable prospect of his being able to pay.

It would seem that these four conditions are satisfied in our case though, as explained, a petition is not possible if an IVA or deed of arrangement is approved.

If United Motor Equipment wished to petition it would need to serve on John a statutory demand, using a standard form. A number of different sorts of forms can be used for different sorts of circumstance. The petition usually would be presented to the Country Court insolvency district, which in our case would be in Exeter. Once the petition has been presented, any actions for recovery of money by other creditors will be suspended. The petitioner may ask at this stage that the official receiver take over the affairs of John while the matter is being dealt with, and the court may authorise this. The official receiver may appoint, subject to the approval of the court, a special manager to run the business. There is no provision for any other creditor to be informed.

Bankruptcy order. The court at this stage can make a bankruptcy order. This order will contain (i) date of the petition, (ii) date and time of the order, (iii) instructions to the bankrupt (John) to attend at a certain time and place, and (iv) notification that all legal proceedings against the bankrupt in respect of his debts are suspended. Two copies of the order are sent to the official receiver and one of these will be sent to John. The official receiver will notify the chief land registrar in Plymouth and the fact of John's bankruptcy will be noted. A notice will appear in the *London Gazette* and the receiver can advertise the fact of John's bankruptcy locally, that is in Exeter.

Meeting of the creditors.   A meeting of creditors will be called and they will appoint a trustee who will then take over from the official receiver. Creditors must be given 21 days' notice of the meeting. It used to be quite usual for the bankrupt to have to attend a public meeting in the court, but this is now rare. At the creditors' meetings, the trustee will provide reports on the affair and at a final meeting he will be discharged. The creditors in our example may accept so much, say 30p in the pound, of the debt owing.

Effect of bankruptcy on the bankrupt

There are a number of effects of bankruptcy on the bankrupt. The main ones include the following:

1 he will lose control of his property,
2 he can only get rid of his assets with the permission of the court,
3 he cannot get credit without disclosing his status,
4 he can only enter business by disclosing his name and the fact that he is bankrupt,
5 he cannot become a member of parliament.

Ending bankruptcy

A bankruptcy may be brought to an end by the court following an application to the court by the bankrupt. If the court is satisfied that a satisfactory arrangement has been made and that all the expenses of bankruptcy have been met, it will grant a discharge. The bankrupt is treated as if he had never been a bankrupt.

Exercise 3

1 Name the four conditions which must exist for a bankruptcy petition to be made.
2 Who may make a petition?
3 State five effects of bankruptcy.

Since the possibility of IVAs was allowed under the 1986 Insolvency Act, bankruptcies are much less common. There is a high cost in bankruptcy, which creditors realise that they will pay, so they prefer to try to get a voluntary arrangement.

16.2 Liquidation

Fortray Coach Tours Co Ltd is a private company operating in the South West of England. In the past the company has been very successful in promoting coach tours to some of the best parts of Devon and Cornwall. However, owing to escalating operational costs and the twin effects of the poor weather and recession the company has a disastrous year and finds that it is unable to meet four very heavy bills:

(1) A petrol account with a local garage, Torbay Garage Ltd, amounting to £12 000.
(2) A repair bill with another garage, Exeter Road Garage Ltd, of £15 000.
(3) Rent for its main booking office in Torquay to Atlantic Properties PLC, amounting to £16 800.
(4) Hire charges to another coach firm of £45 000.

This is very similar to the situation in which John found himself in the previous section, but in this case, because Fortray Coach Tours Co Ltd is a company, it cannot be declared bankrupt. In fact the only way this situation can be dealt with is by liquidation. The law as it relates to liquidation will be dealt with in this section. You will remember from Chapter 14 that a company is regarded as a 'legal person' and because of this its existence can only be terminated by a legal process, the legal process known as liquidation or winding up. Liquidation means making the company's assets liquid or, in other words, turning the assets into money. Winding up, which means bringing to a conclusion the company's existence, is part of the same process.

There are three ways in which a company may be liquidated or wound up.

Compulsory winding up

Fortray Coach Tours Co Ltd may be wound up by the court compulsorily under the following circumstances:

1 It is unable to pay its debts.
2 It is unable to pay its debts and a creditor, for example Exeter Road Garage Ltd, serves a statutory demand (see above, page 231).
3 It fails to hold a meeting as laid down in the Companies Acts, that is a statutory meeting.
4 It does not commence business within a year of its formation or it suspends business for a year or more.
5 The number of members/shareholders falls below the statutory minimum, which you will remember is two (or, under a recent change in company law, even one).

In Fortray Coach Tours' case it is the company's inability to pay its debts which is the problem; usually it is one of the creditors who petitions the court for a winding up order through the issue of a statutory demand.

Exercise 4

1　Explain the terms 'liquidation' and 'winding up'.
2　Under what circumstances may a court make a compulsory winding up order?

Let us assume that Torbay Garage Ltd, who are owed £12 000, ask the court for a winding up order. If the court is convinced that Fortray will be unlikely to pay this debt, it will issue a winding up order. The official receiver is appointed as liquidator and he will ask the directors to prepare a statement. Alternatively Fortray would go to an insolvency practitioner, who will have a function similar to the one he has with bankruptcy. He will try to save the company or will present a plan to the court. The official receiver is often happy to hand over his role to the practitioner, but is not obliged to do so.

The official receiver or the practitioner will sell off the assets which, in our example, were as follows:

Two coaches	£30 000
Office equipment	£ 3 000
Bank account	£ 2 520
Total	*£35 520*

The official receiver's task is to realise the company's assets and distribute them to the creditors. We have seen that, by selling the company's assets, £35 520 will be realised. The receiver will then prepare two lists – list A, the present shareholders, and list B, any shareholder who has held shares with the company in the year before liquidation.

As we have seen, shareholders are only liable to the extent of their shareholding but companies sometimes only require shareholders to pay a proportion of the share, such as 75p in the £1 share; therefore there is 25p unpaid. If still the company debts cannot be paid, list B may be called upon and these former shareholders may be liable for the extent of their former holdings of shares.

Let us assume that all shareholders are fully paid up in Fortray and there is no list B. Then the official receiver or insolvency practitioner declares a dividend to the creditors of 40p in the pound because he can only meet 40 per cent (£35 520) of the debt of £88 800.

Exercise 5

If the liquidator declares a dividend of 40p in the pound, how much will Torquay Garage Ltd get?

Each creditor must prove to the official receiver or the insolvency practitioner the existence of the debt in order to claim a dividend.

Voluntary winding up

Compulsory winding up usually arises as a result of the action of a creditor petitioning the court, but the company can decide to wind itself up because it wishes to discontinue business or amalgamate with another company. If the directors of the company declare that it can meet its debts then the members (shareholders) of the company wind it up; but if the company is insolvent, that is cannot meet its debts, it is the creditors who wind it up.

In both cases a liquidator is appointed who takes over from the directors. He converts the assets of the company into money and uses the money to pay off any debts, paying any balance to the shareholders.

The liquidator then sends a return to the Registrar of Companies. This return is registered and three months after the registration the company is deemed to have been dissolved.

Winding up under the court's supervision

There are certain circumstances where, even though a company is being wound up voluntarily, it is felt that it would be better done under the supervision of the court and the court appoints an additional liquidator to make sure everything is done fairly.

Exercise 6

1 Name the three ways in which a company may be wound up.
2 Peter White, a local printer, is owed £250 for printing done for Chapel Engineering Co Ltd. The company is wound up and a dividend of 30p is declared. How much will Peter get?
3 United Meat Company is sued by a creditor three months after it has been voluntarily wound up. Advise the creditor.

Exercise 7

Answer the following questions which are based upon the two sections of this chapter. If, when checking your answers, you find that you have not understood any particular part, go over that part again.

1 Sterndale Engineering Co is owed a sum of £950 for machine repairs by Fraser Bros, a small partnership. Fraser Bros are heavily in debt and cannot pay this bill. How can Sterndale Engineering Co obtain all or some of its money?

2 What is contained in a bankruptcy order?

3 Who is appointed when a person is adjudged bankrupt?

4 Ashford Machine Tool Co Ltd is facing compulsory winding up. Its lia-bilities are £40 000 in unpaid debts. Its assets are £20 000 for buildings, 16 000 £1 shares (unpaid portion 25p), 200 shareholders who have left the company within the last six months with shareholdings, of £4000, other equipment £2000. Calculate the dividend payable to the creditors.

17 The law and banking

17.1 Cheques

A cheque is a very common method of payment and, besides being used increasingly by individuals, it is also used extensively in business transactions. In this chapter we are going to look at the law as it relates to cheques.

Let us assume for a moment that a small furniture firm, owned by two partners, R. and M. Spencer, trading under the name of Brassingtons, wishes to pay one of its suppliers, Conquest (Furniture) Co Ltd, the sum of £25 430 by means of a cheque. R. and M. Spencer have their account at the Midland Bank and therefore the cheque will carry the Midland Bank Ltd name and symbol. The cheque is dated 28 December 1994.

The legal definition of a cheque as defined in the Bill of Exchange Act 1882 is 'A Bill of Exchange drawn on a banker payable on demand'.

The Bill of Exchange Act defines a bill of exchange which also includes cheques as 'an unconditional order in writing addressed by one person to another, signed by the person giving it, requiring the person to whom it is addressed to pay on demand, or at a fixed or determinable future time, a certain sum in money to or to the order of a specified person or bearer.' This definition is very important. Notice particularly the following points:

1   The order must be unconditional; a mere request to pay is not enough.
2   The order must be in writing; no special form is needed. In practice banks supply their customers with ready-printed cheque forms which are convenient and help both to identify customers and to prevent fraud. However there are no legal rules on the particular form required.
3   The order must be signed by the person making the order, known as the drawer.
4   The order must be addressed by one person to another, known as the drawee. Where a specific person is named the bill is known as an order bill. If the bill is made payable to bearer it is known as a bearer bill. Where the drawer draws a bill on his own account for payment to himself he is both drawer and payee, the person to whom payment is to be made.
5   The order must be payable on demand or at a fixed or determinable future time. If no time is specified, the bill is a demand bill payable immediately. If a special date was given or a determinable future time was specified, such as 20 days after date, the bill is a 'time' bill. A demand bill becomes overdue if not presented within a reasonable time. There is no specific limit for this;

banking practice is to treat cheques as overdue if not presented within six months. A 'time' bill is overdue if not presented on the date given or within three days.

In any cheque transaction there are always three parties:

1   The payee – the person in whose favour the cheque is drawn (here Conquest (Furniture) Co Ltd).
2   The drawer, the person ordering the payment. In this case there are two drawers, R. Spencer and M. Spencer, the two partners in the firm known as Brassingtons. The particular arrangement of this partnership is that there should be two signatories on cheques drawn on Brassingtons' account.
3   The drawee, that is the bank on which the cheque is drawn, in our case Midland Bank Ltd.

Exercise 1

Name the drawer, drawee and payee in the following transaction:

J. Fraser, who has an account with Barclays, pays £210.20 to Rock Base (Garage) Ltd, whose account is with National Westminster.

Cheques must always be payable on demand; this implies that a cheque can be presented to the bank for payment at any time. In fact, however, if a cheque is more than six months old, for example if Conquest Co Ltd presented it on 28 December 1995, it is unlikely to be paid. It would be returned by the bank, marked 'out of date'.

Cheques are usually written thus:

Pay Conquest (Furniture) Ltd or order.

'Or order' means that the Spencers have given instructions to their bank to pay Conquest or anyone else to whom Conquest transfers the cheque. Conquest may transfer the cheque to someone to pay one of its own debts.

If the payee (Conquest Co Ltd) of a cheque wishes to pass it to someone else then he merely endorses it, that is he signs his name on the back.

In the situation relating to Conquest and R. and M. Spencer, Midland Bank is the banker with whom R. and M. Spencer have their account. The relationship which exists between banker and customer is that of debtor and creditor. The bank (the Midland) is the debtor because it owes money to the Spencers, who are therefore creditors.

These days, most cheques are marked 'acc/payee' in the crossing, which means they can only be paid into the account of the payee (here Conquest (Furniture) Ltd).

When the partnership known as Brassingtons, that is R. and M. Spencer, opened an account with the Midland a *contract* was formed between the two parties: the Midland offered banking services which R. and M. Spencer would pay for by means of bank charges. This contract has certain implied conditions. First, Midland will preserve confidentiality in respect of the Spencers' account. This means that the Midland will never disclose information about the account to anyone but the holders, unless of course they are ordered to do so by a court.

The second duty imposed upon the bank is that it must honour (that is, pay out on) any cheque drawn on the Spencers' account, provided:

1 the account is in credit (there is enough money to meet the cheque for £25 430 in the Spencers' account) or
2 arrangements have been made for it to be overdrawn.

If the bank refused to pay out (dishonoured) a cheque and there were sufficient funds to meet it on the account on which it was drawn, then:

1 The bank might have to pay damages to the account holder. The damages would be for breach of contract because the bank has broken one of the implied conditions.
2 Where the cheque is returned to the payee (Conquest Co Ltd) with 'Refer to Drawer' (R/D) printed on it, the bank (the Midland) could be sued by the Spencers for libel. If a cheque is returned in this way this means that it has not been honoured and it can imply that the drawers (the Spencers) have not sufficient money in their account to pay the bill outstanding. This would be a suggestion of libel because:
    (a) it was communicated to a third party, Conquest;
    (b) it named the Spencers by implication since they were the drawers;
    (c) the statement 'R/D', which carries an innuendo that the business has no money, is capable of lowering 'the reputation of the Spencers in the eyes of right-thinking members of society'.

Where business is involved, as in this case, damages could be substantial. In the case of a private individual, damages would be nominal, that is of little value, but designed to make the point that the defendant (the bank) was in the wrong.

In *Pyke* v. *Hibernian Bank Ltd* (1950), it was held that the term 'refer to drawer' is capable of giving rise to a libel action. Claims in respect of dishonoured cheques, it was suggested in this case, could be brought in contract; that is, the bank was in breach of contract for failing to honour its obligations to its client.

The law relating to libel was dealt with in Chapter 12.

Exercise 2

1 Name the two implied duties existing between a bank and its customer.
2 For what could a bank be sued if it failed to keep one or both of the two duties?
3 If Wendy Palmer had an account with National Westminster, who would be the debtor and who the creditor?
4 What does 'refer to drawer' usually mean?
5 When a cheque is not paid by the drawee bank it is said to be what?
6 In the contract between a bank and its customer, what is the consideration?

A bank's authority to pay cheques may be terminated (ended) in various ways. In each of these circumstances the bank will 'stop' the cheque, which means, in effect, when it is presented it is not paid. The following example will help to illustrate this.

Janet Davison runs a small secretarial agency. She has a bank account with Barclays. Janet pays for a computer with a cheque for £1430.29 which she pays to IBL (Office Equipment) Ltd. Barclays' authority to pay this £1430.29 will be terminated in the following ways.

1 If Janet noticed a serious fault in the new computer on the day of delivery and on the day she paid the cheque to IBL she could, if she wished, 'stop' the cheque by instructing the bank in writing or orally that she did not wish them to pay out. Provided notice had been given before the cheque had been cleared (usually three days is the period for clearance) then the bank will not be entitled to debit Janet's account. In fact, if the bank does debit Janet's account by £1430.29, even though the notice has been given, the bank will be liable. It is quite clear that this should be so because the creditor (Janet) can instruct the debtor (the bank) to deal with her money as she wishes and the bank must follow her instructions. It must be remembered, however, that if the cheque is cleared (IBL has already been paid) then Janet could not 'stop' the cheque.

An oral or written countermand is sufficient, but it must reach the banker, as shown in *Curtice* v. *London City and Midland Bank* (1908). If a bank ignores the countermand and pays out on the cheque then it is entitled in law to recover the money from the payee unless the payee in good faith has changed his position and cannot pay. This was summed up in *Barclays Bank Ltd* v. *W. J. Sims & Sons and Cooke (Southern) Ltd* (1980).

2 If the bank (Barclays) receives notification of Janet's death then it will immediately 'freeze' her account: any cheques which have not been cleared will not be paid out on; that is, they will be stopped.

3 If a petition for a receiving order has been made then the account of the person against whom the petition has been made will be 'frozen' and all cheques still uncleared will be stopped.

4 If a receiving order has been made against the drawer (Janet) then the bank must stop all cheques. This is because, as you will remember, the official receiver becomes responsible for all Janet's financial affairs and therefore for her account.

Exercise 3

1 Explain the meaning of a 'stopped' cheque.
2 If a drawer wishes to prevent a cheque being paid, how can he do it?
3 Name the four ways in which a cheque may be stopped.
4 Read the following example and advise the drawer:
  Celia Bennett buys CD equipment from Delta Music Store for £256. She pays this by cheque drawn on Lloyds. Celia feels she shouldn't have spent the £256 and the next day takes the equipment back to the shop and demands a money refund. The shop refuses and Celia writes to the bank telling them to 'stop' the cheque. The bank does not act upon this and Celia's account is debited.

We have already seen that in the contractual relationship existing between the bank and the customer the bank owes to the customer certain implied duties.

Exercise 4

Try to remember the two duties.

The customer also owes the bank certain duties, which the following examples will illustrate.

Jane Smith works as a chief clerk for a firm of accountants. The firm owes her £45 for expenses she incurred on the firm's behalf. Jane is told to prepare a cheque for this amount and she completes the figures but not the words, as shown below:

PAY Jane Smith		or order
		£ 45.00.
		T LUCEY
		LUCEY & PARTNERS
		(Accountants)

The senior partner, Terry Lucey, signs the cheque and Jane fills in the words as 'two hundred and forty-five' and she puts a '2' in front of the figures

45. She then cashes the cheque. Mr Lucey is very angry and sacks Jane and tells the bank that they ought to meet the loss, because after all the bank had paid out the money. However, a duty owed by a customer is that 'he must indemnify the bank against authorised payments made on his behalf'. Terry had been negligent in not insisting that the words be completed; he had through this negligence facilitated the forgery; therefore he, not the bank, is liable. Terry or the partnership must 'indemnify' the bank and therefore the partnership account will be debited by £245.

The first duty owed by the customer, then, is that he must meet the loss if cheques are drawn on his authority when he has perhaps been negligent.

A customer owes a duty to his banker when drawing cheques to take care. Where he does not, the bank is not liable for money wrongly paid out. This is well illustrated by a decided case, *London Joint Stock Bank* v. *Macmillan and Arthur* (1918). In this case Macmillan signed a bearer cheque leaving the space to enter the amount in words blank, and entering £2 in the space for figures. Someone found the cheque which Macmillan had carelessly left lying around and wrote in the words 'one hundred and twenty pounds' and altered the figures accordingly. He presented the cheque and the bank cashed it. The bank was held entitled to debit Macmillan's account because of his negligence.

James Smith has an account with Lloyds and on several occasions his wife had forged his signature on a cheque and obtained cash from his account. She had admitted this to James but he decided to overlook it. Some months later, however, Mrs Smith decided to forge her husband's signature again on a cheque and she drew £250 from his account.

When James discovered this he rang the bank to say that, since they had allowed payment on a forged signature, the bank should stand to lose.

However the second duty owed by a customer to his bank is that he must take reasonable care when operating his account; if he has in the past known of his wife's dishonesty then he had a duty to disclose this to the bank, and if he fails to do so then he will not be able to deny the authenticity of the signature on the cheque. Therefore, in these circumstances, it is James who will lose, not Lloyds Bank.

It is important, however, to remember that a bank is not allowed to debit its customers' accounts in circumstances where the customer has not been negligent. This point is illustrated well in the next section, on crossed cheques.

Crossed cheques

If you have a bank account you will probably find that the cheques you have been issued have a crossing in the middle of them usually, for example,

                     | & Co. |

The meaning of a crossing is that the cheque cannot be cashed across the counter but must be paid into an account. Thus, if Fred Wingfield received a cheque from David Willis for £50 which was crossed, Fred could either pay it into his account or ask someone who had an account to pay him £50. Fred would need to endorse the cheque on the back and then the person receiving it for £50 could pay it into his account.

Usually, however, a cheque will be crossed with the words 'Account Payee' , or 'Account Payee' only:

This means that the cheque can only be paid into the account of the payee; for example:

> *Wendy Thomas (Fashions) Ltd, with an account at the Midland, receives a cheque for £75 from a customer, marked 'account/payee only'. One of Wendy's employees, Brenda, pays the cheque into her own account and her account at X bank is credited to the tune of £75. When Wendy finds out about this she sacks Brenda on the spot and tries to recover the £75 from X Bank.*

In fact X Bank is in the wrong because it did not have an account in the name of Wendy Thomas (Fashions) Ltd, and therefore it is liable to Wendy for £75.

The words 'acc/payee' were not recognised by the Bill of Exchange Act 1882 but are fully recognised by the 1992 Cheques Act which states clearly that such a cheque is only valid between payee (the person to whom the cheque is paid) and drawer (the person/organisation who has signed the cheque). No one else can obtain title to it.

17.2 Negotiable instruments

A cheque is normally regarded as a negotiable instrument. This means that, unless it is crossed 'Account Payee Only', it can be transferred from person to person, provided that it is endorsed in turn by each person transferring it. The person receiving the cheque finally can pay it in knowing that he has good title to it, that is he has a right to it. However cheques sometimes are marked 'Not Negotiable' and if this is the case it means that anyone who accepts it, other than the payee, takes a risk. If the drawer refuses to honour the cheque then there is nothing the holder can do because it has been marked 'not negotiable'; for example:

> In *Wilson* v. *Pickering* (1946), Wilson drew a cheque marked 'not negotiable' and left it for his clerk to complete the name of the payee and the amount. The

clerk, who was in debt, inserted a much higher amount and gave it to one of his creditors, a Mr Pickering. It was held that the clerk had no title to the cheque, nor did Pickering and Wilson was not liable. The cheque was 'not negotiable'.

Frank Brown pays a cheque to Edith Owen for £200 marked 'Not Negotiable'. Edith leaves the cheque lying around and it is stolen; the thief gives it to John Smith in settlement of a debt but when John pays it in he finds that the bank refuses to pay out and, although he accepted it in good faith, there is nothing John can do.

Exercise 5

Read the following and explain the legal position of the person whose name is in italics.

1   *Michael Beresford* is a partner in a firm of wholesalers with an account with Barclays. He is late for an appointment and he signs five blank cheques to be completed by one of his clerks. The clerk, who is short of money, makes a cheque payable to herself for £150 and pays it into her account which, after three days, is credited.

2   *Jim Hough* knows that his son has on several occasions forged his signature. Jim leaves his cheque book lying around and his son completes a cheque made payable to himself and forges Jim's signature. The cheque is for £95 and Jim decides to sue his bank, Lloyds, for cashing the cheque.

3   *Ian Creedland* receives a cheque for £100 from his firm marked 'Account Payee Only'. Ian's account is with National Westminster, but the cheque is stolen and is paid into another bank by the thief, John Green. The other bank cashes the cheque in favour of John.

4   *Roy Goldstraw*, a sub-postmaster, is asked to cash a cheque for £100 marked 'Not Negotiable'. Roy agrees to do this but when he presents the cheque it is not honoured because it has in fact been stolen.

17.3   Protection against forged endorsements

Let us return to our original example in which R. and M. Spencer, operating as Brassingtons, made out a cheque for £25 430 in favour of Conquest (Furniture) Co Ltd. As you will remember, the cheque was drawn on the Midland Bank, known as the drawee or the paying banker. It is known as the paying banker because £25 430 will be paid from an account held with the bank. A paying banker is protected by the Bills of Exchange Act 1882 and the Cheques Act 1957.

The protection given to the paying bank is in connection with forged endorsements. You will remember that, unless a cheque is marked 'Account Payee Only', the payee can pass the cheque to someone else by signing his name on the back. It would be clearly unfair if the bank was made liable for forged endorsements because it would have no way of knowing whether the signature was valid or not. The law therefore provides that, where the bank pays the cheque in good faith and in the 'ordinary course of business', it cannot be made to meet the loss in respect of a stolen cheque and forged endorsement.

'In good faith' means without knowing that it was forged and 'in the ordinary course of business' means during normal banking hours.

A bank, can, however, be held liable where the drawer's name is forged and thus, if R. and M. Spencer's signatures were forged and the bank paid out on the cheque, it would stand to lose unless the bank could show that the account holders had been negligent.

In our example, Conquest has an account with Barclays and Barclays would be known as the collecting bankers. It happens sometimes that cheques which are stolen are paid into a bank. The bank will sometimes in good faith accept the cheque and pay it into the person's account and then collect from the paying banker. The Cheques Act 1957 protects the collecting banker provided he has not been negligent. Negligence could be assumed if:

1 the bank opened an account without taking up references;
2 cheques are collected from a customer but the cheque is drawn in favour of the customer's employee. Thus a bank collecting this cheque drawn in favour of Conquest Co Ltd and paying it into an employee's account would not be protected;
3 a cheque marked 'Account Payee Only' had been paid into an account other than that of the payee.

Exercise 6

Explain the legal position of the bank concerned in the following cases.

1 Michael Field pays one of his employees, Bob Price, by means of a cheque for £150 drawn on the Midland. Bob puts the cheque into his wallet, which is subsequently stolen. The thief endorses the cheque and presents it for payment. The cheque is honoured by the Midland.
2 Barclays pays out on four cheques despite the fact that the signature of the drawer has been forged.
3 National Westminster opens an account for Robert Davies without taking up references. Robert is in fact engaged in fraud and pays 20 cheques which he has stolen into his account. The drawers of the cheques in question decide to sue the bank.

--- Exercise 7 ---

Answer the following questions, which are based upon this chapter. Check your answers and, if you have not understood any aspects of this chapter, read over that part of the chapter again.

1   A cheque dated 6 June 1994 presented on 30 January 1995 will be paid: true or false?
2   Name the two duties owed by a bank to its customers.
3   If a cheque is not honoured by a bank and sent back to the payee marked 'refer to drawer', the drawer could sue the bank in two respects. Name these.
4   If a bank pays out a cheque which has been stopped by the drawer it may be liable for the money paid: true or false?
5   If a drawer is negligent in handling his account and an employee misuses a cheque the bank is liable: true or false?
6   A crossed cheque marked 'Account Payee Only' can be endorsed and paid into any account: true or false?
7   If Bill Brown unknowingly receives a stolen cheque which is negotiable and pays it into his own account, he receives no good title to the cheque and the payee can claim on it: true or false?
8   Explain (a) the protection afforded to a paying bank, (b) the protection afforded to a collecting bank.

18 Business property (I): buying and owning a business

18.1 Buying a business

Reg Pullin has been employed for a number of years in a company producing and printing cardboard containers. As a result of a serious downturn in business, and following a takeover, the company decides to shed staff and, along with a number of colleagues, Reg is offered valuable redundancy terms which he decides, following a discussion with his wife, Lynne, to accept. About the same time he sees the following advertisement in a newspaper.

Village newsagent/general store and Post Office in pleasant Kent village. Attractive detached property with 4 bedrooms (1 en-suite), 2 reception rooms, bathroom, cloakroom. Full gas central heating and part double-glazed. Lawned garden.

Takings per week £2400, plus a post office salary of £12 000 per annum.

Price £160 000

Reg is very interested as he has always wanted his own business and he would like to live near his sister and brother-in-law, who live in Kent. He makes an offer of £158 000 which is accepted by the owners, Mr and Mrs Paul Reaney, 'subject to contract'. Reg sells his own house for £88 000, uses his redundancy money of £32 000 and seeks a mortgage from the Midland Bank of £38 000.

The £158 000 which Reg has agreed to pay is really made up of two elements: the property itself, say, £90 000, and the business itself, with what is sometimes called the 'goodwill', say, £68 000.

In this section we will be looking at the various ways a business is acquired and owned. For example, in this situation Mr and Mrs Reaney could have retained the property and just sold the business, in which case Reg would have to pay a rent. However the Reaneys have decided to sell the property (freehold) and the business for £158 000. This means that, on completion, Reg will own the property and the business. The Reaneys are selling two things: the property at £90 000 and the business at £68 000.

How, then, can the property and business ownership pass from Mr and Mrs Reaney to Reg? It is most likely that both parties will employ the services of a solicitor and, although the property and the business will be sold simultaneously, for simplicity's sake it might be better if we dealt with the two transactions separately.

Property

This is being sold for £90 000 and Reg's solicitor would first raise what are called 'preliminary enquiries'; these are just questions to the solicitor acting for Mr and Mrs Reaney about the property in question, which we will describe as 24 Ramsgate Road, Teynsham, Kent. At the same time Reg's solicitor would make what are called 'local searches' with the local authority. These local authority searches are an attempt to ensure that no plans are being made by the local authority which might affect the property, such as the building of a road.

When satisfactory replies are received from both the seller's (vendor's) solicitor and the local authority, Reg's solicitor will ask Reg to sign the contract which has been sent to him by the vendor's solicitor. Reg's solicitor will send the signed contract with a 10 per cent deposit, that is £9000, to Mr and Mrs Reaney's solicitor, and he should receive back an identical contract signed by Paul and Anne Reaney. This process is known as 'exchange of contracts' and this means that Reg is legally bound to buy and Paul and Anne must sell. Until an exchange of contracts is made either buyer (Reg) or seller (Paul and Anne) may pull out of the deal. Once contracts are exchanged then both buyer and seller are legally bound. Remember that Reg bought the property 'subject to contract', this is the usual case with the purchase of property. The agreement is not binding until the contract, which must be in writing, is signed.

If the buyer (Reg) decided not to proceed following exchange of contracts, he would lose his deposit. If Paul and Anne decided against completing the sale even though they have exchanged contracts, they could be sued for damages and, in some circumstances, the court might award 'specific performance', that is make Paul and Anne complete their side of the agreement.

An example of the sort of contract used by solicitors is shown on pp. 250–2. This is a standard form and the first and final pages of a four page contract have been reproduced. The contract has been completed to refer to the vendors and buyers in our example. Pages 2 and 3 contain standard conditions. Several of these conditions are shown as examples.

Exchange of contracts to completion.

Reg's solicitor must now do five things.

1 He must satisfy himself that Paul and Anne Reaney really own the land they are selling and he will do this by closely examining copies of all the documents relating to the property. The copies will have been supplied to him by the solicitor acting for the Reaneys.

2 Reg's solicitor will have received from the vendor's solicitor what are called office copies. Kent is an area where most of the properties are registered and details are kept at the nearest land registry office which, in the case of Kent, is at Tunbridge Wells. The office copies of properties consist of three registers:

(a) the property register, which describes the property and will have with it a plan describing its location;

(b) a proprietor register, which describes how the property is owned. In our example it would state that Paul and Anne Reaney owned the property jointly in 'fee simple absolute in possession', which means that it is freehold, it lasts indefinitely, can be inherited and left by one person to anyone else in his/her will;

(c) a charges register, which shows any charges on the property, the most usual of which is a mortgage. If Mr and Mrs Reaney still owed money to, for example, the Leicester Alliance Building Society, this fact, with only the original amount of advance, would be shown.

Reg's solicitor would check or 'search', as it is often called, by ensuring that the copies he has received agree with the actual at the land registry. This is really a check to ensure that the Reaneys have not made any changes. Once this check is made, then for a period of time, usually two weeks, the register is protected: that is, no changes can be made until completion.

3 Reg's solicitor would also check the Land Searches Register at Plymouth to ensure that the Reaneys are not bankrupt (see Chapter 16) because, if that were so, they could not sell the property themselves. However it is likely that the search would be returned with the statement 'no subsisting entries'. This would mean that the Reaneys were not bankrupt and, if everything else is in order, the solicitor can proceed.

4 You will remember that Reg is buying the property with the aid of a mortgage of £38 000 and it will be necessary for Reg's solicitor to draw up a mortgage deed, which is a document which creates a mortgage and means that the bank advancing the money has a right to the property should Reg default in his monthly payments.

5 Finally, Reg's solicitor will draw up a transfer which is a document signed as a deed, when signed by both parties, that is Paul and Anne Reaney, the vendors, and Reg, the purchaser, the transfer transfers the property. A copy of a transfer document is shown on pages 253 and 254.

Reg now owns the property, which is mortgaged to a bank, and he will have to pay monthly instalments to the bank for 15 years. Reg is known as the mortgagor and the bank the mortgagee.

AGREEMENT

(Incorporating the Standard Conditions of Sale (Second Edition))

Agreement date : 19th OCTOBER 1994.

Seller : PAUL EDWARD REANEY and
ANNE JOAN REANEY

Buyer : REGINALD FREDERICK PULLIN and
LYNNE MARGARET PULLIN.

Property
(freehold/leasehold) : FREEHOLD
24 RAMSGATE ROAD
TEYNSHAM
Kent.

Root of title/Title Number : K478104

Incumbrances on the Property : /

Seller sells as : BENEFICIAL OWNERS

Completion date : 9th December 1994

Contract rate : 4% ABOVE BASE RATE.

Purchase price : £90,000

Deposit : £9,000

Amount payable for chattels : /

Balance : £81,000

The Seller will sell and the Buyer will buy the Property for the Purchase price.
The Agreement continues on the back page.

WARNING	Signed
This is a formal document, designed to create legal rights and legal obligations. Take advice before using it.	P. A Reaney. a J. Reaney. Seller/~~Buyer~~

SPECIAL CONDITIONS

1. (a) This Agreement incorporates the Standard Conditions of Sale (Second Edition). Where there is a conflict between those Conditions and this Agreement, this Agreement prevails.

    (b) Terms used or defined in this Agreement have the same meaning when used in the Conditions.

2. The Property is sold subject to the Incumbrances on the Property and the Buyer will raise no requisitions on them.

3. The chattels on the Property and set out on any attached list are included in the sale.

4. The Property is sold with vacant possession on completion.

(or) 4. The Property is sold subject to the following leases or tenancies:

Seller's Solicitors   :   *STAUNTONS, High Street Rochester Kent Me1 4XL.*

Buyer's Solicitors   :   *LANSDOWNES Meadow Street Bristol BS2 4QJ*

STANDARD CONDITIONS OF SALE (SECOND EDITION)

NATIONAL CONDITIONS OF SALE 22nd EDITION
LAW SOCIETY'S CONDITION OF SALE 1992

1.   General

1.1   Definitions

1.1.1   In these conditions:
(a) 'accrued interest' means:
   (i) if money has been placed on deposit or in a building society share account, the interest actually earned
   (ii) otherwise, the interest which might reasonably have been earned by depositing the money at interest on seven days' notice of withdrawal with a clearing bank less, in either case, any proper charges for handling the money
(b) 'agreement' means the contractual document which incorporates these conditions, with or without amendment
(c) 'banker's draft' means a draft drawn by and on a clearing bank
(d) 'clearing bank' means a bank which is a member of CHAPS and Town Clearing Company Limited
(e) 'completion date', unless defined in the agreement, has the meaning given in conditions 6.1.1.
(f) 'contract' means the bargain between the seller and the buyer of which these conditions, with or without amendment, form part
(g) 'contract rate', unless defined in the agreement, is the Law Society's interest rate from time to time in force
(h) 'lease' includes sub-lease, tenancy and agreement for a lease or sub-lease
(i) 'notice to complete' means a notice requiring completion of the contract in accordance with condition 6
(j) 'public requirement' means any notice, order or proposal given or made (whether before or after the date of the contract) by a body acting on statutory authority
(k) 'requisition' includes objection
(l) 'solicitor' includes barrister, duly certificated notary public, recognised licensed conveyancer and recognised body under sections 9 or 32 of the Administration of Justice Act 1985
(m) 'transfer' includes conveyance and assignment
(n) 'working day' means any day from Monday to Friday (inclusive) which is not Christmas Day, Good Friday or a statutory Bank Holiday

1.1.2.   When used in these conditions the terms 'absolute title' and 'office copies' have the special meanings given to them by the Land Registration Act 1925

Transfer of Whole to Joint Proprietors (1)	HM Land Registry Land Registration Acts 1925 to 1986	Form 19(JP (Rules 98 or 115 Lar Registration Rules. 192:

Stamp pursuant to section 28 of the Finance Act, 1931, to be impressed here.	When the transfer attracts Inland Revenue duty, the stamps should be impressed here before lodging the transfer for registration.

(1) For a transfer to a sole proprietor use printed form 19.

County and district (or London borough) } **Thanet Kent.**

Title number(s) **K478104**

Property **24 RAMSGATE ROAD TEYNSHAM KENT**

Date **9ᵗ DECEMBER 1994** In consideration of **Ninety Thousand pounds**

(2) Delete the words in italics if not required.

pounds (£ **90,000**) *receipt of which is acknowledged* (2)

(3) In BLOCK LETTERS enter the full name(s) postal address(es) (including postcode) and occupation(s) of the proprietor(s) of the land.

I/We (3) **PAUL EDWARD REANEY and ANNE JOAN REANEY OF 24 RAMSGATE ROAD TEYNSHAM KENT**

as beneficial owners(4) transfer to

(4) If desired or otherwise as the case may be (see rules 76 and 77).

(5) In BLOCK LETTERS enter the full name(s) postal address(es) (including postcode) and occupation(s) of the transferee(s) for entry in the register.

(5) **REGINALD FREDERICK PULLIN (Clerk) and LYNNE MARGARET PULLIN (School Assistant) of 92 QUEENSDOWN GARDENS, BRISLINGTON BRISTOL**

(6) Enter any special clause here.

(7) A transfer for charitable purposes should follow form 36 in the schedule to the Land Registration Rules 1925 (see rules 121 and 122).

the land comprised in the title(s) above referred to (6) (7)

(8) Delete the inappropriate alternative.

(9) If a certificate of value for the purposes of the Stamp Act, 1891, and amending Acts is not required delete this paragraph.

(10) This transfer must be executed by the transferees as well as the transferor(s).

The transferees declare that the survivor of them(8) ___can___ give a valid receipt for capital money arising on a disposition of the land.   cannot

(9) *It is hereby certified that the transaction hereby effected does not form part of a larger transaction or series of transactions in respect of which the amount or value or aggregate amount or value of the consideration exceeds £* 90,000.00 ....

(10) Signed as a deed by

....P.A. Reaney...........................

in the presence of

Name of Witness ..W. Jones........ Signature ..J.Jones......

Address ...14. Margate. Street. Broadstairs. CT.10. 7N.

Occupation .Secretary.................

(10) Signed as a deed by

....A.S. Reaney;..............

in the presence of

Name of Witness ..W. Jones........ Signature ..J.Jones..

Address 14. Margate. Street. Broadstairs. CT.10. 7N.J.

Occupation .Secretary.

(10) Signed as a deed by

..R.F. Pullin.............

in the presence of

Name of Witness .M. DAVISON....... Signature .M. Davison.....

Address 14. BRIDGE STREET. SOUNDWELL. BRISTOL. BS9. 4TZ.

Occupation .Computer. Programmer.............

(10) Signed as a deed by

..L. M. Pullin.....

in the presence of

Name of Witness .M. DAVISON....... Signature .M. Davison....

Address 14. BRIDGE STREET. SOUNDWELL. BRISTOL. BS9. 4TZ.

Occupation .Computer. Programmer.

LR Form 19JP   Stat-Plus Limited, Stat-Plus House, Greenlea Park, Prince George's Road, London SW19 2PU Tel. 081-646 5500 *revised July 1990*

STAT-PLUS Stat-Plus Group PLC

Exercise 1

1 The vendor is not legally obliged to sell property until contracts are exchanged: true or false?
2 Name one reason why the purchaser's solicitor makes a search in the Land Registry.
3 Name the document which transfers ownership of land.
4 If the document transferring land is not signed, as a deed it has no legal significance: true or false?
5 Name the mortgagor and the mortgagee in the following circumstances: Colin Elderson buys a DIY shop with the aid of a mortgage from Commercial Credit Co Ltd.

The property known as 24 Ramsgate Road, Teynsham, is now owned by Reg, although in the transfer he would have had to pay a government tax known as stamp duty. On £90 000 the current rate is 1 per cent, which means Reg would have paid £900. To show that this has been paid the transfer, which will remain with the mortgage until Reg has paid off the loan, will be stamped with an official government stamp.

The business

At the same time as the property is transferred, the Reaneys sell the business. The cost of this was £68 000. This really is the price put on the business by the Reaneys and of course will depend upon how successful the business is. Reg's solicitor will draw up a document known as an 'assignment' which, when signed as a deed, transfers (assigns) the business from Paul and Anne Reaney to Reg. What is being sold is sometimes known as the 'goodwill' of the business. Again the government charge a stamp duty on an assignment which on £68 000 is at present 1 per cent, that is £680. The evidence of the payment is stamped on the assignment. Reg now owns both the property and the business and usually at the same time he buys the stock at cost. Many commercial properties are transferred on a Monday so that the vendor and purchaser can spend the weekend stocktaking. This will allow them to calculate a price for the stock, let us say £10 000. This is a normal sale and does not carry any stamp duty.

Reg is anxious that Mr and Mrs Reaney do not sell the business to him and then start up again nearby because this could seriously affect the business. It is usual, therefore, for the purchaser of a business to require the vendor to sign a covenant that the vendor will not open up a similar business for three years within a three-mile radius of the business they have sold. Courts will, if they regard such a clause as reasonable, enforce it against the vendor. If, however, a purchaser inserts a clause which is too restrictive, for example not to start a business for ten years in Kent, then this would not be enforced; since it could not be enforced the vendors Mr and Mrs Reaney could open up a similar business next door. It is important that a buyer of a business seeks legal advice before drawing up a covenant of this type to make sure it is not too wide. This particular aspect was dealt with more fully in Chapter 6.

Exercise 2

1 How can one check that stamp duty has been paid?
2 Name the document which transfers ownership of a business.
3 The value of stock sold at completion carries stamp duty: true or false?
4 Lewis Williams buys a milk round from Unicorn Dairies Ltd. He requires the sellers to sign a document that they will not deliver milk within a 40-mile radius for ten years. Unicorn sign this but then start competing with Lewis directly. Lewis seeks your advice.

Tenancy of business property

Instead of selling the property, Mr and Mrs Reaney could lease (let) the property and sell the business. The selling of the business would be the same as described above. An assignment would be drawn up transferring the business for £68 000. The property could be leased at a rental, let us say £12 000 per annum for a period of 20 years. The lease would be granted to Reg by means of a document known as a lease which again would need to be signed as a deed. The property would still be owned by Paul and Anne Reaney and if Reg subsequently decided to sell the business he would sell the business by means of an assignment and, provided Paul and Anne were in agreement, he could assign the lease to the buyer.

One of the problems in taking out a lease is that, if the lessee, as Reg would be called, built up a successful business, Paul and Anne Reaney might not renew the lease when it expired in 20 years. This would clearly be unfair to someone like Reg who had worked hard to develop a good business. Fortunately tenants such as Reg are given protection by the Landlord and Tenant Act 1954 which allows tenants who are operating businesses to seek a renewal of their lease, and the courts will often assist in setting the terms of the renewed lease. Landlords (Paul and Anne) can get tenants out only under strictly prescribed conditions. All the following three conditions must exist:

1 the tenant has been unsuitable;
2 a landlord has owned the property for the last five years at least and wants the property for himself;
3 the landlord wishes to make an extensive redevelopment of the property in question.

Generally, however, the Landlord and Tenant Act gives good protection to a business tenant wishing to renew his lease.

Exercise 3

Answer the following questions, which are based upon this section. If you have any difficulty with any of the questions read the section again.

1 Susan Rownes (a hair stylist) buys a hairdressing salon from a firm owned by June Greatorex. Susan obtains a covenant in which the vendor (June) agrees not to work as a hairdresser within a two-mile radius of the shop and for three years. After a year the vendor starts a hairdressing business down the road. Can Susan do anything about this?

2 If a business tenant wished to sell his business he would transfer the lease by means of a document known as what?

3 Name the Act which protects a business tenant from eviction at the end of the lease.

4 Elizabeth Moore is a wealthy landlady who has owned four shops for about three years and which are on lease. One of the shops is run by Franklin Welch, who has a thriving small self-service store. The lease has only six months to run and Elizabeth gives Franklin notice that she wishes the shop for herself and that she has bought adjoining property and wishes to make an extensive development. Is Franklin at risk?

19 Business property (II): patents, copyright and data protection

In the last chapter we looked at business property in respect of the business itself. In this chapter we will be looking at what has been called ' intellectual' property of a business: that is, a product or process that is marketable, such as an invention, a new process, a book, a record or a piece of software. We will also look at the subject of data protection.

19.1 Patents, registered designs and trademarks

John Honeywell works for a small firm operating as a partnership. The firm is a firm of central heating engineers. John has had no formal training but he is quick and has learned a lot on the job. He discovers a very simple device which appears to have considerable potential for fuel saving. In fact simple tests reveal that the device has a potential for yielding a 20 per cent saving in costs. The two partners, Peter May and Ashok Patel, suggest that John joins them in the partnership and, realising that this is a very valuable invention, also advise that John gets the invention patented.

It seems fair that someone who invents a product ought to gain some benefit therefrom and the law, as set out in the Copyright, Design and Patents Act, 1988 does try to do this. Let us for a moment look at the procedure.

The law, as set out in an earlier Act, the Patents Act of 1977, makes it quite clear that an invention made by an employee in the course of his work belongs to the employer but that one made in his spare time belongs to the employee.

In *Electrolux Ltd* v. *Hudson* (1977) it was made quite clear that an invention made by an employee in his own time belonged to him and he had every right to assign if he wished to a company other than the one employing him.

Let us assume that John is very happy to patent his invention through the firm, known as EKHE (East Kent Heating Engineers). The stages are as follows:

1   An application is made to the Patent Office, in either London or Newport. The application must be accompanied by a full specification.
2   The application is examined in detail; because of the pressure on the Patent Office, the decision is likely to take some time.

3   The office will ascertain that the invention is within the categories allowed; that is to say that it is not something obvious that many people would know about anyway. The 1988 Act does not lay down any definition of an 'invention' but it would seem to encompass a product, article, material apparatus or process. The 1977 Act laid down that discoveries would be excluded, so, if you 'discovered' some natural phenomenon like the law of gravity, this would be excluded.

4   The office would then search its records to ensure that no other like invention has been published and patented. The Comptroller-General maintains a register of patents.

5   The office then publishes the invention, giving anyone the right to raise objections. For example, another company may say that they have been using an identical device for ten years and it is not new. There is a procedure for listening to appeals of this sort.

6   If there is no opposition or if the opposition is not upheld at the office, then provided all is well the Patent Office will give EKHE a 20 year right which must be renewed annually on payment of a fee which increases with the age of the patent.

What EKHE have gained is a monopoly in the use of the invention for that period or the right to allow others to use it subject to terms which EKHE set. EKHE can give up their patent rights by assigning them to someone else. If, for example, the firm decided to sell the business, they could at a price assign the patent and the new firm or company could acquire the rights.

What rights does a patent holder have? Consider the following:

Severnside Heating Engineering Ltd is a small Bristol company engaged in the same work as EKHE. They acquire details of the device and copy it and use it without reference to EKHE. EKHE hear of this and take action to prevent this.

The remedy is with the Patents County Court, established by the 1988 Act, which replaced in the main jurisdiction of the Patents Court within the Chancery Division. EKHE would seek damages and also an injunction preventing the Bristol company from using the invention. However the patent law does not apply outside the UK and a German firm could use the device, though, of course, not in the UK. Under the European patent convention which came into force in 1978, an applicant can apply to the European Patent Office in Munich designating those European countries he wants included in a 'bundle of national patents'. The national laws of each signatory nation to this convention mean that a European patent designating that country should be treated as a national patent. Thus, if EKHE applied to Munich and its application was accepted and it named Germany, a German firm could not use the invention in Germany.

One of the problems with inventions made by employees in the past has been there has been no safeguard to ensure that they are remunerated adequately. The 1977 Act ensures that, where the invention turns out to be of outstanding value to the employer, the Comptroller-General or the court can award the employee compensation.

A contract of employment which seeks to limit the rights of employees in respect of inventions is unenforceable in court. In other words, an employee cannot by agreeing to terms 'sign away' his rights, as it were. In our example, John was quite happy to join the partnership but, if the two other partners had tried to deprive him of some of the benefits of his invention, at least he would have been afforded some protection under the 1977 Act.

Designs

Designs may also be registered at the Patents Office; the law is laid down in the Registered Designs Act of 1949 and the 1988 Copyright, Design and Patents Act. The following example may help to explain the law.

Rosemary Stevens has completed a degree in art and design and she sets herself up as a freelance designer. She is very talented and produces a design for chinaware which is taken up by a leading chinaware manufacturer, Trent Potteries Plc. Anxious to protect their design, they decide to register it. Rosemary is paid a fee and she agrees to accept a percentage of profits from the sale of goods with this design.

Trent would apply to the Patents Office to have the design registered and, if agreed following a similar procedure to that explained above, protection would be given for five years, extendable up to a period of 25 years under the 1988 Act. If another company tried to use the design then Trent could sue them in the Patents Court and, if successful, gain damages and an injunction. The damages will often amount to the value of the profit gained by the offending business by using the invention on contravention of the patent law. In *Dawson* v. *Palter* (1984) the defendant had to pay as damages the profit he had earned.

There is also some protection under the 1988 Act against firms' drawings being copied – and therefore their designs. This is an automatic right known as 'new rights items'. The right need not be registered and gives a 25 year protection. Those items which relate to the fitting of an item are excluded. It excludes those items/parts such as produced by car manufacturers which they then claim must only be used for that particular make of car. This attempts to deny rights to other manufacturers who could easily copy the design and sell the product more cheaply. This exclusion does prevent what many regarded as a restrictive practice. In other words, a distinctive shape could be protected, but not the way it is fitted.

Exercise 1

1   How long may a patent last?
2   How may a patent be acquired by someone other than the inventor?

3   For what length of time must a patent be published to allow possible objections?
4   How is an employee who invents a valuable product protected?
5   What is the procedure for registering a design?
6   What court usually now hears cases of design or patent infringement?
7   What sort of 'new rights items' will not be protected?

Trademarks

When next you are drinking a glass of Mackeson's stout or Gilbey's gin, or if you are eating Kit-Kat for your break or maybe for your health taking a spoonful of Seven Seas cod liver oil, look at the bottle or container to see if you can spot the trademark. In each of the products mentioned the trademark is registered. Trademarks are registered on the A or B parts of the register. New products will be registered as a part B and only when they are more established can they be registered as A.

The protection afforded by A registrations is greater, in that companies or businesses improperly using the trademark have no defence, whereas in B there is the defence that the use of the mark did not mislead. A company which believes its trademark has been improperly used will seek the assistance of the court in getting an injunction to prevent the offending firm continuing the improper use. Trademarks are not only represented by logos but could in fact be names, such as Britvic, Formica or Hoover.

The 1984 Trademarks (Amendment) Act 1984 extended the trademark legislation to services. The Lloyds Bank black horse is very well known, as is THF, the Trust House Forte trademark.

Activity

See if you can find other examples of trademarks and whether they are registered.

See also if you can find some other examples of trademarks used in the service sector.

There is an interesting dispute between Coca-Cola and Sainsbury about the production of coca-cola in identical bottles by Sainsburys. Try to find out more about this.

(Coca-Cola tried in a 1985 application to have the distinctive shape of their bottles and containers registered as a mark. The application failed.)

We have already examined, in Chapter 12, the law relating to ' passing off'. If a business or company does not register its trademark, and many do not, they cannot sue for any infringement of the trademark but only on the tort of passing off, which has been shown to be more difficult.

19.2 Copyright

Producers of literary, dramatic, musical or artistic work are protected by the Copyright, Designs and Patents Act 1988. Protection is also given to sound recordings, film, and sound and television broadcasts. The following example may assist an understanding of the law as it applies to copyright.

> *New Music Discovery Co Ltd is a small but very prosperous and expanding company which has concentrated upon recording new music groups, often giving them a chance with their first recording. A number of top stars have been launched with the New Discovery label. The two directors of the company, Bob Bown and Toby Edwards, are well versed in the copyright law and they get each group or singer to sign an agreement which gives them a set commission on sales. Attracted by the success of the company, one of the employees, David Pryce, forms a partnership known as David Pryce Associates (Musical). David continues to work for New Music Discovery Ltd but takes home taped recordings which he records and makes his own records, which he sells under his own label. This proves a very lucrative business and begins to threaten New Music Discovery Co Ltd's sales and profits.*

The legal position is quite straightforward. When New Music Discovery Co Ltd negotiated with the singers and obtained their signatures which provided for a commission to the singers of 6.5 per cent of the value of the sales, in return the singers vested the copyright in New Music Discovery Co Ltd. Copyright under the 1988 Act lasts the lifetime of the author/producer/singer and 50 years following his/her death. The only way in which David Pryce Associates could produce a record from this source is by licence from New Music, which clearly was not the case.

New Music Discovery Co Ltd could sue David Pryce Associates for the infringement of the copyright and could obtain damages and an injunction.

Copyright for 50 years is also available for literary and dramatic works in addition to musical work. Thus it is an infringement of copyright to:

1 reproduce the work;
2 publish the work;
3 perform the work in public;
4 broadcast the work;
5 make any form of adaptation of the work;
6 allow it to be recorded for transmission to subscribers, for example through a video recording service.

Painters also can gain protection for their work through copyright and for artistic work it is an infringement of copyright to:

1   reproduce the work;
2   publish the work;
3   include the work in a TV broadcast.

A good deal of work is covered by copyright and before anyone attempts to copy or reproduce someone else's work it is always wise to see whether copyright is being infringed. Copying BBC material would certainly be an infringement because the British Broadcasting Corporation is entitled to 50 years' copyright on any television or sound broadcast. Copyright laws do not extend to a person's home and it is quite safe to reproduce material at home for home consumption. If this were not the case then people with video recorders would be breaking the law every time they made a recording of any television programme. However, if these recordings are made available to the public, copyright has been infringed. There are certain other exemptions possible but recently educational establishments have been shown that their activities are not beyond copyright. Oakham School in Leicestershire has had to pay extensive damages for copying sheet music which was covered by copyright.

Activity

Look at records or books to see if you can find statements expressing the copyright which exists.

A common form used in books is as follows: 'All rights reserved. No part of this publication may be reproduced or transmitted in any form or by any means including photocopying and recording without the written permission of the copyright holder, application for which should be addressed to the publisher. Such written permission must be obtained before any part of this publication is stored in a retrieval system of any nature.' If you look at the front of this book you will find a notice to this effect which protects the publisher.

The EU is attempting to harmonise the law regarding copyright and a directive about to be issued suggests raising the limit from 50 to 70 years. You should note that, unlike patents, designs and trademarks, there is no need to register a copyright.

The question often arises when a person is in employment and, for example, writes a book or produces a piece of music, whether the copyright belongs to the employer. The position is well summed up in what is quite an old case.

In *Stevenson, Jordan and Harrison Ltd* v. *Macdonald and Evans* (1952) the author sold to the publisher his manuscript on business management. It appeared that part of the work was based upon the author's public lectures and the other part he had done as a project for his employer. The employer claimed the copy*right*, but it was held that they could only restrain the publication of the part relating to the project.

This particular problem could often occur when a lecturer employed by a college uses his lecture notes to produce a book. Do they belong to the college or him/her? It seems that courts will interpret the law in relation to the extent to which the writing of the book or music was part of his/her contractual duties or was done in his/her own time. You can see it is quite hard to separate these two aspects.

Computer software

The 1988 Act, which has consolidated much of the law relating to patents, designs, trademarks and copyright, also followed the Copyright (Computer Software) Amendment Act of 1985, which extended the same protection to computer software producers as to producers of books. The following example will assist in explaining the law.

> *Rachel Tennant works as a computer manager for a large firm of accountants, whilst her sister-in-law, Audrey James, works in her own business as a solicitor employing four other solicitors and a number of administrative staff. Audrey is anxious to use the most up-to-date software for her business and consults Rachel, who recommends Microsoft Office and the Lotus 1-2-3 Organiser. Rachel tells her sister-in-law that it would be a waste of money buying the software and gets her a copy from her company which is copied onto the hard disc of the 10 486 PCs which Audrey's business has. One of the solicitors, Mr Morgan-John, aggrieved that he was not promoted to senior solicitor in the firm, writes to both Microsoft and Lotus pointing out that the firm is not licensed to use the software.*

Audrey must, of course, be aware that she is breaking the law since she is in breach of copyright. Both Microsoft and Lotus could sue Audrey and the result would be likely to be damages and an injunction restraining the use of the software. It is likely that the two companies would persuade Audrey to purchase the software and instal it legally, rather than sue her, but what they do would be a matter for the companies concerned.

It is, of course, quite easy to copy software and software producers do have a great deal of difficulty in detecting infringements and therefore in enforcing the law. The law is quite simple, however: if one uses software which is not licensed then one is infringing the copyright law.

Exercise 2

1 How long does copyright last?
2 What change is proposed by the European Union?

3   If an employee produces some work as part of his job, to whom does the copyright belong?
4   Is it legal to copy BBC productions?
5   Examine the following and advise whether you think the person in italics has infringed copyright.
    (a) *Mrs Linda Brazier* often works late at a local supermarket and, not wishing to miss her favourite programme, records ' Eastenders'.
    (b) *Modern Art Publications Ltd* has published a book of contemporary art, many of whose illustrations have been taken from art exhibitions across the country.
    (c) *Dr John Hartley* is writing a scientific article and he wants to use a diagram from a book. He writes to the publisher and he is given written permission.

19.3   Data protection

Credit Services Plc is a company which has been set up to collect information on behalf of client companies who may wish to know whether or not to grant credit facilities to individuals. Mark Lendley wants to buy a new car and needs to finance the purchase with a loan which he seeks from United Finance Ltd. United Finance Ltd, who keep data on all their customers following the completion of application forms, make an enquiry about Mark from Credit Services Plc and find that there have been a number of County Court debt proceedings against him. United Finance write to Mark regretting that they cannot fund the loan. Mark, who has a very well paid job, is angry and mystified as to why he has been refused.

It is a fairly common practice for companies such as Credit Services Plc to collect data on a computer which, for a fee, they will make available to companies who wish to find out information. This sort of situation is of course a threat to one's privacy, in that personal data of this type are available to applicants. Computers, of course, because of their ability to process large amounts of information, can increase the risks to one's private affairs.

It was for this reason that the Data Protection Act (DPA) 1984 was passed, though it did not become fully operational until 1987. The Act identified five terms, which we will explain by reference to our example:

1   *data*: data which is processed automatically – the data on Mark would come into this category;
2   *personal data*: data about an individual who is living and can be identified by name or indirectly by number – again Mark comes into this category;
3   *data user*: a person (or organisation) who holds the data and controls them. A company holding personal data on its staff or customers would be a data

user – thus United Finance Ltd is likely to hold data on its customers or potential customers and would be a data user;

4   *a computer bureau*: this holds data on behalf of data users – Credit Services Plc would come into this category;

5   *a data subject*: the person who is the subject of the data – Mark, in our example.

The DPA which brings the UK into line with Europe (in 1981 the UK became a signatory to the Council of European Convention on Data Protection).

It is necessary for all data users or computer bureaux to register with the Data Protection Register using DPR 1 (long form) or DPR 4 (short form) – suitable for small businesses. The form must be accompanied by a fee, currently £75. Successful registrations are valid for three years. The application must contain details as follows:

1   name and address of the data user,
2   nature of the data held and the purposes for which they are held,
3   sources from which data are obtained,
4   persons to whom data are disclosed,
5   transfer of data overseas,
6   address/es to which requests for access to the data might be made.

Firms using data just for payroll purposes do not need to register. Other data users must by law register and then are subject to a number of data protection principles, including the rights of individuals to be informed that data exist on them and that, at reasonable cost, they can gain access to it.

___ **Activity** _____

The Office of the Data Protection Registrar publishes a series of guidelines and guidance notes. These are available from the Data Protection Registrar, Wycliffe House, Water Lane, Wilmslow, Cheshire SK9 5AX.
Try to get a copy of these documents and identify the eight principles in the Act.

The Data Protection Registrar can:

1   refuse applications for registration (an appeal against a decision can be made to the Data Protection Tribunal);
2   serve an enforcement notice requiring compliance with the Act;
3   serve a deregistration notice;
4   serve a prohibition of transfer notice which prohibits transfer of the data abroad;
5   apply to a circuit judge (see Chapter 1) to get a warrant to enter and search premises.

The DPA gives important rights to data subjects like Mark Lendley:

1 He can gain access to his personal data by submitting a written application and sending a fee, which must not be more than £10. The information must be sent within 40 days.
2 If the data subject, Mark, suffers damage because of an inaccurate entry, he may be entitled to compensation. For example, if, because of wrong information supplied by Credit Services Plc, Mark had to get a loan from a more expensive source, he might be compensated. In addition Mark can apply to the court to get an order to rectify or erase the error.
3 If the data are lost or sent to an unauthorised person or company, then again Mark may be able to claim compensation.

Computer misuse

The Computer Misuse Act 1990 establishes three new offences:

1 unauthorised access to computer material – this is to criminalise the activities of 'hackers', either external or internal, who illegally gain access to a computer. The offence is triable summarily and subject to a maximum of a £5000 fine or 6 months' imprisonment;
2 unauthorised access with the intention to commit or facilitate a further offence. This is triable by a Magistrates' or Crown Court;
3 unauthorised modification of computer material. This offence is subject to a maximum prison sentence of five years and an unlimited fine. It is triable at either Magistrates' or Crown Court.

Exercise 3

1 List the protection given to data subjects under the DPA 1984.
2 What data can a company collect not subject to the DPA?
3 What three offences were created by the Computer Misuse Act 1990?
4 What steps can a data user take if the Registrar refuses his application for registration?

⟨20⟩ Review

We have now covered a number of important business law topics. However, in an introductory book of this sort, it is not possible to deal with these topics in any great detail. You may be interested in learning about more business law or you may be interested in learning more about one or two particular topics. There are many excellent business law books available and at the end of this volume there is a list of books which cover the topics more thoroughly.

This chapter is intended as a review of the various business law topics that have been dealt with in other chapters. It consists of a number of review exercises. Try to do these exercises without looking back at the relevant chapter or section. If you find you do have difficulty with any of them, then refer to the text. At the end of each set of review exercises there is the chapter number which indicates the part of the book which deals with the topic which is the subject of the exercises in question.

Exercise 1

1 For each of the examples outlined below say: (a) whether it is civil or criminal law; (b) what court is likely to hear the case.
  (i)   Mrs Gardener has been convicted by magistrates on a charge of drinking and driving; she decides to appeal.
  (ii) Michael Pavey refuses to sell his house, value £100 000, to a buyer despite the fact that contracts have been exchanged.
  (iii) Jean Mitchell is injured while coming down the stairs of the college where she works. Her solicitor advises her to claim £100 damages.
  (iv) The Inland Revenue has successfully prosecuted a wealthy business man for tax evasion. Such, however, is the importance of the case that it is heard on appeal in the highest court in the land.
2 Name four civil courts.
3 Name four criminal courts.
4 What does 'triable either way' mean?
5 What do you understand by the 'small claims court'?
6 Give three examples of 'tribunals'.
7 What is the name of the European Court?
8 How many judges has this court and where does it meet?

Reference: Chapter 1

___ **Exercise 2** ___

1 Why is a statutory instrument referred to as 'delegated legislation'?
2 Give another example of delegated legislation.
3 Name three rules that judges might use in interpreting Acts of Parliament.
4 What does the term '*ratio decidendi*' mean and why is it important in the UK legal system?
5 Why is *C (a minor)* v. *Director of Public Prosecutions* (1994) such an important case?
6 In European Community law, give an example of secondary legislation.
7 What has to be proved to establish a custom in English Law?
8 Explain the term '*ultra vires*'.

Reference: Chapter 2

___ **Exercise 3** ___

1 What change took place in English law as a result of the Commercial Agents (Council Directive) Regulations 1993?
2 What principle exists in the European article 48?
3 In his application for a higher degree course in Belgium, Ted Westlake indicates he has a B.Sc with honours in physics. The university refuse him a place, saying they do not recognise English degrees. Is the university acting illegally?
4 Decisions of the European Court of Justice are binding on English Courts: true or false?
5 If France, Germany, Italy and the UK vote against a European Union proposal, it does not become law: true or false?

Reference: Chapter 3

___ **Exercise 4** ___

1 All Queen's Bench Division cases begin with what?.
2 What do you understand by the term 'discovery process' as used in relation to civil cases?
3 What is a 'garnishee order'?
4 In County Court actions, what are interlocutory or preliminary proceedings?
5 What happens if a debtor does not reply within 14 days of a County Court summons?
6 What do you understand is the situation where a County Court bailiff places a 'lien' on goods?

7 What is a stipendiary magistrate?

8 Are both barristers and solicitors liable for negligence?

9 Who in the English legal system is head of the courts and Speaker of the House of Lords?

10 What issue was raised in the article, 'A Law unto Himself'?

Reference: Chapter 4

___ **Exercise 5** _____

1 Why are the following *not* legally binding contracts? In each case state the element which is missing.

(a)   David Stuart is writing a book and he offers his wife £50 if she will do the typing for him.

(b)   Michael agrees to buy a suit from Easiwear priced at only £12.50; the salesman, who has priced it wrongly, refuses to sell.

(c)   Tony Bendrey accepts a post as foreman motor mechanic with Super Motors Ltd but demands £250 per week, not the advertised wage of £220.

(d)   Andrew Martin (aged 14) signs a complicated hire-purchase agreement to purchase a new cycle.

(e)   Under threat of violence, Mrs Ward sells her seventeenth-century house, worth £250 000, for £55 000.

(f)   Brian Webster agrees to work as hard as possible if he gets a rise of £30 per week.

2 If an offeror agrees to keep an offer open to an offeree for three days then he (the offeror) is bound by his promise: true or false?

3 Name three ways in which an offer can come to an end.

4 Under what circumstances will a promise of a gift be enforced?

5 Name the five rules of consideration.

6 A boy of 16 has, in English law, full contractual capacity: true or false?

7 Stanley Oldham enters into a verbal credit agreement with a garage to buy a motorcar for £12 500. Stanley defaults on payment and the garage decides to sue him. Does the garage have a good case?

8 Explain the three circumstances where *consensus ad idem* may not exist.

Reference: Chapter 5

___ **Exercise 6** _____

1 Give an example of an Act of Parliament which provides for implied terms in a contract of sale.

2 Terms and conditions which are written are known as implied terms: true or false?

3 Explain the difference between a condition and a warranty in a contract.

4 Do you think the following contract is breached?

Computer Power Ltd agree to deliver a mini-computer, together with various software packages, to Safe Sure Insurance Co. On 31 August 1994. The delivery takes place on time but one item of software is delivered three days late, on 3 September 1994.

5 Explain to the proprietor the significance of the notice below:
   M. & G. (Groceries) Ltd cannot accept liability for loss or damage to customers' property while they are shopping in this store. Nor can the company be liable for personal injury to customers.
6 Name four ways in which contracts may be discharged.
7 Specific performance is always available to a plaintiff in a breach of contract case: true or false?

Reference: Chapter 6

Exercise 7

1 Contracts of employment must always be in writing to make them valid: true or false?
2 The Employment Protection (Consolidation) Act 1978 lays down that a statement must be given to an employee within how many weeks of his employment?
3 Is the following situation legal, and if not why not?

Kanwar Singh applies for a job as a driver with United Haulage Co but is turned down because company policy does not allow the employment of foreigners.

4 List the four terms which are implied in a contract of employment in respect of the employee.
5 List three of the terms which exist in a contract of employment in respect of the employer.
6 Explain the legal position of Dual Accounting Services Ltd in the following situation:

Alex Hall is an accountant with Dual Accounting Services Ltd. He has a poor record in terms both of attendence and of the accuracy of his work. He applies for a job as chief accountant with an engineering firm and, on the strength of a good reference from Dual Accounting Services, who are anxious to get rid of him, he obtains the post, but three months later he involves his new company in heavy losses as a result of unsound financial and accounting practice.

7 Tony Bendrey (48) has been a motor mechanic with Bowdens (Bristol) for ten years at a wage of £180 per week. Owing to a heavy fall in trade, Tony is given a week's notice and £350 bonus. Is Tony entitled to more than this and, if so, how much?

8 James Street has been employed at a firm of motor suppliers for ten years. Following a firm audit it is discovered that James has been stealing from the firm to the tune of about £2500. James is dismissed instantly and he decides:
  (a)   to appeal against unfair dismissal;
  (b)   to claim redundancy;
  (c)   to claim the statutory notice period or money in lieu.

Do you think James would be successful in any of the above?

Reference: Chapter 7

Exercise 8

1 Identify the principal and agent in the following:
  (a)   Kenny Dalglish, Manager of Blackburn Rovers FC, signs a player from a first division club for £200 000.
  (b)   Ward & Co buys machinery on behalf of Kent Engineers plc.
  (c)   Mr Y contracts for a famous pop group to appear in a pop festival in Sheffield.
2 List three ways in which an agency is created.
3 List two duties owed by a principal to his/her agent.
4 All partners in a partnership are agents for each other: true or false?
5 Contracts entered into by agents for their principals are always avoided by the other party: true or false?
6 A person who leaves an agency having been an agent is never entitled to commission from sales he had negotiated: true or false?

Reference: Chapter 8

Exercise 9

1 In each of the following cases advise the party in italics of his/her position in law.
  (a)   *Peggy Kerr* buys an antique for £500 from Disdale Bros in a small antique shop. A few weeks later the police call at Peggy's house saying the antique has been stolen and it is handed back to its rightful owner. Eric Disdale, the owner of Disdale Bros, tells Peggy he did not know it was stolen and says that unfortunately it is Peggy's loss.
  (b)   Richard Partridge buys a stereo record player for £350 from *Good Bargain Radio Supplies Ltd*. He finds that after a few weeks the

stereo develops a fault which can only be put right at a charge of £150. Richard demands his money back.

(c) *John Martin* buys a Christmas cake from United Bakeries for £10.50. He selects from a range of cakes displayed. He is given a cake already packed but when he unpacks it he discovers it is completely unlike the one he chose. He demands his £10.50 back.

2 (a) Which Act of Parliament makes it illegal for shops to wrongly describe goods?

(b) Double pricing is a criminal offence: true or false?

3 When a person buys a car on hire-purchase he/she owns the car on payment of the first instalment: true/false?

4 Examine the following cases and advise the party italicised:

(a) *Jeff Evans* buys a car for £12 500 on hire-purchase. Although he signs a form at the car showroom he never receives a copy and refuses to pay the five instalments.

(b) *Susan Murgatroyd* signs an agreement to buy a washing machine. She signs the agreement at her house but the following day changes her mind and notifies the firm, *Household Supplies Ltd.* The firm threatens her with legal action.

5 A customer is only protected for goods, never services: true or false?

Reference: Chapter 9

___ **Exercise 10** _____

1 Which of the following risks are non-insurable? Fire, theft, failure to make profit.

2 Insurance companies take on large numbers of risks at quite modest premiums. This is known as what?.

3 In the following situations advise the party in italics and say what insurance principle is involved.

(a) Michael Jones's hobby is stunt motorcycling. In an insurance against accidents he omits to mention this. Michael is injured while stunt riding and the *Star Insurance Company* refuses to pay out.

(b) *Surety Insurance Ltd* refuse to pay out any compensation to Michael Hunter, who has taken out insurance on his friend's house, which is destroyed by fire.

(c) *Frank Brown* insures his car (value £10 000) with two separate companies. Following an accident which completely wrecks his car Frank claims a total of £20 000.

4 What is the meaning of the term 'subrogation'?

Reference: Chapter 10

___ **Exercise 11 and 12** _____

1 Name the three elements which must be proved in any negligence action.
2 A duty of care is never owed to a trespasser: true or false?
3 State four defences that might be used by a defendant in a negligence action.
4 Name of three kinds of trespass.
5 Libel is the written form of defamation: true or false?
6 Do you think the party italicised would have a good case in defamation? Give your reasons.

When she comes to work *Marlene Wardle*, the office supervisor, sees a notice on the noticeboard which reads:

'It is strictly against company policy to use the firm's telephone for making private calls and this includes Mrs M.W.'s calls to New Zealand. Signed F. Jones, Managing Director.'

7 What was decided in the case, *Deeny and others* v. *Gooda Walker Ltd and others* (1994)?
8 How has the Environmental Protection Act 1990 assisted victims of nuisance?

Reference: Chapters 11 and 12

___ **Exercise 13** _____

1 The Health and Safety at Work Act 1974 has introduced a new range of criminal offences: true or false?
2 Under the Health and Safety at Work Act, what is a prohibition order?
3 State three duties imposed upon employees by the Health and Safety at Work Act.
4 Employees injured at work can sue for negligence or for breach of statutory duty. To what Act of Parliament does this statutory duty apply?
5 If an injured employee cannot prove negligence or breach of statutory duty, can he still get compensation?
6 Explain what 'vicarious liability' means.
7 State the four common law duties imposed upon an employer.

Reference: Chapter 13

___ **Exercise 14** _____

1 In a partnership what is a sleeping partner and a salaried partner?
2 Name three types of business organisation which have legal status.
3 A company which acts outside the powers laid down in its memorandum of association is said to be acting in what way?

4 What does the word 'limited' imply for a shareholder in a company?

5 What is the maximum and minimum number of partners allowed in a partnership?

6 What is important about *Spicer (Keith) Ltd* v. *Mansell* (1970)

7 Is it possible for one person to form a company?

8 Under what Act are company names controlled?

Reference: Chapter 14

Exercise 15

1 When a public corporation is privatised what legal form does it usually take on?

2 What is the function of a 'regulator' in respect of companies that have been privatised?

3 What must firms do if they want to show a 'restrictive practice' is in the public interest?

4 What Act attempts to regulate monopoly?

5 Which European Union articles try to deal with monopoly and restrictive practice?

6 What was the decision in *IAZ International Belgium NV* v. *the Commission* (1983) and what was the reason for it?

Reference: Chapter 15

Exercise 16

1 What is an insolvency practitioner?

2 In an IVA, what is a proposal?

3 With regard to a deed of arrangement, what Act regulates it and what is a 'composition'?

4 Why do you think that a copy of a bankruptcy order is sent to the Chief Land Registrar?

5 Companies are never bankrupt, but in the circumstances of being unable to meet their debts they are what?

6 After a company is wound up, creditors may be offered 20p in the pound: what does this mean?

Reference: Chapter 16

Exercise 17

1 In a cheque transaction who is the drawer, the drawee and the payee?
2 State the two duties owed by a bank to its customer.
3 A bank refusing to 'honour a cheque' could be liable in libel: true or false?
4 How can a cheque be drawn so that it can only be paid into the account of the person in whose favour it is made?
5 In respect of cheques what does 'negotiability' mean?
6 State two circumstances where a bank might stop a cheque.
7 When was the term 'acc/payee' recognised?

Reference: Chapter 17

Exercise 18

1 A buyer of a business property is not legally bound to buy until there is an exchange of contracts: true or false?
2 If a business such as a shop is sold but not the property, what is being sold is known sometimes as what?
3 Fred Bellamy is selling a lucrative restaurant. He signs a contract with the purchaser that he will not operate a restaurant for 20 years in the UK. Within a year Fred has opened a restaurant in the same street. Could the purchaser do anything to stop him?
4 A landlord who owns the property from which a business operates can evict the tenant at any time: true or false?
5 Name the three registers for each property registered with the Land Registry Office.
6 Why would a solicitor acting for a purchaser of property want to examine the Land Searches Register?
7 Documents transferring property must be 'signed, sealed and delivered': true or false?
8 What is a stamp duty?

Reference: Chapter 18

Exercise 19

1 In what court are disputes about patents resolved?
2 How can a person try to ensure that the patent on his invention applies to Europe?
3 What is the difference between trademarks registered in the 'A' and 'B' register?
4 Is trademarks legislation only available to producers of goods?
5 In what year was copyright protection extended to computer software?
6 What is a data subject, as defined by the Data Protection Act (DPA) 1984

Reference: Chapter 19

◯ Answers

Chapter 1

Exercise 1

1 Criminal law could be defined as being concerned with conduct of which the state so strongly disapproves that it will punish the wrong-doer.
2 Civil law could be defined as being concerned with settling disputes between individuals and providing a remedy to the person wronged.
3 (a) The other party in a criminal case is known as Regina or Queen and in some cases the police.
   (b) The other party in a civil case is known as the plaintiff.

Exercise 2

1 This is a dispute between Brenda and the shop and would be a civil case.
2 This is a dispute between David and the garage and would be a civil case.
3 Deborah has committed a minor wrong but one of which the state disapproves. It would be a criminal case.
4 This is a good example of a crime and would be a criminal case.

Exercise 3

1 This would be a good example of an appeal 'on a case stated' and would be heard by the Divisional Court of the Queen's Bench Division.
2 Peter would be tried for this minor driving offence in the Magistrates' Court.
3 John would be tried in the Crown Court.
4 Jennifer's appeal would go to the Court of Appeal (Criminal Division).
5 Because of its legal importance, James Johnson's further appeal would go to the House of Lords.
6. The Appeal would be heard in the *Crown Court*.

Exercise 4

1 Peak Building Supplies is the plaintiff and Woodruffe Renovations is the defendant.
2 A default summons is issued by the plaintiff for the recovery of money, whereas an ordinary summons relates to other types of claims.

3   There are many examples you could have mentioned, such as recovery of money, claims for compensation for injury, bankruptcies, undefended divorces or disputes relating to housing.

Exercise 5

The three divisions are the Queen's Bench Division, the Chancery Division, the Family Division.
   The Queen's Bench Division deals with contract and negligence.
   The Chancery Division deals with bankruptcies, mortgages and company affairs.
   The Family Division deals with divorces and family matters.

Exercise 6

1   The first case is a civil case and it is most likely that it will be heard in the County Court.
2   This is again a civil case. It is likely it will be heard in the Queen's Bench Division of the High Court.
3   This would be a criminal case heard in the Crown Court originally but with the appeal being heard in the Court of Appeal (Criminal Division).
4   This is a criminal case heard orginally in the Magistrates' Court and therefore the appeal against sentence would be in the Crown Court.
5   This is a very serious criminal case which would be heard in the Crown Court.
6   This is a civil case. It provides a good example of 'leapfrogging'. The case has gone to the highest court in the land, the House of Lords, and missed out (leaped over) the Court of Appeal Civil Division.
7   Jenny would have a case which would go to the industrial tribunal.
8   Provided it was allowed for in the business contract, then the dispute could be settled by arbitration.
9   This case would be heard in the European Court of Justice.
10   This would be heard in the Social Security Appeals Tribunal.

Chapter 2

Exercise 1

1   The three main sources are legislation, precedent and European Union law.
2   It is important that a reason is given because the decision of one judge may be followed by other judges in similar cases.
3   The decisions of the House of Lords are binding on all other courts.
4   Ministers, local authorities (district councils), nationalised industries.
5   House of Commons, House of Lords and Royal Assent.
6   Treaties, secondary legislation and decisions of the European Court of Justice.
7   Because it is based very much on case law.
8   That it had existed from time immemorial.
9   The European Court of Justice.

Chapter 3

Exercise 1

1 Unanimously, by simple majority, by qualified majority.
2 For the UK the two commissioners are Sir Leon Brittan and Neil Kinnock.
3 The European Parliament can only advise on the law – it never makes the law.
4 You might have answered 'Statutory Instrument' and 'Directive'.

Exercise 2

1 Three or five.
2 Regulations apply immediately they are passed, directives must be brought in by national legislation and decisions apply only to one person, company or country.
3 It is introduced by the Commission, it is then approved by the Council of Ministers, sent to the European Parliament and then voted on by the Council of Ministers.
4 She could take her case to the European Court of Justice because this is in contravention of article 48.
5 Françoise could also go to the European Court of Justice because she is clearly being discriminated against.
6 The four basic economic freedoms are: free movement of goods, free movement of persons, free movement of capital and free movement of services.

Chapter 4

Exercise 1

1 A statement of claim, a defence, a defence to the counter claim.
2 Chancery and Family Division.
3 Fieri facias, charging order, garnishee order, writ of sequestration, appointment of a receiver, bankruptcy order.
4 A procedure whereby each party must supply each other with the documents and written evidence that he/she intends to produce in court.
5 This is where a defendant makes a claim against the plaintiff.

Exercise 2

1 When the claim is for less than £1000.
2 The district judge will deal with arbitration matters and will try cases where the amounts involved are relatively small.
3 Because it is expensive.
4 The employer is required to deduct money from the defendant's wages just as he does income tax.
5 False: in a company, shareholders can only lose what they invested, that is why companies are referred to as limited.

Exercise 3

1   The stipendiary magistrate is paid, other magistrates are not: they only receive their expenses.
2   The Lord Chancellor.
3   The clerk.
4   (a) The Law Society.
     (b) The Bar Council.
5   False: they can be sued.
6   The High Court judge sits in the High Court and can try class 1 offences in the Crown Court. The circuit judge hears cases in the County Court and can try less serious cases in the Crown Court but never class 1 offences.
7   The jury gives the verdict 'guilty' or 'not guilty'.
8   13; from each member state; three to five.

Chapter 5

Exercise 1

1   False – the majority of contracts are made without the help of a solicitor.
2   False – most contracts are not written.
3   A contract is an agreement which the law will recognise.

Exercise 2

Alan is the offeree and Ian is the offeror.

Exercise 3

The shopkeeper would not be in breach of contract because it is the customer who has made the offer which the shopkeeper could and most likely would refuse.

Exercise 4

There would be no contract between Frank and his employee because, as we have learned, consideration must be two-way. A gift is only a one-way consideration. Frank is supplying consideration but the employees are not. Except in rather special circumstances, a court of law will never enforce the promise of a gift.

Exercise 5

John is the offeror; Good Deal Motors is the offeree; consideration is the car and the £8900.

Exercise 6

The list should have included offer, acceptance, two-way consideration, capacity and legality.

Exercise 7

A clause which contains words such as 'binding in honour only' is likely.

Exercise 8

You should have in your list: offer, acceptance, consideration, capacity, legality, *consensus ad idem* (meeting of the minds), legal intent and form.

Exercise 9

1 This agreement is lacking in the essential element of legal intent. It is a domestic arrangement and it is assumed that there is no legal intent unless there is a specific statement to the contrary.
2 All hire-purchase agreements must be in writing. The agreement between Keith and the garage is not in the required form and is not therefore legally binding.
3 All contracts need to be supported by two-way consideration. In this case the customer is giving no consideration and therefore it is only one-way consideration.
4 Since Michael is unaware of the reward there is no offer to him and since all legally binding agreements must start with an offer this is the element lacking here.
5 Although John and his wife have written to book a room, this is only an offer which the hotel has not accepted. There is no acceptance and therefore no contract. In a situation such as this, John should have contacted the hotel before he and his wife set off.
6 There is no 'meeting of the minds' between Graheme Brown's company and Low Peak Co Ltd. Graheme has persuaded Low Peak to buy by misleading them; therefore there is no contract.
7 Young people below the age of 18 have limited contractual capacity. They have no capacity in respect of credit agreements. This agreement lacks capacity in respect of Carol.
8 Courts will never enforce agreements which are based upon an illegal act. This agreement is not legally binding by reason of illegality. John could never recover the £2000 through the courts because there has been no breach of contract because no contract exists.

Exercise 10

1 Acceptance and withdrawal or revocation.
2 Acceptance.
3 By the offeree paying a sum of money to the offeror.

Exercise 11

1 Acceptance, withdrawal, rejection, lapse.
2 (a) A counter-offer. (b) Roger would be the offeror.
3 Expiry of time and death of offeree.

Exercise 12

1 True: acceptance must match the offer completely.
2 False: postal acceptance takes place when the letter is posted.
3 False: the offeree must accept in the manner suggested by the offeror.
4 False: withdrawal takes place when the letter has been received.

Exercise 13

Commercial Supplies Ltd are supplying consideration in the form of a laser printer and Highgate Televisions Ltd are supplying consideration in the form of £1200.

Exercise 14

If you examine this situation carefully you will see that there are two separate agreements:
1 East Credit Ltd lend Mary £400. Mary agrees to pay this back, plus 20 per cent over 20 months. Therefore there is two-way consideration.
2 East Credit Ltd agree to give up the interest. Mary, however, only agrees to fulfil an existing obligation and therefore no consideration exists.
   Since only the first agreement is supported by two-way consideration it is the only one legally binding and therefore East Credit Ltd could sue for recovery of the £80.

Exercise 15

1 Consideration must be two-way.
2 Consideration may be future or present but cannot be past.
3 Consideration cannot be an existing obligation.
4 The courts are not concerned with the adequacy of considerations.

Exercise 16

1 Marchant Machine Tools must keep the offer open to Sterndale Engineering Ltd because they have received the £1500 consideration. Sterndale could sue Marchant Machine Tools for damages.
2 Deepdale Cash Registers Ltd have made an agreement with the Palace which became effective when the letter was sent, provided the letter was prepaid and correctly addressed.

3   The promise of the gift cannot be enforced against Harpur Builders Ltd because it is an agreement based upon one-way consideration. A written statement is not sufficient. Only a deed will make the agreement legally binding.

4   You will have noted the word 'past'. Paul's offer of a week at his cottage is merely an offer of a gift since the solicitor's consideration is past, and past consideration is not consideration.

5   Reg could not recover the car. Although £6000 is far too low a price, provided the agreement had been entered into freely it is legally binding. This comes from the rule that the courts are not concerned with the adequacy of consideration.

6   Julian could recover compensation as a result of the Road Traffic Act 1972.

Exercise 17

1   Contracts for necessaries.
2   Contracts for employment, apprenticeships and education.

Exercise 18

1   Agreements relating to necessaries, apprenticeships, education and employment.
2   Agreements relating to non-necessaries and credit.
3   Agreements in respect of leases, partnerships and shares.

Exercise 19

1   False, because some agreements, for example, football coupons, take out this legal intent.
2   False : the sender could not sue in the court because no contract exists between him and the Post Office because the legal intent has been removed by Act of Parliament.
3   True : domestic agreements, because they are usually binding in honour only, are not legally enforceable.

Exercise 20

1   (a) Misrepresentation, (b) duress, (c) undue influence.
2   (a) Agreement to commit a criminal act, (b) agreements involving sexual immorality, (c) agreements affecting public safety, (d) agreements to defraud the Inland Revenue, (e) agreements tending to the corruption of public life.
3   Where an agreement is made to sell the goods of only one supplier and it is illegal if it is unreasonable.

Exercise 21

It means that the house is sold but the agreement to buy and sell cannot be enforced until a written contract is drawn up – sold, therefore, subject to a written contract being drawn up.

Exercise 22

1   This is a document signed as a deed.
2   Leases of three years or more; conveyances or transfers of land; agreements supported by one-way consideration.
3   Agreements to buy company shares; agreements to buy certain goods by instalments; agreements to insure ships.
4   Agreements to buy a house.

Exercise 23

1   You should have: acceptance; revocation (withdrawal); rejection; lapse.
2   Acceptance takes place at the time of posting; therefore if Alan withdrew his offer after the letter was posted this would be too late, for offers cannot be withdrawn after they have been accepted.
3   (a) False : consideration can never be past.
     (b) False : courts are not concerned with adequacy.
     (c) True : a promise to fulfil an existing obligation is never consideration.
4   Bob need not worry because this is a credit arrangement and, since Bob is not yet 18, he has no capacity to enter into this sort of arrangement.
5   Misrepresentation; duress; undue influence.
6   (a) True.
     (b) Because they are regarded as being 'in honour only' and therefore there is no legal intent.

Chapter 6

Exercise 1

False: expressed terms must be stated (expressed) in some way, but this can be verbally or in writing.

Exercise 2

1   The most likely term to be regarded as a condition is term 4, which stipulates that the ownership of the goods in question passes to the buyer. Any attempt by the company to interfere with the buyer's ownership would be regarded as a breach of condition and would affect the very basis of the agreement.
2   (a) A warranty is a term which is not so important as to go to the heart of the contract.
     (b) The plaintiff could sue for breach of warranty, not breach of contract.

Exercise 3

If you have applied the test 'does the breach go to the heart of the contract?' then it is clear that:

1 John is in breach of warranty – his failure to attend one practice does not fundamentally affect the contract. Note the connection between this and *Bettini* v. *Gye*.
2 Michael is in breach of a condition since playing for the team is the essential part of the agreement. To miss six games is very serious indeed. Remember *Poussard* v. *Spiers & Pond* (1870).
3 Although the absence of a programme will cause Andrew some inconvenience it is not so essential and Andrew could sue for breach of warranty.
4 It would seem that the tipping facility is something which goes to the heart of the contract. Indeed this is why H. & G. ordered the vehicle. Certainly the manufacturer is in breach of a condition and therefore in breach of contract.

Exercise 4

1 Rachel could sue because the new motorcar is not of 'merchantable quality'.
2 Precision Engineering could sue because there is an implied term that the lathe will be suitable.
3 Mr and Mrs Goldstraw would recover the £150.50 because being rat-infested suggests that the premises are not fit for human habitation. Real Estates is therefore in breach of an implied term.

Exercise 5

1 An exclusion clause is also known as an indemnity clause or disclaimer clause.
2 False – it need not be part of a signed document.
3 False – an exclusion clause can only be introduced before the contract is made.

Exercise 6

1 Veronica would be successful because the exclusion clause must be introduced at the time the contract is made. If it is introduced during the flight it gives Veronica little chance to disagree with the terms and change her mind.
2 Francis could sue because the Unfair Contract Terms Act prevents businesses from excluding liability for personal injury arising from negligence.
3 It is unlikely that Electrical Components would be successful. They have agreed to the exclusion clause which is in respect of loss or damage of equipment. Though the court would look at the charges imposed by County Store Ltd if the charges were high, the exclusion might be regarded as unreasonable.

Exercise 7

1 Discharge can take place by: (a) performance; (b) agreement; (c) frustration; (d) breach.
2 Law Reform (Frustrated Contracts) Act 1943.
3 *Krell* v. *Henry* (1903).

Exercise 8

1   Since Nigel cannot play football as a result of the unfortunate accident, the contract is discharged by frustration. The very basis of the contract has been destroyed.
2   Provided that Timber Supplies Ltd agree to release Stanley's firm from the contract, the contract is discharged by agreement.
3   Both sides, Precision Engineering Ltd and Western Machines Ltd, have fulfilled their respective sides of the bargain and the contract has been discharged by performance.
4   Leather Supplies Ltd are clearly in breach of contract since they have failed to deliver the goods in time or reasonably near the time. The contract is discharged by breach.

Exercise 9

1   The court could never adequately supervise an employee to see if he was fulfilling his agreement.
2   It would not make sense to force an unwilling person to work somewhere he did not want to.

Exercise 10

1   Damages, specific performance, injunction.
2   False – specific performance orders will never be awarded for contracts of a personal nature and employment is of a personal nature.
3   An injunction is an order requiring someone **not** to do something.
4   This means that the court can award an injunction or a specific performance order if it wishes. The court need not make such an award, it can use its 'discretion'.

Exercise 11

1   In the first case John Bennett would receive damages but not for £9500. He would receive £500 so that he would be in the same position as before the contract was breached.
2   It is possible that the court would grant an injunction preventing Chris from playing for the second club. Remember *Warner Bros* v. *Nelson*.
3   Since the furniture is rare Tony would not really want damages and it is likely that the court would grant a specific performance order ordering United Antique Dealers Ltd to sell the furniture at the agreed price to Tony.
4   It is unlikely that Mr and Mrs Disdale would obtain a specific performance order. More likely they would receive damages of £3000 so that they could buy a similar property or to compensate them if they had bought the property from another company.

Exercise 12

1   This act lays down rules:
    (i) parties can choose the law applicable to their contract
    (ii) if not the contract will be governed by the law of the country with which it is most closely connected
2   It is likely to be the law of contract prevailing in Germany.

Chapter 7

Exercise 1

1 A legally binding contract has not come into existence because there is an absence of two-way consideration. Only Matthew is giving consideration. It could also be argued that this is a domestic agreement and therefore the assumption in the courts will be that it will lack legal intent.

2 No offer has been made to Vic and, therefore, there is no acceptance. Since these two elements are lacking there is no legally binding contract.

3 It would appear here that Keith has no authority to bind his company to an agreement with Roy Spencer. Keith does not possess the capacity to make this contract and, therefore, it is not legally binding.

4 There is no doubt that the purpose for which Michelle entered into this agreement was illegal. Therefore, it is not legally binding.

5 A contract of employment, like any other contract, must be based upon reality of consent. Therefore, if one party was persuaded to reach agreement because it based its decision on false information provided by the other party, then the party misled has a right to avoid the contract. The possession of an HGV licence is essential and, therefore the agreement is not legally binding.

6 Even though there has been nothing in writing between Frances and Trenchard Industrial Holdings, nevertheless a legally binding contract is in existence and Frances could be sued for breach of contract.

Exercise 2

1 Peter could not treat this contract as breached because the absence of these particulars does not affect the validity of the contract. Indeed, the firm could sue Stephen if he left without giving the minimum notice agreed.

2 In this case, the written particulars supplied to Audrey by Boston Furnishings Ltd do have the weight of law because they have been endorsed by an industrial tribunal and, therefore, Audrey can challenge the firm because of the change in her conditions of employment.

3 The law states quite clearly that, under the Race Relations Act 1976, no discrimination must exist in arrangements made for selection; and since here discrimination does exist, Vivian has a case to take to an industrial tribunal.

4 The Sex Discrimination Act 1975 makes it illegal to discriminate on grounds of sex or marital status and Anne could take this case to an industrial tribunal.

Exercise 3

1 The need to obey lawful and reasonable instructions.
2 The need to work competently and carefully.
3 The need to conduct himself/herself in the interest of his/her employer.
4 The need to show good faith to his/her employer.

Exercise 4

1   To provide a safe system of work.
2   Not to discriminate on grounds of sex, race or union membership.
3   To reimburse employees for any expenses incurred while they are on the firm's business.
4   To deduct PAYE and national insurance contributions.
5   To provide reasonable management.
The following case is a good illustration of this implied duty. In *Donovan* v. *Invicta Airways Ltd* (1970), a pilot was, three times in rapid succession, put under pressure by management to take abnormal risks on flights. On two occasions there were passengers aboard. He refused each time. Relations with management deteriorated and he left the company. Although the decision to leave was his, he was held to have been dismissed, and received £900 damages for breach of contact. This provides a good example of constructive dismissal.

Exercise 5

1   Burlow Road Building Supplies are clearly in breach of what was probably an express condition of their office manager's contract of employment.
2   Michael is not in breach of an implied condition to obey reasonable and lawful orders. It is not reasonable to expect a development engineer to engage in painting and decorating.
3   Margaret is in breach of faith in respect of her employers since her position demands that she does not discuss this sort of information.
4   An implied condition is that an employee must not misconduct himself. Stealing from the firm is a clear case of misconduct and John is in breach.
5   Since a contract of employment requires that employees work competently it would appear that Philip is in breach.
6   It is an implied duty resting upon an employer that an employee is reimbursed for expenses incurred. Therefore Midland Dairy Food, in refusing Richard's claim, are in breach of this implied condition. Provided Richard can show that the money was spent in the course of his work, Midland Dairy Food are in breach.
7   Fashion Textiles were clearly in breach of the implied condition that requires employers to provide a safe system of work.
8   Unfortunately for Reginald it is not an implied condition of employment that an employer provides a reference, and TV Rentals Ltd are not therefore in breach.

Exercise 6

1   Reg would be entitled to 12 weeks' notice or £3600 in lieu of notice.
2   Carol would be entitled to one week's notice or £120 in lieu of notice.
3   Ken would not be entitled to any notice under the Act because he has only been in employment for three weeks.
4   Tracey would be entitled to two weeks' notice or £240 in lieu of notice.

Exercise 7

1   Frederick is not entitled to redundancy because he is a government employee which is one of the categories not entitled.

2 Bob is entitled to 2 years at 1 week = £280
and 4 years at $1/2$ week   = £280
He is entitled to a total of £560. His first two years of employment will not count.
3 Frank, unfortunately, is not entitled because he has reached retirement age.
4 Rita is entitled to 20 years' service.
9 years at $1 1/2 \times$ £205   = £2767
11 years at 1 wk $\times$ £205 = £2255
A total of   £5022.

Exercise 8

1 The loss of status for Dr Morris is so considerable as to make the alternative offer unsuitable. Dr Morris could justifiably refuse this and still claim redundancy.
2 This would seem a suitable offer; Deborah is offered the same post only ten miles away. She could not really refuse this and still claim redundancy.
3 This would not be regarded as a suitable offer. A move from York to Torquay for a married man with a family is a big move and Fred could justifiably turn it down and still claim redundancy.

Exercise 9

1 The three stages are as follows: (a) complaint to the industrial tribunal; (b) a copy of the complaint to ACAS; (c) hearing before an industrial tribunal.
2 (a) Basic award; (b) compensatory award and (c) additional award.
3 52 weeks, but for a small firm with less than 20 employees 104 weeks.
4 (a) Adam would be unlikely to be successful because of the serious nature of his misconduct.
  (b) Jane would be successful even though she has only been with the firm for two weeks because being a member of a union is not a fair reason for dismissal and if an employee is dismissed for joining a union he does not need to have the 52 weeks' qualifying service to appeal against unfair dismissal.
  (c) Roy would be successful because the Codes of Practice would have required that he be given a warning. In fact a poor month on top of two years' success would probably not be regarded as a sign of incompetence.
5 The trade union would take heavy penalties for forcing the employer to sack Roy.

Exercise 10

1 False: contracts of employment need not be in writing.
2 True: apprenticeship contracts must always be in writing.
3 Written particulars must be provided within 13 weeks.
4 An employer has no legal duty to provide a reference.
5 An employee with 15 years' service is entitled to 12 weeks' notice.
6 The employee is entitled to £1920, that is 5 years at $1 1/2$ weeks and 5 years at 1 week.
7 False: employees may turn down offers if they are not considered suitable and still claim redundancy.

8   52 weeks, or 104 weeks in the case of a firm employing less than 20 employees.
9   Provided Mary gives notice of her intention to leave at least 21 days before leaving, she is entitled to return within 29 weeks of her confinement.
10   Until 1987, Michael had no rights in this respect, but now he must be given the information within 40 days.

Chapter 8

Exercise 1

1   Alex is the agent acting on behalf of his principal, Manchester United FC.
2   Business Property Services is the agent acting for Janet Baker (Fashions) Ltd, the principal.
3   Derek Butterfield is the principal, the stockbroker is the agent

Exercise 2

Authorisation; by implication, apparent authority, ratification, necessity.

Exercise 3

1   (a) To act in good faith.
     (b) To work skilfully and show reasonable care.
     (c) To act personally.
     (d) To obey the principal's instructions.
2   (a) Death.
     (b) Insanity.
     (c) Lapse.
     (d) Performance.

Exercise 4

1   Geoff cannot avoid the payment: Sheila acted on his authority and if she made a bad deal that is Geoff's loss. He is bound by her agreement.
2   Kent Sports plc would be obliged to pay because Sports Equipment plc could not possibly know of this instruction. This is a good example of agency by implication.
3   Greenfield (Stockbrokers) Ltd are in a difficult position. This is hardly a necessity and, anyway, they could have contacted Sir Roger. It seems that there is no agency between Greenfields and Sir Roger in respect of this deal, and action would be to Greenfields.
4   Following the death of his principal, John is no longer the agent. The agreement to sell the property is not valid and the beneficiaries could avoid it.

Chapter 9

Exercise 1

1 Leisure Supplies Ltd's sale of a music centre to Philip is a consumer sale.
2 Since John is reselling the furniture this is not a consumer sale. Also it is not for his private use.
3 Although United Food Ltd are selling in the course of business the grocery chain is buying with a view to resale and not for private consumption, therefore this is not a consumer sale.
4 Malcolm is not selling in the course of business, therefore it is not a consumer sale.

Exercise 2

1 That the buyer has the right to sell.
2 That the goods are of merchantable quality.
3 Goods sold by description must correspond to it.
4 Goods sold by sample must correspond to it.
5 Goods supplied must be fit for the purpose.

Exercise 3

1 David could sue because the racquet is apparently not of 'merchantable quality'.
2 Brian could possibly sue despite the 12 months' warranty, which can only add to his rights. A £12 500 car should not need such attention after only 14 months.
3 Muriel could sue because the goods do not correspond to the sample.
4 Caroline could sue because the car she has purchased does not correspond to the description.
5 Philip relied upon advice and he could sue because the goods supplied are not fit for the purpose.
6 David could sue because of the implied condition that the seller had the right to sell them.

Exercise 4

1 False: the Trade Descriptions Act 1968 created criminal offences and contravention could lead to prosecution.
2 (a) False description of goods; (b) double pricing; (c) false description of services, accommodation and facilities: (d) importation of goods bearing a false indication of origin.

Exercise 5

1 Alan Harrison has imported goods bearing a false indication of their origin. West Germany is certainly not regarded as a Third World country.

2   Torbay Holiday Flats Ltd have made a false description in respect of accommodation and therefore broken the law.
3   The answer would hinge on whether the full price was charged for a 28-day period during the last six months.
4   Country Kitchen Bakery have falsely described the goods as being 'home-made', which is not the case.

Exercise 6

As a result of the Consumer Protection Act 1987, Michael Moss does have a case against Mecca TV Plc.

Exercise 7

1   A secured loan is one where the creditor regains some interest in property of the person seeking the loan. In an unsecured loan no such interest exists.
2   False: the goods become the property of the debtor immediately.
3   False: the goods remain the property of the creditor until the last instalment is paid.

Exercise 8

1   This agreement is not regulated because it is made with a company.
2   Loans to buy houses are exempt and in any event this exceeds the £15 000 limit.
3   This would be a regulated agreement.
4   This would not be regulated because it exceeds the maximum limit which at present is £15 000.

Exercise 9

1   Secure Finance Ltd could face criminal prosecution and a court may not enforce the agreement against Jane because the company is *not* licensed.
2   All agreements of this sort must be in writing to be enforceable. John will never be forced to pay.
3   Ian can withdraw because this is a 'cancellable' agreement. His so-called 'cooling off' period lasts for five days after receipt of his copy of the agreement.
4   50 per cent could be regarded an 'extortionate' rate of interest and the court could require John to repay the loan but could change the agreement to reduce the interest.

Exercise 10

1   True: the hirer is also the debtor.
2   The maximum proportion of the hire-purchase price payable on termination is one-half.
3   The finance company has broken the law since it needs a court order to 'snatch back' the goods. In this instance two-thirds of the hire-purchase price has been paid and, as we have seen, the goods are protected.

Exercise 11

1 Unfortunately, since this is a private sale, Bob can do very little unless his friend misrepresented the condition of the machine.
2 Deborah could sue under the Sale of Goods Act 1979 because the goods she obtained did not correspond with the description.
3 Wainwrights (Domestic) Ltd are contravening the Trade Descriptions Act 1968 and could be prosecuted.
4 Again this is an example of a contravention of the Trade Descriptions Act 1968. The Magistrates' Court has the power to award compensation to the parties affected by the false description and Mr and Mrs Taylor may get some money back.
5 This agreement can never be enforced in the court because the debtor must receive a copy of her agreement.
6 Audrey is allowed a five-day 'cooling off' period from the receipt of the copy of the agreement, since the agreement was signed away from the business premises. Whether she could cancel depends upon when she received the copy agreement.
7 It is likely that the court would regard the rate of interest as extortionate.
8 This false information could take Sure Credit PLC to face criminal prosecution.

Chapter 10

Exercise 1

1 A proposal form.
2 Insurance companies cannot estimate the number of claims for this sort of risk.
3 Pooling of risks.

Exercise 2

1 Hang-gliding is apparently a very dangerous hobby and it is essential that in any life insurance this hobby is mentioned. Roger's widow could not really recover the £50 000 from Security Insurance.
2 It is vitally important for the company to assess the risk that Brian mentions, both the past burglaries and his rather irregular practice with the back window. The insurance company could refuse to pay out.

Exercise 3

1 Michael could not really claim an interest in the boat despite the fact that he has borrowed it occasionally. Michael could take out insurance for the period when he was using the boat because he might be liable if the boat was damaged.
2 Mrs Yeomans does have an interest in her husband's life.
3 Victor could claim an insurable interest in what is his own car.
4 Sheila could under no circumstances claim an interest in her best friend's life in the sense that she would suffer no financial loss as a result of her friend's death.

Exercise 4

1   Indemnity means that the insured will be indemnified (compensated) for his loss.
2   Because no one can measure the value of life.
3   Overinsurance exists where the insurance cover is more than the value of the property. Underinsurance exists where the insurance cover is less than the value of the property.

Exercise 5

1   Carole cannot get double compensation because of the principles of indemnity and contribution.
2   (b) Subrogation.

Exercise 6

1   John could find that the insurance company in the event of a claim will refuse to pay out. This fact of epilepsy is most relevant. Remember insurance contracts rely upon utmost good faith.
2   Again Bob should have disclosed this very important fact.
3   The money Michael gets from the sale of the carpets legally belongs to the insurance company because they have paid out in full for his loss.
4   In the event of loss, Pat could only claim up to £65 000, as that is the value of the cottage.
5   Anne has no insurable interest in her neighbour's life.
6   Bob is liable to pay back the value of one claim and the two companies would share the cost of the other.

Chapter 11

Exercise 1

1   'Wrong': from the French.
2   Sheila as plaintiff.
3   False: negligence is civil.

Exercise 2

1   Richard Huyton would be the defendant in this instance and David Pritchard the plaintiff.
2   Drivers of vehicles on the public highway owe a duty of care to all pedestrians and other road users who might be affected by their acts or omissions; thus Richard clearly owed David a duty of care.
3   The clue as to whether the duty of care had been broken lies in the phrases 'in a hurry' and 'far too fast'. It would suggest that the standard of care exercised by Richard was not that of a reasonable person.

Exercise 3

1 The three elements are: (a) duty of care; (b) breach of duty; (c) loss arising from the breach.
2 £400 plus an assessment of the amount to compensate George for pain and discomfort.

Exercise 4

1 Buxted Engineering Co owe no duty of care to Michael because he is a trespasser and Michael would be unsuccessful.
2 Low Peak District Council owe a duty of care to all lawful visitors. Mary is a lawful visitor. Low Peak have breached their duty and Mary is injured. She would be successful.
3 Alan clearly owes Rachel a duty of care but Alan is a careful driver and has maintained this high standard during his journey down the main street. Alan has not broken this duty and Rachel would therefore not be successful. He can explain the skid.
4 Although the hospital owed Margaret a duty of care which had clearly been broken by the existence of loose floor covering, it is likely that Margaret would have died anyway and her death probably did not arise from the breach. It is unlikely John would be successful.
5 Michael would not be successful, for although there was a duty of care which had been broken, there was no loss because Michael did not suffer any injury.
6 Although Andrew is a trespasser, because of his age Easibuild Co Ltd would owe him a duty of care which has been breached and injury has resulted. David Knowles would be successful.

Exercise 5

1 The defendant may claim: (a) no duty of care existed; (b) no breach; (c) no loss or injury arising from the breach; (d) consent; (e) contributory negligence.
2 False: since the passing of the Unfair Contract Terms Act it is no longer possible to use as a defence a disclaimer notice disclaiming liability for death or personal injury.

Exercise 6

If we apply our three essential elements then there is little doubt that the hotel was negligent. Having a member of staff with a known police record who has access to guests' rooms is very questionable. The notice in the room could not be used as a defence because it had been introduced too late. To be relied upon by the hotel it needs to be shown to guests at the time they book in, that is at reception. The hotel, however, could argue that Alan should not have kept such valuable equipment in his room but should have left it at Reception. It is possible that full compensation would not be awarded and that Alan would bear some of the cost. You may have remembered the case, *Olley* v. *Marlborough Court* Ltd [1949].

Exercise 7

1   Duty of care, breach of duty and damage or loss from the breach.
2   Remoteness of damage
3   False: under the Consumer Protection Act 1987 the person injured can sue.
4   Vicarious liability.
5   False: he is liable for the acts of his employees.

Chapter 12

Exercise 1

An injunction is an order saying not to do something. In this instance it would be an order saying to Rachel and Doreen, 'Do not continue to walk through the timber yard.'

Exercise 2

1   Burlow Motors could not prosecute because trespass is a civil offence.
2   Provided Marc used a minimum of force to eject the man then Weaving could not be sued.
3   Although probably unwelcome visitors, the health inspectors would be considered lawful visitors and therefore could not be trespassers.
4   Bill started as a lawful visitor but has clearly acted in a way which makes his presence unwelcome. After being asked to leave he becomes a trespasser and the fact that he has paid for his ticket is really immaterial.

Exercise 3

1   The three types of trespass to person are: (a) assault; (b) battery; (c) false imprisonment.
2   (a) Ray could rightfully claim he was preventing a greater evil and Mike would have little chance in a trespass case.
    (b) This is more difficult and it would be for the court to determine if this comes within the normal interpretation of parental authority.
    (c) Probably John could use as his defence that he was acting in self-defence.
    (d) If no offence had been committed at this time either by Nick or someone else then Phil could be sued for trespass to person, that is false imprisonment.
    (e) It is within one's rights to use minimum force to eject a trespasser provided he has been requested to leave. This might be regarded, however, as excessive use of force, in which case Michael might be successful.
    (f) Jack really could not sue successfully because he has consented by implication to be battered by taking part in games such as rugby, where injuries are a distinct possibility – unless he could prove his opponent had acted completely outside the rules.

Exercise 4

1   Graham has been negligent since this was an accident. Trespass to goods must be wilful. The neighbour could sue in negligence.

2 The firm could sue Mary for conversion since Mary is denying the firm's ownership of the books by trying to sell them.

Exercise 5

1 Public nuisance is a crime and it is something which affects a number of people. Private nuisance is a tort and is concerned usually with an individual or family.
2 (a) The pensioners would have little chance because once a year would not be regarded as unreasonable.
   (b) If the noise and smells are excessive then Frances would be successful; it is no defence to say it has always been the same.
   (c) John might be successful; necessity as claimed by the vet is no defence.

Exercise 6

1 (a) Libel; (b) slander.
2 (a) The statement must refer to the plaintiff; (b) the statement must be communicated to a third party; (c) the statement must be capable of lowering the plaintiff's reputation in the eyes of right-thinking members of society.
3 If we apply our three rules: (a) the statement has been communicated to a third party; (b) Paddy was named by inference (note the spelling of the word 'byrne') (c) but Paddy's reputation is not lowered in the eyes of right-thinking members of society because to give the game away is, despite his friends' view, the right thing to do. Therefore he would have no case in defamation.

Exercise 7

1 Mary would be unsuccessful because, provided Associated Metals did not write the reference with malice, the firm has protection.
2 Mr Green is privileged, that is absolutely protected against a defamation action. If he repeated the allegation outside Parliament then this would be quite a different matter.
3 The *Bristol Times* could not use as a defence the offer of amends and the printed apology because the statement about Brayshaw had been printed intentionally.
4 Jennie would have little chance because the statement was in fact true and the fact of the conviction would make it easy for the *Kent Times* to prove it. The newspaper also has a defence in that it has privilege in respect of fair, accurate and contemporaneous reporting of court proceedings.

Exercise 8

1 Local Authorities can visit the scene of a nuisance and may issue abatement notices.
2 (a) The plaintiff was referred to. (b) The statement was made to a third party. (c) The statement lowered the plaintiff's reputation in the eyes of right-thinking members of society.
3 Absolute protection is given for statements in court or Parliament. Qualified protection is given for references.

4   Trespass to land; trespass to person; trespass to goods.
5   Because trespass is usually a tort and not a crime.
6   False: it must be more than merely 'unfair': the statement must be untrue, made maliciously and cause economic loss.
7   Misrepresentation, in the course of trade, made to customers or potential customers, calculated to injure business, and does damage or threaten to damage plaintiff's business.

Chapter 13

Exercise 1

1   False: the Act introduces a new range of criminal offences.
2   'Enabling Act' means that ministers can add to the Act by issuing regulations which have the force of law.
3   Workplaces must make improvements within a certain period of time.
4   The maximum fine at present is £2000.

Exercise 2

1   There is little doubt that such a sad accident record would lead to a Prohibition Order taking this particular piece of machinery out of action.
2   The Hotel Regal could face criminal action because it has not provided sufficient 'information, instruction, training or supervision' in the use of these new stoves.
3   This constant skylarking makes it debatable whether a safe system of work is being provided. If the company cannot deal with it then they must, in the interest of safety, terminate the employment of the two apprentices. Both of the employees involved could face legal action because they are 'not cooperating with the management in the interests of safety'.
4   It is a duty of the employer to provide a safe and healthy environment. Victoria Laundry clearly is not doing this and the inspectors will either simply recommend or perhaps issue an Improvement Order.

Exercise 3

(a) The existence of a duty of care.
(b) The breach of that duty of care.
(c) Injury or loss as a result of the breach.

Exercise 4

1   Ben has a good case; Peakdale Engineering Co owe him a duty of care; this has been broken and Ben is injured.
2   North West Builders are liable to Fred despite their claim to the contrary. Employers are vicariously liable for the torts of their employees. Therefore North West Builders are liable for the tort of the site foreman.

3   It is no defence for Hotel Sceptre to blame the supplier. The Employers' Liability (Defective Equipment) Act provides that an employee such as Adam can sue his employer even though the fault may lie with the supplier.

Exercise 5

1   Factories Act 1961.
2   False: he/she may be compensated by the state for industrial injuries.
3   Linda would not be successful in negligence but the industrial benefit scheme has defined employment as anything arising out of an employee's presence at work. The works canteen would come within this category.
4   Common law duty.

Exercise 6

1   David Hogg is liable for prosecution under the Health and Safety at Work Act 1974 because he is under a duty to take care for the health and safety of himself and fellow employees, and also to cooperate with his employer in health and safety matters.
2   John can inspect the factory and will be termed a lawful visitor and therefore not a trespasser. If he is of the opinion that a particular process is dangerous he can issue a prohibition order ordering it to be discontinued.
3   Philip could sue his company in negligence and as we have seen the Employers' Liability (Defective Equipment) Act 1969 prevents the employer denying liability or trying to shift liability to someone else.
4   Maureen could apply for industrial injuries benefit because this is likely to be one of the prescribed diseases in the 1980 regulations. She might be successful in a negligence action.
5   John may not be able to claim in negligence against his company but he could claim industrial injuries benefit.
6   The apprentice could sue for a breach of statutory duty which makes it necessary for machines to be fenced. The company could not deny liability by blaming Bob Brown because, as we have learned, companies can be vicariously (indirectly) liable for their employees' actions.

Chapter 14

Exercise 1

John could lose his house because his liability is not limited to the £50 000 of his original investment.

Exercise 2

1   A sleeping partner is one who has invested money but takes no part in the running of the business.

2   Unlimited liability means that a partner may be liable for debts over and above his/her initial investment.
3   Partnership Act 1890; Companies Act 1985.
4   By expressly informing firms that he has retired and/or by publishing his retirement in the *London Gazette*.
5   Unfortunately Linda cannot plead ignorance; she is bound by any agreement made by her partner, Christine.
6   A salaried partner is paid a salary and is found in firms of solicitors or accountants. He/she does not usually get a share of the profits but can be liable for debts.

Exercise 3

1   'Dissolution of a partnership' means bringing it to an end.
2   Partnerships may be dissolved (a) by order of the court; (b) by the partners themselves according to the agreement, or if no agreement exists, by methods laid down in the Partnership Act 1890.

Exercise 4

[Statutory] refers to anything which has been laid down by statute, that is, Act of Parliament.

Exercise 5

1   The two differences are: (a) a public company must have a minimum share capital; (b) only public companies can sell their shares to the public.
2   That the shareholders in the company have their liability limited by the amount of their total shareholding.
3   Articles of association.
4   The objects are the reason why the company is operating.

Exercise 6

1   (a) Nominal capital is £1 million; (b) issued capital is £500 000.
2   (a) Unicorn Motor Supplies Co Ltd has full legal status and it is the company not the managing director who will be sued.
    (b) SE Touring Co Ltd can no longer claim this because our laws in this respect have been brought into line with EU regulations.
    (c) Unfortunately for Palatine, the football club could refuse payment and payment could not be enforced because supply of sports equipment is outside its objects.

Exercise 7

1   John could stand to lose the £1000 because it is a legal requirement that anyone trading under a name other than his own needs to display this.
2   Partnership Act 1890.
3   Minimum two, maximum 20.
4   David could not be made to pay. The company, not David, would be sued.

5 Certificate of incorporation.
6 A company acting '*ultra vires*' cannot use this as a reason for not meeting their contractual obligations.

Chapter 15

Exercise 1

1 A public corporation is owned by the state, whereas a public company is owned privately but its shares are available to the public.
2 The powers of a public corporation are laid down in an Act of Parliament and if the corporation exceeded these powers it is said to be acting 'ultra vires' – beyond its powers.

Exercise 2

1 Monopoly, restrictive practices and resale price maintenance.
2 When 25 per cent or more of the supply of a product is in the hands of one organisation.
3 Where a supplier insists on the price at which a product must be sold to the public.
4 'That the restriction does not affect materially competition to any relevant trade or industry' is one example.
5 The Secretary of State can issue a prohibition order preventing the merger from going ahead.

Exercise 3

1 Articles 85, 86 and 87.
2 If the benefit of the practice went to consumers.
3 It became law in 1990 and allowed the European Commission to deal with mergers.
4 The Commission could intervene in this situation.
5 It would seem that, under regulation 4064/89, the Commission could intervene.

Chapter 16

Exercise 1

1 The supervisor supervises the voluntary arrangement.
2 No, because this is not 75 per cent, assuming all the creditors voted.
3 This is to ensure time for the person threatened with bankruptcy to come up with a proposal.

Exercise 2

Because creditors 1, 2, 4 and 6 would not make 50 per cent of the value.

Exercise 3

1   The person was carrying on a business, it was in England and/or Wales, the petitioner is a creditor or the debtor himself, the debtor cannot pay or does not seem to be likely to pay his debts.
2   A creditor or the debtor himself.
3   Loss of control of property, inability to get credit without disclosing bankruptcy, inability to become an MP, loss of control of assets and inability to start a business without saying he/she was a bankrupt.

Exercise 4

1   Liquidation – turning the company's assets into money. Winding up – bringing the affairs of the company to an end.
2   (a) The company cannot pay its debts; (b) the membership falls below the legal minimum; (c) the company does not hold the statutory meeting; (d) the company has not operated within a year of its setting up or has suspended business for a year or more.

Exercise 5

£2400 × 60p = £1440.

Exercise 6

1   (a) Compulsorily; (b) voluntarily; (c) under the court's supervision.
2   £75.
3   The creditor cannot sue the company because it no longer exists.

Exercise 7

1   Sterndale can petition the court for a bankruptcy order.
2   Date of petition, date and time of order, instruction to debtor to attend at a certain time and an instruction that all legal proceedings against the debtor should stop.
3   A trustee.
4   Ashford Machine Tool Co assets are as follows:

Buildings	£20 000
Equipment	£ 2 000
Un-paid up shares	£ 4 000
List B	£ 4 000
Total	**£30 000**

Liabilities = £40 000; assets = £30 000. A dividend of 75p in the pound is likely to be given.

Chapter 17

Exercise 1

Drawer: J.Fraser; drawee: Barclays; payee: Rock Base Garage) Ltd.

Exercise 2

1 (a) To keep confidentiality; (b) to honour cheques drawn on the customer's account.
2 Breach of contract and the tort of libel.
3 Wendy would be the creditor, the bank would be the debtor.
4 It usually means that the creditor has insufficient funds in his account to meet the cheque.
5 Dishonoured.
6 (a) The bank charges charged by the bank to the customer. (b) The keeping of the account by the bank for the customer.

Exercise 3

1 This is where the bank does not pay out on the cheque.
2 He may instruct the bank provided that he does this before the cheque is cleared.
3 (a) By the drawer; (b) when the bank is notified of the drawer's death; (c) where a petition for a receiving order against the drawer has been presented; (d) where a receiving order has been made against the drawer.
4 If Celia could show that her instructions to the bank had been received before the cheque was 'cleared' then the bank would be liable and would not be entitled to debit Celia's account.

Exercise 4

1 To preserve confidentiality on the customer's account.
2 To honour all cheques.

Exercise 5

1 Michael must meet the loss of £150 because he has a duty to his bank if a cheque is drawn on his authority and this one was.
2 Jim will lose the £95 because he has been negligent in the handling of his own account.
3 Ian could sue the other bank for recovery of the £100 because the cheque was marked 'Account Payee Only' and should not have been honoured by the bank.
4 Roy cannot do anything; the cheque was marked 'Not Negotiable' and therefore he can claim no title to it.

Exercise 6

1   The bank is protected because it cannot be expected to recognise forged endorsements.
2   Barclays is not protected unless it can show that the account holder had been negligent.
3   The National Westminster, by not taking up references, had been negligent. It thus could not get the protection afforded by the 1975 Act and could be liable to all 20 drawers.

Exercise 7

1   False: if a cheque is more than 6 months old it will not be paid.
2   (a) To maintain confidentiality in respect of a customer's account; (b) to pay cheques for customers on demand.
3   The drawer could sue the bank for breach of contract and libel.
4   True: provided the cheque has been stopped in time; that is, before payment the bank could be liable.
5   False: the drawer who has been negligent is liable.
6   False:it can only be paid into the payee's account.
7   False: because the cheque is negotiable, Bill Brown does receive good title and therefore the payee cannot claim.
8   (a) The paying bank is protected if it pays out on false endorsements. (b) Provided it has not been negligent the collecting bank will be protected if it accepts a stolen or forged cheque.

Chapter 18

Exercise 1

1   True: a vendor is only legally obliged to sell after exchange of contracts.
2   To make sure that the seller is not bankrupt because, if he is, he will have no right to sell.
3   Transfer.
4   True: this is an example of a contract which must be in deed form, that is, signed as a deed, before it can be legally binding.
5   Colin is the mortgagor. Commercial Credit Co is the mortgagee.

Exercise 2

1   It is stamped on the transfer or assignment document.
2   An assignment.
3   False: stock sales are not affected by stamp duty.
4   Lewis could do very little because the court will not enforce a clause which is so wide. Forty miles and ten years is far too wide.

Exercise 3

1   Susan could get a court order enforcing what is a reasonable covenant against June.
2   An Assignment.

3   Landlord and Tenant Act 1954.
4   Franklin is not at risk because, although the Landlord and Tenant Act does allow a land-lord to repossess property where (a) the landlord wants the property for herself/himself and (b) the landlord wishes to redevelop it extensively, the landlord must have owned the property for at least five years, and this in Elizabeth's situation is not the case.

Chapter 19

Exercise 1

1   20 years.
2   By being assigned to the other person by the holder.
3   Three months.
4   The employee can be granted compensation by the Comptroller-General or the Court.
5   An application is made to the Patents Office in London or Newport.
6   Patents Court.
7   Items related to the fitting of an item, such as spare parts of a car.

Exercise 2

1   50 years.
2   To raise the 50 years to 70 years.
3   It will depend on the extent to which the work was part of the employee's duties.
4   Not unless permission has been obtained, or it is in a person's own home.
5   (a) No, because it is in her own home.
    (b) It is likely that Modern Art Publications has breached copyright.
    (c) No, because John has got permission.

Exercise 3

1   He/she can gain access to any personal data, he/she can get compensation for damage suffered because of inaccurate entries and if data are sent to an unauthorised source or lost then the data subject can get compensation.
2   Payroll data.
3   Unauthorised access, unauthorised access with the intention to commit a crime or fraud and unlawful modification.
4   An appeal to the Data Protection Register.

Chapter 20

Exercise 1

1   (i) Criminal law. It is likely that the appeal would be in the Crown Court. You will remember that appeals from the magistrates go to the Crown Court unless it is on a point of law, in which case it goes to the Queen's Bench Divisional Court.

(ii) Civil law. This is a case of breach of contract and, because of the amount involved, the case will be heard in the High Court, Queen's Bench Division.

(iii) Civil law. This would be heard in the County Court because only a small sum is involved.

(iv) Criminal law. The highest court in the land is, of course, the House of Lords.

2　Four examples of civil courts are: County Court; High Court; Court of Appeal (Civil Division); House of Lords.

3　Magistrates, Crown Court, Court of Appeal (Criminal Division) and House of Lords.

4　This means that the case can be tried in the Magistrates' or Crown Court.

5　This is a court for claims of £1000 or less and the proceedings, which are informal, are known as arbitration.

6　Tribunals include the following: industrial tribunal, Social Security Appeal Tribunal, Lands Tribunal and Criminal Injuries Compensation Board.

7　European Court of Justice.

8　13, Luxembourg.

Exercise 2

1　Because it is power delegated through an Act of Parliament.

2　Bye-laws or Orders in Council.

3　Literal, golden and mischief rules.

4　'The reason for the decision'. It is important because of the UK system of case law.

5　Because it indicated that children aged between ten and 14 are capable of committing a crime.

6　Directives, regulations or decisions.

7　That the custom existed from 'time immemorial': in practice within the memory of an old resident.

8　It means 'beyond its powers' and often refers to companies acting outside their objectives.

Exercise 3

1　Agents who had terminated or had their agency terminated were entitled to commission on income which resulted from their efforts.

2　That countries may not discriminate against nationals of other member countries.

3　Higher education qualifications gained through three years' study or more should be recognised, therefore the university in Belgium is acting illegally.

4　False: these decisions are only persuasive.

5　If the voting is by qualified majority, then 30 votes from these four countries would block the legislation.

Exercise 4

1　A writ.

2　This is the process whereby each party in the case must provide the other with copies of any written evidence that they intend to use in the court.

3　This is an order by which any money owed to the defendant is paid to the plaintiff.

4   This is where the district judge clears up any matters relating to the case before the hearing.
5   The plaintiff may ask for judgement.
6   This is where the bailiff enters the business premises of the defendant and lays claim to items of his property by placing a 'lien'.
7   A magistrate who is paid a salary.
8   Only solicitors are liable for negligence, though a barrister may be liable for statements made outside his court work.
9   The Lord Chancellor.
10   The independence of judges.

Exercise 5

1   (a) No legal intent because this is a domestic arrangement.
    (b) There is no acceptance. Michael made the offer having been invited to do so by the shop.
    (c) Tony's acceptance is conditional; in fact, it is a counter-offer and therefore there is no acceptance.
    (d) No capacity – minors (persons not yet 18) cannot make agreements in respect of credit.
    (e) There is no *consensus ad idem* (meeting of the minds). Mrs Ward only agreed to sell because she was under threat.
    (f) There is no two-way consideration. Brian has only agreed to fulfil an existing obligation.
2   False: an offeror can withdraw an offer at any time before acceptance, even though he has made a promise to keep it open.
3   Any three of the following: withdrawal (revocation), rejection, lapse, acceptance.
4   A gift can only be enforced if it is on a document, 'signed, as a deed'.
5   (i) Consideration must be two-way. (ii) It must not be an existing obligation. (iii) It must not be past. (iv) It must be of value but not necessarily adequate. (v) Only the party supplying the consideration can sue.
6   False: a boy of sixteen has only limited contractual capacity.
7   The garage has no case against Stanley because contracts of hire-purchase, credit and so on must be in writing, otherwise they are void.
8   Where duress, undue influence or misrepresentation has existed.

Exercise 6

1   Sale of Goods Act 1979.
2   False: if they are written or spoken they are known as express terms.
3   A condition is an essential part of the contract. It goes to the heart of the contract. A warranty is a minor part. A breach of condition is the same as a breach of contract.
4   It is unlikely that any court would treat the contract as breached. Failure to deliver just one minor part would be a breach of warranty.
5   M. & G. (Groceries) Ltd could rely on the first exclusion clause which relates to loss and damage of property but, since the Unfair Contract Terms Act 1977, the company cannot rely on the second part, which relates to personal injury.
6   Performance, breach, agreement, frustration.
7   False: this remedy is discretionary; the court can award it if it wishes.

Exercise 7

1   False: a contract of employment may be verbal, though in practice offers of employment are confirmed in writing.
2   13 weeks.
3   The Race Relations Act 1976 states that it is illegal for firms to discriminate on grounds of race, colour or ethnic origin in selection for employment, so rejecting a man because he is foreign is illegal.
4   (a) To obey lawful and reasonable instructions; (b) to work competently and carefully; (c) to conduct oneself in the interest of the employer; (d) to show 'good faith' to the employer.
5   You could have included any three of the following: (a) to provide a safe system of work; (b) not to discriminate on grounds of sex, race or union membership; (c) to reimburse employees for expenses while they are on the firm's business; (d) to deduct PAYE plus National Insurance contributions; (e) to operate a reasonable system of management.
6   Since the engineering firm has lost money owing to Alex's bad work and since they relied on a 'good' reference from Dual Accounting Services in employing Alex, the engineering firm could sue Dual Accounting Services for negligence.
7   Tony is entitled to ten weeks' notice or £1800 in lieu and £2430 redundancy pay (7 weeks × £100 × $1^1/_2$ + 3 weeks × £180 × 1).
8   James has misconducted himself and can be dismissed *without* notice. His appeal against unfair dismissal is not likely to be successful and he certainly has not been made redundant.

Exercise 8

1   (a) K. Dalglish is the agent, Blackburn Rovers FC is the principal.
    (b) Ward & Co is the agent, Kent Engineering plc is the principal.
    (c) Mr Y is the agent, the pop group is the principal.
2   You could have listed: express authorisation; implication; statute; necessity; ratification.
3   To pay him for his duties and to reimburse him for expenses.
4   True: each partner binds the others by his/her actions.
5   False: most often they are binding on the other party even though they had been entered into by the principal himself.
6   True – under a European directive now part of English law he could be entitled to commission.

Exercise 9

1   (a) Under the Sale of Goods Act 1979, it is an implied term that the seller has good title to the goods. Therefore Disdales would have to give Peggy her £500 back.
    (b) The Sale of Goods Act 1979 implies that goods bought from a shop must be of 'merchantable quality'. It does not seem that this was the case here. Good Bargain Radio Supplies Ltd would have to give Richard a refund.
    (c) John Martin could get his money back because the Sale of Goods Act implies that goods sold by description must correspond with the description and the Christmas cake did not.

2 (a) Trade Descriptions Act 1968.
  (b) True: this is one of the offences under the Trade Descriptions Act and criminal proceedings can result from double pricing.
3 False: the goods are hired and become the property of the hirer on payment of the last payment.
4 (a) Jeff is fortunate because, if he can prove he has never received a copy of the agreement, he cannot be forced to pay the final five instalments because the court will never enforce an agreement where the hirer (Jeff in this case) has not received a copy.
  (b) Susan is given up to five days to 'cool off'. She can withdraw from the agreement since it was signed at her home as long as it is within five days. Household Supplies Ltd can do nothing.
5 False: protection is available in respect of services.

Exercise 10

1 Failure to make profits is non-insurable.
2 Pooling of risks.
3 (a) Star Insurance Company need not pay out because Michael Jones has not obeyed the principle of 'utmost good faith'.
  (b) Surety Insurance need not pay out because Michael Hunter has no 'insurable interest' in his friend's house.
  (c) Frank Brown, in receiving £20 000, would be getting more than the value of the car. He can only claim £10 000. This principle is known as indemnity.
4 Any property, after an insurance claim has been met, belongs to the insurance company.

Exercises 11 and 12

1 A duty of care; breach of that duty; damages or loss arising from the breach.
2 False: in some instances, especially in the case of children, a duty of care can be owed to a trespasser.
3 That no duty of care was owed; that the duty was not broken; that no loss damage or injury resulted; that the plaintiff had agreed to take the risk (consent).
4 Trespass to land, persons and goods.
5 True.
6 Mrs Wardle would have a good case in defamation. She is referred to. The statement is communicated to a third party. The statement is capable of lowering Mrs Wardle's reputation in the eyes of right-thinking people. After all, telephoning New Zealand at the company's expense is not what one would expect from a supervisor.
7 This showed that courts were willing to accept negligence claims for financial loss.
8 The victim can seek the assistance of the local authority, whose officer may issue an abatement notice.

Exercise 13

1 True: the Health and Safety at Work Act is concerned with criminal offences.
2 This is an order which forbids the use of equipment or a process which the Health and Safety inspectors feel is dangerous.

3 (a) To take reasonable care for the safety of other employees; (b) to cooperate with employers in safety matters; (c) not to interfere with anything provided for safety.
4 Factories Act 1961.
5 He may apply for industrial benefit which is paid by the state.
6 This is where an employer might be liable for the torts of his employees.
7 To ensure a safe place of work, a safe system of work, safe fellow employees and safe equipment.

Exercise 14

1 A sleeping partner is one who invests money but plays no active role in the partnership. A salaried partner receives a salary but no share in the profits.
2 Private companies, public companies, nationalised industries.
3 *Ultra vires.*
4 A shareholder stands to lose only the value of his shares–his liability is limited to his shareholding.
5 Maximum 20; minimum two.
6 In this case it was established that a partnership could only exist when business had commenced.
7 Under new European legislation, it is possible for one person to form a company.
8 The 1985 Companies Act.

Exercise 15

1 A public company.
2 To balance the interests of the consumers against the needs of the shareholders.
3 They must get through one of the 'gateways'.
4 The Fair Trading Act 1973.
5 Articles 85, 86 and 87.
6 The agreement that only dishwashers made in Belgium could be fitted to the mains supply was judged illegal because it restricted competition.

Exercise 16

1 An accountant who assists a debtor facing bankruptcy.
2 IVA is an Individual Voluntary Arrangement, and a proposal is a plan put forward by the debtor, setting out how he intends to deal with his creditors.
3 The Deed of Arrangement Act 1914. A composition is a plan setting out how the debtor will seek to settle his debts.
4 In order that land/property owned by a bankrupt cannot be sold unless it is of benefit to the creditors. It serves as a warning to the solicitor acting for the buyer.
5 Liquidated.
6 The creditors will get 20p in every pound they are owed.

Exercise 17

1 The person paying out is the drawer, the bank is the drawee and the person whose name appears after 'pay' is the payee.

2 (a) To maintain confidentiality in respect of a customer's account; (b) to honour all cheques drawn.
3 True – by refusing to honour a cheque, a bank could be liable in libel.
4 Cross the cheque and mark it 'Account Payee Only'.
5 Negotiability refers to the fact that the cheque can be transferred from person to person.
6 A cheque may be stopped: (a) under instructions of the drawer; (b) if the bank is notified of the drawer's death; (c) where a receiving order has been made; (d) where a petition for a receiving order has been made.
7 By the Cheques Act, 1992.

Exercise 18

1 True: a buyer is not legally bound to buy until contracts are exchanged.
2 Goodwill.
3 The purchaser unfortunately could do nothing because the clause '20 years anywhere in the UK' is far too restrictive and the courts will not uphold it.
4 False: the tenant is protected by the Landlord and Tenant Act 1954.
5 Property, Proprietorship and Charges Register.
6 To make sure the seller was not bankrupt.
7 False: they must be 'signed as a deed'.
8 A tax payable when properties are sold or businesses are sold by an assignment.

Exercise 19

1 Patents Court within the Chancery Division.
2 By applying to the European Patents Office in Munich.
3 Protection for businesses on the 'A' register is greater than for those on the 'B' register. New products can only get on the 'B' register initially.
4 No, trademarks are available to producers of services, also.
5 1985, by the Copyright (Computer Software) Act.
6 A data subject is the person who is the subject of the data.

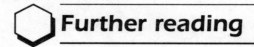 **Further reading**

General

Make sure that you always obtain the most recent edition of these books.

KEENAN, D.J., *Advanced Business Law* (Pitman).
KEENAN, D.J., and RICHES, Sarah, *Business Law* (Pitman).
MARSH, S.B. and SOULSBY, J., *Business Law* (McGraw-Hill).
READ, P.A., *General Principles of English Law Case Book* (HLT Publication).
SCHMITTHOFF, C.M. and SARRE, D.A., *Charlesworth's Mercantile Law* (Stevens and Sons).

European Community law

LASOK, D. and BRIDGE, J.W., *Introduction to the Law and Institutions of the European Communities* (Butterworths).
PEARSON, E., *Law for European Business Studies* (Pitman).

Contract

DAVIES, F.R., *Law of Contract* (Sweet and Maxwell).
SMITH, J.C. and THOMAS, J.A.C., *A Casebook on Contract* (Butterworths).

Tort

BAKER, C.D., *Tort* (Sweet and Maxwell).
BRADBURY, P.L., *Cases and Statutes on Tort* (Sweet and Maxwell).

Sale of goods

ATIYAH, P.S., *The Sale of Goods* (Pitman).

Agency

FRIDMAN, G.H.L., *The Law of Agency* (Butterworths).

Consumer credit

DIAMOND, A., *Commercial and Consumer Credit: An Introduction* (Butterworths).

Industrial and employment law

SELWYN, N., *Law of Employment* (Butterworths).
SELWYN, N., *Law of Health and Safety at Work* (Butterworths).
WHINCUP, M., *Modern Employment Law* (Butterworth/Heinemann).

Index